To my Ride or Dies:
Rachelle Lee, Harli Jade, and Chase Allen.

In It for Life

San Bernardino,
California
1986

Launched

I FOLLOWED MY brother out the apartment door, not bothering if it banged behind me. My sister was sleeping and my mom was either at work or passed out in her room. I didn't know where we were going, but it didn't matter. I just followed Eric, knowing it was better to be outside on a cool night, walking around with our friends, floating from street to street, seeing what's up.

At twelve, I was younger than most of the others. Sure, at a party I might see someone my age, a *chica* playing hopscotch, or a kid bragging about his Atari. Sometimes I'd go inside to play Pitfall for an hour until Eric pulled me out finally at midnight because we had to go home.

That was our night, strutting around, lords of the neighborhood, kings of San Bernardino. We knew everyone who should be there. If we saw anything out of the ordinary, a strange man, a strange car, we'd know, and we'd take care of it.

Sometimes we'd break into parked cars; we called it jockey-boxing. Sometimes we'd climb the fence and check for open windows around the private school which bordered the apartment complex. They rarely had anything worth stealing but there was something peaceful about the grounds at night, the way our footsteps echoed in the classrooms. And the vandalism, the destruction, honestly, it was an afterthought.

We had no beef with the school; we were just there, and the desks were just there, or the window, or the garbage or whatever it was: it was just there, and it felt good to knock it over, toss it around, and leave a mark.

But we weren't breaking into anything that night; that night was for walking and hanging with our homies. My brother, Eric, was talking about Sheila, a girl he liked. He described their last encounter, and I was laughing with them even when I didn't understand. But then he told us she had invited him to a party coming up the next week. It was going to be wild, she'd said; someone was bringing some serious drugs, and Eric wanted us all to go.

Aaron stopped laughing. He was seventeen, same as my brother, and they were good friends. Both were lean, almost skinny, but quick and hard. Both slicked back their hair and wore Cortez shoes and Sureño blue. My brother grew a thin mustache he'd smooth as he talked. Aaron had hungry eyes and would be jumped into the set soon. They saw the world in mostly the same way except Aaron didn't like to leave the neighborhood.

"That's almost on the north side," he said.

Eric was broader minded. Plus, he wanted to see the girl.

"They got some *vato* coming with some good shit."

Aaron shook his head. "This *vato*, where's he coming from?"

"I don't know."

"He comes around a lot?"

"Why you asking?"

With a slow grin, Aaron said to my brother, "Could we jack this fool?"

His question changed the energy of the night. I felt it, even if I didn't understand it. The two of them started talking more seriously. They got quieter so Rocco and I walking behind them couldn't hear their words. Rocco was Aaron's brother and my best friend. He was smaller than me, always wore his sunglasses on his forehead, but even at twelve he had a slow way of looking at someone, giving the impression he might pounce. We were heading back towards our apartments, skirting the park near my middle school.

"I don't know, *homes*." My brother's words floated back. "I know these people. I know this *chica*."

I was the little brother and didn't like not being part of things. I said, "We talking about a jack move?"

They laughed at me.

"Yeah, Brad, it's a jack move."

"What are we taking?"

Aaron grabbed the back of my neck and shook me. "Some good shit," he said. "Kind of like candy, like a big bag of tootsie pops."

This burned. I could take some teasing but I wasn't a little kid. I knew about drugs. I'd smoked a little weed. I'd had a few beers. Not a lot, but here and there as I followed my brother around. And I'd stolen for them already - at the private school, in grocery stores and gas stations. I had a baby face the clerks never suspected. I knew what I was doing.

"We should do it," I said.

"Hear that," Aaron said. "Brad's in. Come on, *homes*, nut up."

There was a hard edge under my brother's laugh.

IT WAS EARLY, AROUND NINE, AND WE HAD NO PLANS so I was hanging out in my brother's room. He had no furniture in there except for a mattress on the floor. The only light came from a desk lamp next to it. A nerf basketball hung from the back of his door and I was taking jump shots from the corner.

"Yeah, I hear you, I hear you." Eric shrugged the phone to his ear. "Sounds cool."

He leaned against the wall. As he talked he sketched Magic Johnson with the stub of a pencil, copying from a page he'd ripped out of a magazine.

"We'll be there, Sheila, like I told you."

My brother sounded so smooth with this girl. He spoke low and cool, like everything he did. He was my big brother, seventeen years old and he watched out for me. I had clung to him ever since my dad left for Portland.

It was better with him gone. Popps drank too much and would get rough with all of us, my mom especially. But Eric had been there, protecting me. He'd sit on my bed, whispering with a hand on my neck, saying I should stay where I was, saying it was going to be okay even with Dad screaming on the other side of the door.

Eric was my world, the whole thing, and he always knew what he was doing.

"Hey, who is this *vato* you buying from?"

Eric said it so smooth I barely knew what he was talking about.

"You said he's got good shit. We were thinking of getting hooked up with him too, you know."

It clicked what he was doing. He was following Aaron's plan from a few days ago, setting it up. I grabbed the ball and dunked again. I tried to act normal, natural so Eric didn't think of kicking me out for this part.

"Nah, nah, nah, but you know how to..."

I sneaked a glance at Eric. He grinned at me, and I knew he was in control.

"Yeah, but could - could he hook us up?"

I tossed up a fadeaway jumper and the nerf ball bounced wide.

"Me and my boy, Aaron."

I stepped across the bed to get the ball, my feet tangling in the blankets. My brother slapped at my calf as I hopped off.

"Come on, Sheila, help me out."

Eric nodded big and scribbled a number down on his notebook. He circled it a few times as they talked about something else. I dribbled quietly, my brother listening on the party line as others talked. Outside the room, the apartment was quiet. Our sister, Melissa, huddled in her own room doing her thing. She was eleven, a year younger than me, and the only girl. Mom was at work.

"That's right," Eric said.

San Berarndino breathed through the window: cars humming down Lugonia Avenue, voices drifting muffled from other apartments.

"Come on, Sheila, you know me."

I mouthed, 'We good?' but Eric glared at me to shut up.

With a shrug I leaned against the wall and slid down to sit. I rested my feet on my big brother's bed, happy to be there, ready for anything.

THE BALL THWACKED AGAINST PLYWOOD THEN slapped against my palm. The sun beat down. Sweat beaded on my forehead. The Fourth of July came on a Friday that year and my best friend, Rocco, and I spent the morning playing handball against the garage outside the apartments. We barely kept score, caring more about the plan for that night: a barbecue with the family. We wanted to see the fireworks, blow things up. We were still kids.

My brother walked up with Aaron. He didn't even look at me, but I always felt different when he was around, like nothing could touch me.

The two leaned their heads towards each other. They were talking seriously about something, but a hot wind whipped through the cars and pushed their voices the wrong way. Rocco and I stopped to watch. Aaron pointed to different places around the parking lot, but Eric shook his head and patted his hand down, like he was telling Aaron to stop.

Finally, they stepped close enough for me to hear.

"Listen, *homes*," Eric was saying, "in the middle of the day? Naw."

Aaron grinned at him. "What's the problem?"

I bounced the handball against the asphalt and caught it without thinking. Squeezed it anxiously against my palm. They were talking about jacking the dealer, I'd figured that out. I knew it'd work out right if Eric was in charge, and I needed to be a part of it.

"All right. Shit." Eric said. "But what if we scatter up, run it like play, you know?"

"Yeah, yeah," Aaron said, "You're getting it. We scatter like that, block a couple times, it's no problem."

"If there's a couple of them."

"If there's two it'll be easy."

"But if he's got a whole crew with him?"

"He won't."

My brother shook his head. "I don't know about this."

"Easy money. You worry too much." Aaron turned towards us and nodded. "You two fools ready for this?"

I glanced at Rocco and we shared a slow smile. The day had grown brighter, more electric.

"Yup." I nodded with my whole body. "Let's do it."

Eric laughed. "He don't even know what it is yet."

"I know what's going on," I said. "Easy money."

My brother laughed at that and gave me an affectionate slap on the back of the neck. Aaron brought us into a loose huddle and explained the plan, pointing around the parking lot. Eric corrected him as he spoke, talking through, pointing to a different spot. He had lost his hesitation and had a grin in his eyes. When the time came, he said, you just gotta run like hell.

The plan sounded fine. Not brilliant, but I knew it would work. My part would be easy: grab the bag and go. I could do that. They gave me the longest run but my brother said it was because I was the best runner. I felt pride in that. And all I has to do was make it to the park.

No problem.

MY BROTHER WARNED ME TO NOT ACT OBVIOUS, TO stay loose, so I took my time, kicked a pebble down the sidewalk, ran my fingers against the rough brick walls. I wondered if the others could see me, if they saw how cool I was acting. I was jacking a drug dealer, and working with Aaron so I was working for the set. He was with Los Dukes. It was a Sureño gang. If I did this right maybe they'd jump me in a little early.

I shook my head roughly. No, that was stupid. I was getting distracted over stuff I shouldn't be worried about right then. I had to focus on the job.

I found my spot but I couldn't see what was going on so I stepped forward about twenty feet. A few minutes passed, not long, before the dealer showed up. He drove a boxy white car; it had a little rust on the side. I tracked it through the parking lot, the top gliding through the cars and past the dumpsters. It stopped next to Aaron and he leaned in to talk through the passenger side window. Eric slouched on the other side with his hands shoved in his pockets. I stared at the windshield, but the glare of the sun kept me from seeing through it. We'd planned for two of them, but if there were more it could be a problem.

An argument in Spanish tumbled through a nearby window and fed the nervous energy building in my legs. I shifted from foot to foot, thinking I should move into position, but I stayed where I was. I had to watch.

Aaron straightened and peered into a brown paper bag. He dug into his pocket as if going for money then sky-hooked the bag to Eric.

It arced over the car as the driver barked out a curse.

It was time. I scurried back towards the building, trying to play it cool, but my heart was already thumping. My legs were ready to run. I heard more yelling, a shouted "Hey! Hey! Hey!" and the screech of tires.

It cranked me up, but I had to wait. Aaron would pass the bag to Rocco. Rocco would pass the bag to me. My brother would hang back to block any fool who gave chase while I sprinted to the park and got lost.

A few moments, then footsteps patted on the concrete, and Rocco skidded past the corner. Breathless, he pressed the bag into my hands.

I launched my body down the sidewalk, legs churning, gulping air already. I couldn't see the white car or the dealer or anyone, but still I sprinted between two buildings, then cut though cars to the alley alongside the apartments. I leaned forward, eyeing Lugonia Street ahead of me, the most dangerous part.

I felt it rumble in my knees first, then heard the gravel crunching behind me under a whining engine. The dealer's car, it sounded close and was gaining.

I ran faster, super-speed, hurtling forward to the curb as a flash of white streaked by my elbow, the car fishtailing into the middle of the intersection.

Not thinking, I shot away from the sidewalk into the street, angled away from the dealer's car. I ignored the screech of tires until it made contact. A furious vibration launched me off my feet and tossed me into space.

I floated for a heartbeat before impact. A flash of pain. The world spun. I laid on the concrete staring up into a bright blue sky. My body felt heavy and strange. I blinked at the sun.

THE SKY SWIRLED AROUND ME. I COULDN'T MOVE. I wanted to close my eyes but I knew that was wrong. Everything was wrong.

A voice. "You okay, kid?" A middle-aged man crouched near my face. "You've been hit by a car. Are you okay?"

Then Rocco was close, his face next to mine, screaming, "You're okay, Brad! You're going to be okay!" The panic in his voice told me that this wasn't true. "Just don't look down, *homes*. Don't look down."

I was dazed half out of my mind and could barely move, but now I had to look down. I lifted my head but all I saw was a twisted mess of dark red, torn cloth and what looked like macaroni pouring out of my shorts. Unable to make any sense of it, I squeezed my eyes shut. A terrible throbbing, not pain exactly, but an alarm started screaming through my body.

My brother called my name, and I tried to hold on to his voice. Eric was there so it had to be okay.

He said, "We gotta get him out of the street."

The man said, "No, no. You need to let the ambulance come."

Eric ignored him. He knew nothing about neck injuries and his kid brother's blood was creeping across the pavement. He dug his hands under my shoulders, Rocco grabbed under my waist, and they lifted me up. I screamed when my leg moved, crying, begging them to stop, but they hauled me over until they could set me on the grass.

I closed my eyes. A distant siren pierced through the street noise. I wanted to pass out, but someone leaned their head close to mine and said something. I couldn't understand the words but I recognized his voice: Aaron. He pulled at my shorts, sending jolts of pain through my legs. My eyes startled open to see him standing over me. He gripped the paper bag, having just dug it out of my pocket.

My brother and Rocco stayed squatting nearby as Aaron hurried away. I tried to find Eric's face, but my eyes wouldn't focus. I tried to ask, "How did this happen?" but no words came out.

The sirens grew louder until the ambulance arrived followed by a police car. As the paramedics checked my body, a cop leaned in too close. "Who did this to you?" I felt his breath against my ear.

The drug dealer we jacked had tried to murder me with his car, but, even hurt and dazed, I knew what to do.

"I don't know what happened." I breathed for a long second. "I was running to the store... I think a car maybe hit me."

The paramedics worked around my body. Their voices and movements grew farther and farther away. I closed my eyes, ready to drift down into sleep until they strapped my head to the stretcher. Fresh pain screamed through my skull. I begged them to loosen it.

"I'm sorry," they said. Their voices were serious but not unkind. "It's only a couple blocks to the hospital."

The ambulance pulled away down the street. The ride only lasted a few minutes, but every breath, every moment, every bump was torture.

I WATCHED FROM THE BALCONY AS MY FRIENDS TOSSED the football back and forth. I'd been watching them for four weeks. Sometimes Eric would join them and they would remember to wave up at me. Sometimes I tried to pretend I was an emperor or something, reigning over all I surveyed, but that fantasy wouldn't last. And that afternoon all I could do was stare out stupidly, thinking nothing.

My sister, Melissa, made noise in the apartment behind me. I was sick of her and she was sick of me, but we couldn't do anything about it. Our apartment was up two flights of stairs and my leg was wrapped in a cast from hip to ankle. I wasn't going anywhere.

But I had grown tired of the balcony so I pushed my wheelchair into the living room. Melissa pretended not to notice as I struggled to get my back wheel over the bump. It was only after I finally rolled onto the carpet that she looked up, acting annoyed. I had an insult ready, but before I could say it, my brother walked through the door.

"How you doing, Brad?" He gave me puppy-eyes and leaned in too close and over eager. I looked away.

A month to think about it and I still couldn't figure what happened. It had been Eric's plan so it shouldn't have gone wrong. The fool who hit me had got away. Cops had asked a few more questions in the hospital, but we told them we didn't get a good look at the car. We said we didn't know the driver. We didn't know anything. The cops dropped it, the dealer didn't get arrested, but we kept the drugs. It was a good arrangement for Aaron and Eric. Even Rocco got his cut. Me, I got a broken leg.

"Hey Brad, want to go outside?" He put his hand on my shoulder and grinned down at me. "Check out the park, see what's up?"

I was hurt and angry, but anything was better than that apartment. I shrugged into it and let Eric push me out.

Aaron was waiting for us at the top of the stairs. He grabbed at the

11

front wheels and helped carry my chair down. Then they took turns pushing me down the alley. We followed the same path as the drug dealer had when he chased me. Neither of them said anything when we crossed the intersection.

When we entered the park, Eric started clowning, trying to get me to laugh with him, but I wasn't in the mood. At the basketball court we found the homies. A few were playing a loose game. Others squatted on basketballs, or leaned against the fence, fingers curling around the metal. A few girls sat on the bench.

Everyone smiled when they wheeled me up. The girls cooed, and some of the bigger homies came over and clapped me on the back.

Big Wheez laid his massive hand on my shoulder. A huge Mexican man, shiny-bald and a little fat, he was older than Eric and though he wasn't the big homie yet, he would be within the next year. He said, "What you doing in that chair, *ese*?"

Wheez had never talked to me before; he'd never looked at me before. I croaked out something like, "I dunno."

"Nah, you don't need that thing. Come on, get over here and play ball."

"Damn, Big Wheez, I could beat you sitting down."

The homies laughed around me and Big Wheez nodded. "That's funny. That's good, but listen. We heard what you did. Aaron told the story. Heard you did good with the cops."

The whole thing, the girls looking at me, the homies paying attention, Big Wheez talking to me like this, it warmed me up and made me light-headed.

Wheez said, "Aaron get you your share yet?"

"Naw, not yet."

Big Wheez looked up and Aaron brought out a wad of bills.

"There it is."

He placed it in my hand. I wanted to bring the money to my face and sniff it or something, but I played it cool.

"That's eighty bucks there. For your work."

It seemed an impossible amount, like it would pay for a lifetime of video games, pizza, or anything else I wanted.

"You did good out there," Big Wheez said. "You kept your mouth shut."

All the homies were listening to Big Wheez as he said these things about me. Everyone nodded along except my brother. Eric had his head turned down, staring at the cracked concrete.

The basketball game started up again. The homies started clowning about something. I sat in the sun and took it in. I watched Eric slide up to a girl. I watched him talk her up, act smooth, but I couldn't help noticing my big brother didn't seem quite as big as he used to be.

Especially compared to Big Wheez.

Gilbert Hall

Three months later

ROCCO NUDGED ME, close, arms touching, and passed me the dope. It had been a hot day, Southern California heat, but a cool night and the door was open into the Godfather's Pizza. Outside, older homies cruised in their lowriders and trucks, turning around in the strip mall parking lot; they'd pull up next to each other to drink or get a little high before cruising the loop again.

I shoved the fat bag of weed in my pocket without thinking. We'd sell it later or pass it to another homie, whatever, but Rocco didn't feel like carrying it any more. It put a bulge in his pocket, scratched at his leg and he wanted me to deal with it. I was playing Afterburner, shooting down bogies in an F14 so I didn't care.

After I'd been hit by one too many missiles, I hunted through the little arcade for my next game. Maria leaned against the gumball machine, her hair gelled straight up, makeup slapped on thick. I laughed a little louder when I saw her, clowning hard with Rocco as I weaved through the crowd. I heard the shouting outside but didn't think anything of it.

Some of the older homies from my clique nodded at me as they pushed through the door and I glanced at Maria to see if she noticed. I was known as a tough kid since I got flattened by a car and kept my mouth shut about it. It had earned me a dent in my thigh and a little respect. It didn't seem a bad deal.

I started into Street Fighter and was choosing my character when I heard the sirens. I kept playing - I didn't want to lose my quarter - but the screaming kept growing louder and the arcade emptied around me until I couldn't ignore it. With a curse, I abandoned the game and hurried to the door.

Police lights lit up the parking lot as cars streamed out. Younger kids scattered like dice. I moved on instinct, not thinking, and ran down the line of shops. Immediately, I saw I'd made a mistake: I got myself in an area where there was no place to move.

Still, I kept running. I figured the cops had no reason to bother with me. I was just a shit kid, nobody to notice. I had a clear path and no fear until a blue smudge blurred in the corner of my vision. I braced for the impact a moment before it landed and hit the ground hard, my shoulder scraping along the cement and into the dirt.

The cop yanked me up before I could catch my breath. He gripped my arm, what there was to it; I was small for thirteen. I tried pulling away but the cop squeezed harder.

"Where you going, kid?"

I looked at my feet and kept my mouth shut. I went flat, didn't even shrug. I'd done nothing but play a couple video games so I figured there'd be no problem. They had been called because of a fight and I'd been nowhere near it.

"What were you running from?"

Everyone ran; it meant nothing so I said nothing.

"What are you doing here?"

I saw some of my homies watching from across the parking lot. I had an audience and it warmed me up. I glared at the cop. "Fuck you, *chota.*"

"What's that?"

"You heard me."

The cop yanked my arm, making me stumble, and he shoved me towards the cruiser. I was tiny; I weighed nothing so I slammed my elbow against the trunk harder probably than the cop had meant.

He dug his hands into my pockets and pulled out the weed. The baggie bulged in the cop's hand when he showed it to me. I gaped at it, more surprised than anything. I had forgotten it was there.

15

My stomach dropped but I wasn't freaking out, not yet. I figured it would be a hassle; I'd get in a little trouble from my mom, but no big deal. I lost the smirk and the attitude, but even as the metal pinched into my wrists, even as the cop twisted my shoulder into the car, even as the door slammed me inside, I hoped my homies were watching. I'd get respect for this: my first bust.

No big deal.

THE COP TOOK ME STRAIGHT TO THE JUVENILE HALL on Gilbert Street. He drove through a gate in the barbed wire fence and spoke into a dented receiver, "One for processing." He led me through a series of heavy doors until a man in regular street clothes took off the handcuffs. I rubbed at my wrists as the man led me to an interview room. He directed me to one of the four off-colored plastic chairs, then left. The door shut and locked.

I leaned forward and traced my finger along the grooves and gashes carved in the table. Above me, the lights gave off a low buzz which grew louder as the minutes passed. With no one watching, the gangster thrill I got wearing handcuffs in the parking lot was gone. The guard had been bland and almost polite which made me feel more lost than bad-ass. Sitting alone in that room, a small part of me, a part I wanted to shove away, wanted my mom. I wanted her to hold me and tell me it was going to be okay.

I started to fidget. Time oozed too slow and I began to pace. Paint covered old graffiti on the wall and I spent a few minutes trying to make out what it used to say, who had tagged it, but I soon lost interest. I needed to move.

I needed to get out of there. I needed to get back to the street, find Rocco, see what was going on. I figured the door would open any second, but thirty minutes passed, then an hour. The flickering light made me feel sick. I heard a banging sound from some other part of the building and I flinched away from the wall. I didn't want to see my mom any more; I didn't want her anywhere near this place.

I pounded on the table; the vibration moved up my fist into my wrist but didn't do anything. I paced furiously, back and forth. I was a skinny kid, small boned, tiny, and I didn't belong there. I banged on

16

the cinderblock but it didn't give at all and no one seemed to hear. I wanted my mom again but I was afraid she'd show up.

I slumped back in the chair. I wanted to throw it and the table against the mirror, but the table was heavy and I was tired. I had no idea what time it was. I lowered my head on my arm and squeezed my eyes shut.

The sound of a giant key in the lock - *ka-chunk* - startled me. I sat up straight as the jailer pushed open the door. He had a bland face, a plaid shirt, beige pants. As he sat down across from me, the ID badge hanging from his neck hit the table.

"How you doing, Brad? You doing all right?"

"Yeah, yeah," I said, but I was already retreating. I knew by instinct not to trust men who could move through locked doors.

He opened a folder. "Do you go to school, Brad?"

"I go to Clemont Junior High."

"Yeah? What kind of things do you do in your free time?"

"Play basketball, I guess."

"You a Lakers fan?"

I was waiting for a trap but this seemed safe. "Yeah," I said.

"All right. Why don't you tell me what happened today."

"I don't know. I was playing video games and heard some noise going on so I went outside to check it out and there were police."

"Mm-hmm. And an officer found an ounce of marijuana on you."

I raised up my chin. "I don't know nothing about that."

"Want to tell me where a kid like you got that much weed?"

It felt like a test that I knew I was about to ace. I leaned back and stared the man down.

"I told you I don't know nothing about that."

Then the man said, "We talked to your mom." This got my attention. "She says you been getting in trouble a lot."

I knew that already but his tone of voice was getting to me.

"Listen, Brad. Your mom?" The bland face smirked. "She's not coming to get you."

I tried to slouch like I didn't care but it didn't work. I turned away, bit down every emotion, and said the words in my head, *Fuck it.*

"She says she doesn't want you home right now. She wants you to stay in jail."

17

Fuck it, I thought again, but without energy. My forehead fell forward like it was attached to a weight.

"All right, Brad." The man's voice softened which made it worse. "We'll dress you down. Maybe get you something to eat."

After he left, I stared at the wall. Without his bland smile tamping me down, my insides started to burn. I screamed out and shoved at the table with all my strength, but it didn't budge.

Only a few minutes passed before there was another *ka-chunk* and the door opened. A kid entered in a green jumpsuit. He held a tray with a peanut butter sandwich and a glass of juice.

My heart was thudding hard enough to hurt but I hardened my face. This kid had me by at least three years and fifty pounds but I stared him down. I was concerned, that's what I told myself. I was a little worried, no big deal. I flicked my eyes to the jailer in the doorway.

"Don't I get my phone call?"

The kid with the tray smirked but screw that fool.

"My free phone call?"

The jailer said, "No, that's not how this works."

"What?"

"Just eat your sandwich and we'll dress you down."

I didn't know what that meant or what would happen next but I hadn't eaten for hours. I took a bite. The bread tasted stale, my mouth was dry and I almost choked as I swallowed it down.

THE JAILER LED ME INTO A SMALL ROOM AND SHUT the door behind us. I stared stupidly at a bench where a folded jumpsuit laid next to a pair of thin sandals, a bed roll, and a bar of soap. I had no idea what was expected of me.

The jailer nodded at the jumpsuit. "Get undressed." He sounded bored.

For a moment I felt an overpowering need to cry out for my mom, and I had to stand very still until the moment passed.

"Come on, let's go."

"Ain't you going to leave?" I hated how small my voice sounded.

"I have to make sure you don't have any contraband."

"What?"

"Make sure you don't have anything you aren't supposed to."

I could see no way out besides doing what the jailer said. I knelt down and took my time with untying my shoes and pulling off my socks. I felt the man's eyes on my skin, and my face grew warm, but I kept moving until I was down to my underwear.

"All the way now. Come on."

I dropped down my shorts and kicked them off. The room was cold and I felt all skinny arms and legs.

The jailer began offering instructions and it was a strange relief to focus on the commands. I shut off my brain and kept moving, doing whatever was asked. I lifted up each foot, ran my fingers through my hair and around my mouth.

"Turn around," the man said. "And again. Now lift your testicles." I did, the man watching all this until he finally said, "You're clean. Come on now, get dressed," and he turned to the side, looking away, a little kindness. I pulled on my underwear as fast as I could.

The jumpsuit scratched against my skin. The jail sandals pinched my toes. We waited outside a heavy door as the jailer talked to a man on the other side of one-way glass. I took the chance to study myself. The mirror warped my face and I looked shriveled in the green uniform, like a kid wearing one of his dad's shirts.

After the door buzzed open, the jailer led me down a long hallway. Cinderblock walls painted peanut-butter brown made the space feel narrower than it was. I struggled to breathe normally. I didn't know where I was heading. I didn't know how long I'd have to stay. I wasn't sure if my family really knew I was there.

I couldn't figure out what happened. When I woke up that morning I'd had no plans except to hang out with Rocco. We had just been playing video games, like almost any other day. Then somehow I was in jail.

We turned a corner and walked down a hallway lined with doors the color of ketchup. Through scratched plexiglass I saw faces staring out. Their voices were muffled, but I could hear them well enough. Some were calling to the jailer but most yelled towards me. They rattled at the doors, calling me fish, new fish, telling me to come closer, playing me to see if I'd crack.

It was a long-ass hallway.

We stopped at the end, room nine, and a man's face appeared behind the scratched window: my new cellmate. It could be anyone, a monster, a murderer, a pedophile. I worried I might throw up.

The door opened and my cellie grinned down at me. He was maybe sixteen years old, still a kid, but he had big bones covered in muscle. He had rolled down his jumpsuit so he was shirtless wearing what looked like green pants.

The door locked behind me and I braced myself to fight. I was small and figured I'd get a beat down, but I hoped to go down swinging.

"What's up, *ese*? Where you from?"

I said I was Brad. I told him my neighborhood and he said he was from the other side of town. His name was David.

"This your first time?"

I nodded.

"Yeah, yeah. Listen, it's all right, *homes*."

Something in me released. All the tension and fear I'd been holding drained out, but too fast and again I worried I might cry. I went silent and barely kept it together as David helped me set up my bunk. He talked for awhile, running down what to expect in the morning, but it was late and he quickly grew quiet. The light turned down, never dark but dimmer. The building muted, never silent but not as loud.

I stared at the ceiling and listened to David snore. I wanted to move but worried I'd wake him so I laid as still as I could. The hours passed slowly. I wondered where my mom was and if she was thinking of me. I figured I'd find out tomorrow when I went home.

I slept an hour, maybe two before the light finally brightened and David started to move. My body hurt when I swung my legs out from the bunk. David began talking, telling me what was going to happen. The door would open, he said, and we'd wait in the hall before going to chow.

I followed instructions and stood outside the cell when it was time. Other inmates lined the hall. These guys were twice my size and I could no longer pretend I was only a little concerned. I was scared. I didn't know what was going on; I couldn't figure how I got there. I was thirteen years old. My mom was nowhere around, nor my big brother. I was alone. Everyone else was older, tougher, with hard eyes mean-mugging me. Down the hall, a few called out, calling new fish, watching how I'd react.

Another instinct clicked in with the fear and I made myself as tall as I could. I felt small, but I knew these *vatos*. I didn't know their names, but I knew them. I was from their world. They were like me. They were like my homies. I had to represent my clique. I had to act tough. For the neighborhood. For Big Wheez.

I raised my head and stared each of those fools down one by one.

WE WERE IN LOCKDOWN, SITTING IN OUR BUNKS. I'D been there a week and spent a lot of the time doing nothing, wondering what was going on. I hadn't talked to anyone in my family. I heard my dad had called but didn't get a chance to talk to him. There'd been no word from my mom at all.

She hadn't even come to the hearing. No one had. My third day there I had stood before the judge and twisted my neck to check the gallery only to find it empty except for a man named Montoya. He was a gang counselor who I'd met the day before. He had leaned against the table in the multi-purpose room, and asked after who I knew in the neighborhood. Montoya acted like a homie, but I knew not to trust him when he got up and walked through a locked door.

At my hearing, he'd stood from the gallery and told the judge my mom couldn't be there because she was working. He said she was a single mother doing the best she could. The judge nodded at this then gave me 30 days. It all happened fast and I didn't even know when it was over. I had waited for him to bang a gavel but he didn't. None of it was like the movies.

When I'd stood up, I had felt unsteady, like I was standing near the edge of a high roof. Pressure built in my chest and pushed against the back of my eyes, but I swallowed it down. Don't stress, I told myself, I had homies. Palone and Weasel from my clique had showed up the day after I did. I had stepped out of my cell and found them both grinning down at me. And my cellie was solid. These bigger homies had my back.

I didn't need my mom. I didn't need my family. It had been three days since the hearing, and I kept saying this to myself. I didn't need my brother. I didn't need nobody but my homies. When I was outside my cell in the classroom or in the multi-purpose room, it worked all right, but during lockdown the words felt like a lie. I laid on my bunk, my head turned towards the wall. I didn't think I was going to cry, not then, not with David in the room, but I wasn't sure.

The sound of a door opening somewhere down the hall came muffled through the cinderblock. A few moments later, I heard a man's voice and figured I knew who it was. The voice grew louder as he worked his way closer to my cell; it was the Gideon like I'd thought. He came around every couple days, talked to us through the cell door. I didn't fully understand what a Gideon was, but he acted like a priest. I hopped off my bunk, eager to talk to somebody. I stepped around David who had dropped to the floor to do his pushups.

The voice came closer. The man was asking the guys in each cell if anyone needed prayer, if they wanted to come to Mass on Sunday, if they had a bible.

I grabbed the books I got from the library and put them on the ground by the door, then stepped up on them so I could reach the window. It was scratched and hazy but I could see enough. The Gideon had a soft face, like someone who stayed out of the sun, like someone who had never been in a fight. He knocked gently at my cell door.

"Hello," he said. He turned his head slightly to speak through the crack.

"Hey, Father."

"How are you today?"

"I'm all right."

"Anything I can pray for you?"

"Nah, that's alright."

"Anything you want to talk about?" His voice was thin as paper. On the streets I'd do nothing but clown on a man like this, but he came at the wrong time and I had heat in my chest and couldn't help it. The words came up without meaning to.

"I'd like to talk to my mom."

He nodded.

"I don't know if... I'd just like to talk to her is all."

"Have you spoken to her since you've been here?"

"Naw, she... no."

"I'll see what I can do."

"Thanks, Father."

"I'll try to call her for you."

"Yeah, yeah, good."

"And see what I can do."

I was done with him but the fool wouldn't leave; he wanted to draw me out, ask more questions. I shrugged and grunted until he grew tired of trying. Then I fell back to my bunk, slouched against the wall and tried not to think too much.

SATURDAY WAS VISITATION DAY. I WAS HANGING OUT with my homies in the multi-purpose room, talking to Little Weasel. I was clowning about something when a guard called my name.

It had to be my mom. I hurried over. I expected she'd yell at me; I'd get the talk about how I had to straighten up, but that'd be all right. Maybe my brother came too. Or my sister. I'd sit through a lecture to see them.

The guard didn't say anything as he led me through the doors. We passed the mirrored glass I remembered from the first night and I checked myself out. I thought I looked tough. I imagined Eric seeing me like this and wanted the guard to move quicker.

We came into a room I didn't know. Parents sat around plastic tables with inmates. I scanned the faces, not bothering to hide my smile. I couldn't find my family, but this didn't bother me. I figured they were out in the hallway waiting to be called in.

I kept smiling even as the guard led me to a table with a man already sitting at it. I didn't look at him, not really, not at first.

"Brad, have a seat."

It was Montoya, the gang counselor. I had no beef with him. He was fine, easy enough to talk to. The other homies liked him all right, but I didn't want to bother with him right then.

"I wanted to talk to you a bit, just you and me."

I stared towards the door, waiting.

"Brad?"

A sick feeling rose into my belly.

"I wanted to talk to you a bit."

Inside, I started to crumble. I asked, "Are you my visitor?"

He nodded. "I talked to your mom, Brad. She's worried about you."

I lowered my head and sunk into the chair.

"She's having a tough time. Working hard. Why are you making it harder for her?"

"I don't know," I mumbled. "I'm just doing my thing."

"Your mom is really worried about you."

"I'm just living, *ese.*"

I felt Montoya staring at me so I grabbed the edge of the table and twisted at it, pushing the flesh of my thumb into a shard of plastic.

"That's all you got?"

My mom hadn't come. My brother and sister hadn't come. All I wanted was to get out of that room.

I said, "I don't know, *ese.* I'm just living."

Montoya shook his head and gave me the speech about changing my life. When he was done, anger carried me back to the unit. I figured the Gideon messed me over, sold me out to Montoya. I figured I should never have talked to him; I should never have said anything to anyone about my mom. She wasn't coming. My family wasn't coming. I was on my own.

Back in the the multi-purpose room, the homies called my name. I forced a wide smile and slapped Little Weasel's outstretched hand.

THEY SAT ME DOWN ON ANOTHER PLASTIC CHAIR against a desk scratched to hell. Cinderblock on all sides, I pressed the phone to my ear and it smelled a bit like eggs.

"*Mijo*, it's so good to hear you." Hers was the first woman's voice I'd heard in a month; it triggered an emotion, a softness I had to fight back.

"Hi auntie." My voice echoed back to me.

"Are you calling from jail?"

"Yeah."

She was quiet for a moment then said, "Are they treating you good?"

I took a moment to think about how to answer. A week ago some NorthSide Redland fool slammed his tray against the back of Palone's neck. My homie's face went bright red as he spun from the table and jumped on the *vato*. With the rest of the homies, I leapt up and swung wildly at the nearest NSR fool, but I was too small to be worth much. I barely brushed him back before he pinned me down. I took a hard knee to the gut before the guards dragged him off me. We were in lockdown for several days, but the next time I saw Palone he told me I did good.

"It's all right," I said to my aunt, "but I want to go home."

There was another stretch of silence.

"They say I can go home but only when an adult picks me up."

"Didn't they tell your mom?"

They did. I had been scheduled for release two days before. I had barely slept I'd been so excited to get out. I rolled up my bedroll and told everyone at breakfast, all of the homies excited for me. I had held my own. I wasn't Verdugo yet but I had acted like one, they said. I grinned at them, feeling full of myself and ready to head back to the neighborhood.

Then I'd sat in the cell when everyone else went to school and felt each minute until finally an officer came down the hallway. The man started to pass my cell and I had to call through the crack, "Hey! Come to room nine! Hey! Room nine for Strain!"

"Yeah, Strain, what's up?"

"I'm supposed to be released today."

He had checked a clipboard. "It looks like that's right." He lifted his radio near his face and spoke into it. I couldn't hear what was said until he turned back to me. "Looks like we're waiting on your guardian."

"My mom's not here?"

"No one's here to pick you up. We can't release you unless you have a legal guardian or a parent to come and get you."

All the air left my lungs. I had sat on my bunk, lowered my head and waited. Morning passed into afternoon. That night I had to join my homies at chow, feeling stupid to still be there. I'd slapped on a smile and clowned about it, but inside I felt forgotten, rejected by my family. It didn't seem fair. My brother had been into the same things but he wasn't left to rot in jail. Somehow I was different. I was the throwaway kid.

Now, to my aunt I said, "Mom didn't show up."

She chewed on that for a long moment.

"Ok *mijo*. Let me talk to her."

"Could you come get me?"

"I'm not... I don't know how that would work."

"You're family."

"I know, but I... I'll have to look into it."

"I want to go home, Auntie. I'm not supposed to be here anymore." I said it with anger but also something else, something pathetic and weak that I hated.

"I know, Bradley. But with the holiday coming up, it might take a little time."

The holiday. Christmas was coming in a couple days. I knew this of course, but like a hazy memory. And one I didn't want to think about.

I returned to my cell and waited. The next day I called my aunt but she wasn't home. I left her a message. She called back at a time when I wasn't allowed to take the call.

Christmas came, but no one talked about it.

Finally, two days later, seven days after I was supposed to be released, I stepped out of the facility into the hot sun. My mom wasn't there, but my aunt held me close. She kissed me and left my cheek smeared with her tears.

She took me to a Jack in the Box and bought me a burger. She smiled sadly in a way that made me feel small. Then she pushed the empty wrappers to the side, wiped the table with her napkin and leaned onto her elbows. After a slow, serious shake of her head, she started in on another version of the talk. Mom was a single mother. She was trying hard and just couldn't handle it. I needed to clean up and change my ways.

All things I'd heard before, but I said, "I will. I promise. But I'd like to go home now."

She took a deep breath. "I'm sorry *mijo*, but you can't. Not today. You mom needs a break. But you could come stay with me for awhile."

I sucked on my straw and tried to shut down, but it was all too close. I wouldn't be going home. My mom didn't want me there anymore. I was a throwaway kid.

Luis

Two years later

WHEN I STEPPED off the airplane the heat blasted me so I could hardly breathe. I followed the line of people across the steaming tarmac into the terminal where the air conditioning hit me as hard as the heat.

My brother called, "There's my homeboy!" My mom said, "*Mi novio!*" My sister grinned and they all gave me hugs. Mom kissed me and squeezed me close and it all felt right. I was fifteen and hadn't seen any of them since before I was arrested for the dope. I'd spent the last year and a half living with my dad and grandma in Portland - but I didn't think about any of that. I was just happy to be back.

We drove back to the same neighborhood, the same apartment, and my mom made me tamales. We ate together as a family before Mom had to get to work.

After Mom left and my sister disappeared into her room, Eric leaned back from the table. He looked smaller than I remembered; he didn't seem to have the same swagger, the same weight, but he was still my big brother. He said "I got a surprise for you. You ready?"

"You know me." I grinned back; I was always grinning, "I'm ready for anything."

I followed him out into the night. We walked through the familiar streets; everything looked the same but a little different too - the trees a little bigger, new paint on some of the houses. As we walked, I talked, telling him about my time in Portland. Eric and I were half brothers so I told him about my grandma. She was a special woman, and living with her had mellowed me out. I told him about my friends Shawn and TJ, how we'd sneak beer and Playboys into a clubhouse we had tucked behind the paper factory. I told him about the trouble we'd get into. We'd steal car ornaments and tag the neighborhood, nothing big, just idiot kids having a good time.

Eric listened quietly, nodding sometimes. He didn't have much to tell me, which I expected. I already knew he'd moved out of the neighborhood. He was living with some white boy a few miles away. He had never been jumped into the set. Somewhere he had lost interest in the gang life, which made no sense to me.

I figured my big brother had gone soft, but then we turned the corner. Three houses down was Big Wheez's place. It was the heart of the set, where Wheez lived with his brother, Little Weasel.

"A few of the guys wanted to get together. Welcome you back." Eric showed me his grin again, pleased with himself. I smacked him on the shoulder with a whoop.

Music thumped from the garage. Their chihuahua spotted us and started yapping. I stepped across brown grass onto the cracked driveway. I took in the noise, the paint flaking from the siding, the dead bushes. Some fool was pissing against the fence. It felt like home.

The homies, most of the set, called out to me and waved me over.

I went first to Big Wheez. He was a brick wall, a bald Mexican man with a little fat starting to replace prison muscles. He was the big homie now, and had been for the past year. He ran the house and called the shots for our set, Los Dukes.

Big Wheez cocked his head and smiled real slow. "Little homie, you came back to us."

"You know it."

"That's good, *homes*. That's good."

He handed me a beer and I drifted, drinking, smoking and talking. My old friends slapped me around, listened to my stories, laughing about everything.

A few beers later I sat on the couch in the garage and one of the homies used a needle and a piece of string to give me a cross tattoo on my fist - it stood for brotherhood. I winced as he pinched the ink into my skin and cried out, clowning about the pain.

Aaron had showed up with Rocco, and they laughed with me. My old best friend said, "Hey Brad, how long you with us?"

"Forever, *homes*. I'm not leaving."

"Yeah?" Big Wheez had overheard. He said, "You going to be Verdugo?"

The Sureños was a Mexican gang run out of prisons. It was split up into geographic areas, mostly in California. We were in Verdugo, which spread inland from East L.A. Then this was split up into smaller neighborhood groups called sets. Ours was Los Dukes.

To Big Wheez, I said, "Yup. You know it."

The homies laughed and joked about jumping me in right then, everyone but Eric; he stared at the ground, looking sour and too sober.

But I didn't care about that. I had another beer and watched some homies play bones at the couches, hoping for a chance to get in on it, but they were all older than me so I needed to wait for one of them to leave.

"Hey Brad, good to have you back." Some man I didn't know was standing too close to me. He was older, in his early twenties; had a dark face, with a thin mustache. He was skinny as hell, some called him Flacco but he introduced himself as Luis.

"Good to be back."

"That's right," he said. "I heard about you. Aaron told me all about the car wreck. Sounds like it laid you out."

"Yup." I pulled up my shorts and showed him the dent. Behind him, more girls climbed out of a little truck.

"Heard you're down, *ese*," Luis said. "Heard you're solid."

"That's right, I am."

"Know not to talk to cops about shit they don't need to know about."

I didn't know where he was going with this but I continued to nod. He said, "You like cars?"

"Of course."

He gestured with his head and I followed him out front. A Monte Carlo with sweet rims had been parked in the middle of the driveway.

"How do you like my ride? I just got it last week."

I admired it, looking through the window. The steering wheel box had been ripped out and a bandana hung out from the lock, but I didn't say anything about that.

"It's a nice ride."

"Well, shit, if you like this, there's a car show coming up this weekend we should check out." Luis had a slick way of talking, low and smooth, kind of like my brother.

"Yeah, yeah, I'd like that."

I shrugged off and found my way back into the yard and pissed in the dirt. I looked over the house as I zipped up. The place was a hole. Everything was broken, or falling apart. The cops drove by slowly a couple times an hour. Still, it felt like home. With these guys it felt like home.

THE SUN CAST NO SHADOWS; IT WAS HIGHER AND hotter than I'd seen it in two years. The four of us were back together - Me, Eric, Aaron and Rocco - playing handball in the parking lot. The satisfying thunk against the garage door, hassling each other, giving my big brother a hard time, all of it like no time had passed.

The low thump of a a subwoofer echoed against the apartments and mixed with the whine of a beater car. We watched it cut through the parking lot; the brakes squeaked as it stopped next to us. Luis leaned out the window, grinning. He nodded at me; asked how we were doing. The four of us stopped the game and drifted over.

"What's this piece of shit?" I asked. "Where's the Monte Carlo?"

Aaron started laughing. "Brad, did this *vato* tell you that Monte Carlo was his? Come on, Luis ain't got no cars."

"What?" I said, playing it up like I was surprised.

"He steals that shit."

We were all laughing, Luis too. "Come on, *homes*. Why you gotta talk like that?"

I leaned on the car as the others shook their head and shuffled back.

"Hey," Luis said, "the expo's today. We need to check out the lowriders."

"Yeah, yeah," I said, "that'd be cool."

"We need to hang out, *ese*. You should check if your boys want to go."

"All right."

Luis drove off and I rejoined the handball game. We started it up again, the four of us playing, everything all right.

"That *vato*, Luis," I said. "He's all right."

"Yeah, he's cool."

"He was saying we should go to that car show. Maybe get the homies together and get out there, you know, check it out."

Aaron and Rocco nodded, but Eric went quiet.

I said to him, "What do you think?"

"Yeah," he said. "Sounds good." But his heart didn't seem into it. "Yeah, that's cool."

A few hours later we rolled up to the expo with some of the homies. Little Weasel and Miguel, with Eric, Aaron and Rocco. We parked, then walked through the hot sun, the bunch of us dressed out in Sureño blue, music playing around us. We passed through the crowd, mostly car guys out with their families. We checked out the lowriders, just out to have a good time, causing no trouble.

We walked the length of the show, then draped ourselves on a picnic bench near the food carts. We talked through the different cars, comparing the ones we liked, bragging about the one we'd someday own. Eric had slouched off to the bathroom when Luis showed up, skinny as hell and grinning under his mustache.

"There's the fool," Rocco said. "What you driving today?"

"I got something nice, I'll have to show you." And then to me, "Hey *ese*. What do you think?"

"It's good. I like it."

"What did I tell you? Listen Brad, we got to hang out some time."

"Yeah, yeah. I'm up for anything."

I was always up for anything and Luis seemed like someone who'd know how to find some trouble. I'd hang out with anyone who promised some chaos.

"Let's do it tonight."

I said, "Yeah, yeah, I'd be down for that," and we shook hands as Eric came back, glaring over at us, giving me the dead eye, not happy.

I shrugged him off. This *vato*, Luis, had some crazy in his eyes and he seemed to know some things that I was eager to learn.

31

I turned away from Eric and said, "Let's do it."

LUIS HAD ONE HAND ON THE WHEEL, THE OTHER ON the forty in his lap as we cruised through quiet neighborhoods. He had turned us off the main road twenty minutes earlier, but didn't say what we were doing. I had been doing most of the talking. I told him about the car accident, working the story. I made the whir of the engine in my throat. I pumped my arms when I described my sprint down the alleyway. Luis laughed at the right places, said, "Oh shit," when the car slammed into me. I told him about lying to the cops, and he nodded.

"Yeah, that's right, Strain. That's right."

He pulled into a McDonald's parking lot.

"So you know..." He glanced over at me. "I'm into stealing cars."

A light burst inside me. Like that, the stakes had just been raised. I was eager, ready to get into it, but played it cool.

"Yeah, I kind of figured that out."

"You did, huh?" He nodded at the restaurant. "You want something?"

"I could eat."

He pressed some bills into my hand and told me to order whatever I wanted. I grabbed us a couple burgers and some cokes. He didn't ask for the change.

I ate as he drove, circling blocks. I watched the way he examined parked cars as we passed. I didn't know exactly what he was looking for, but it didn't matter. I felt like a predator hunting for prey.

"You ever steal a car?"

"I did some jockey boxing, that's about it."

"This is better. You don't just get a little pocket change and some shitty ass stereo. You get the whole car."

"Hell ya."

We pulled down a street I didn't know. Palm trees towered over us. The houses were in good shape. The lawns were mowed and green. I opened my window and tasted the desert air. It was dark, quiet, and we cruised, not too slow, taking it easy and talking. Finally, Luis pulled into a dark spot far from any street lights.

"All right, follow me."

I hopped out without asking any questions. I was happy to go along wherever the night took me, curious more than anything about what was coming.

We cut through a yard, trotting through the darkness. Luis ducked under a clothesline and gestured to watch out. We hopped a low cinderblock wall, crossed the alley then the next wall into another yard. Luis scaled a short chain link fence and I followed, shoving my foot into a low hole and swinging my foot over. I moved quickly, all while trying to make as little noise as possible.

I worried about dogs, listening for them, but mostly felt light and a little giddy. This was what I wanted: real gangster action.

About six blocks from where we parked, we stopped near a Honda Prelude covered in shadow. The windows in the nearest houses were dark.

Luis said, "Watch this." And he showed me a quick flash of white. "It's from a spark plug," he said and he whipped it at the window. With a sharp thunk, cracks spiderwebbed across the glass. I gave a low whistle. It was as satisfying as a magic trick.

Luis pushed at the window. He started delicately, almost gentle with it until the glass shattered under his fingers. Shards scattered into the car, and the alarm began to wail. Brake lights flashed in the empty street. I flinched back, not fully understanding. Luis was already running. He was almost to the corner before my brain kicked in.

Luis whisper-screamed back, "Let's move, *homes*. We gotta go."

A shot of fear pumped through me. I followed him back to the chain link fence and leapt over it. I crossed the alley and hurdled the cinderblock wall, then glanced back. I saw the flashing lights, heard the horn, but no sirens. In the shadows, I felt safe, but still, I sped up, sprinting across a lawn until I spotted Luis duck a half-step ahead of me. I lowered my head right before a clothes line took it off.

A few blocks later we jumped into his car. Luis leaned against the headrest and gasped for breath.

"Listen, *homes*," he panted, "that's not how it's supposed to go."

"Yeah, yeah."

"That was fucked up. Shit."

Luis was embarrassed and I was disappointed. This *vato* didn't know what he was doing; he was just another drunk fool with nothing to offer. He pulled away from the curb, taking it easy now, in no hurry. As we drove, I became more than disappointed. I could have gone to prison for that, for nothing. It had been stupid to come.

"We'll have to try again."

"Yeah, yeah." I said. "Another night."

As we pulled onto the street which would lead us back home, I heard a police siren from several blocks away.

HEADLIGHTS DRIFTED THROUGH THE LOT, THEN stopped right outside. Luis leaned out of an older sedan, the third car I'd seen him drive.

"Hey, Strain, what you got going on tonight?"

I was sitting on the weight bench in Rocco's garage. I'd been back for only a few weeks and it was still a novelty hanging out with my friend, talking about whatever came up in my head, drinking a little, smoking a little, but mostly chilling. We kept the door open and a little breeze cut through the heat.

I turned to Rocco. "We got anything?"

He shrugged.

"All right, *homes*. I'm going to kick it with Luis a little bit."

Rocco shrugged again. I shuffled towards the car, but as I reached for the door, I heard Eric's voice behind me.

"Brad, where you going?"

He was standing under a street light in the parking lot. He had his hands shoved in his pockets but he looked tense.

"I'm heading off with Luis."

"Well shit, you better make sure you're back early."

"What the hell you talking about?"

Eric scratched at his head. "Mom's home tonight. You gotta get in early."

I stared at my brother, confused. He no longer lived there, and what he was saying made no sense. Mom was probably working but if she was home she'd be on her pills, prescription medicine for anxiety which knocked her out. Either way she wouldn't notice no matter where I was.

"Just... don't stay out too late."

"All right, big brother," I said it slowly, not sure what we were talking about. I felt his eyes on me until we pulled out of the parking lot.

We drove a few minutes and I quickly forgot about Eric. Soon we stopped at a fast food restaurant where Luis gave me money to buy some burgers. From there, we didn't wander around side streets like the first time. Instead, Luis drove like he knew where he was going.

And I was quieter. I felt tense and uncertain. It had been about two weeks since the disaster with the Honda and I hadn't seen Luis at all in that time. I didn't trust him, not fully, but I was willing to see where the night was going to go.

We pulled into a nicer neighborhood. Our car didn't belong on the street and it didn't seem smart. The tension spread into my chest, but I kept my mouth shut as Luis pulled down a dark corner and parked.

Again, we crept through the shadows, block after block, maybe a half mile until we paused under a tree. Luis nodded towards a Cadillac parked under a car port. It looked new, expensive, and I found myself grinning, my criminal brain responding like a wolf creeping up on a deer.

Luis trotted across the street, no cars coming, everything quiet, the house dark. He stopped next to the car and rested his hand on the window, peering in. I stood next to him, watched with mounting excitement as he pulled a wire hanger and a door stop out of a little bag and started to work.

As he went, he described what he was doing in a loud whisper. He pried a space between the window and the door and shoved the wire hanger down. To my eyes, he seemed an expert, perfectly in control of the situation and I laughed when the door popped open like a miracle.

Luis grunted back and gestured me in. I shuffled over to the passenger seat and Luis hunched down behind the wheel, closing the door softly. Both of us low, he shoved a dent puller under the ignition - again explaining every step. He yanked down so the bottom panel came off the steering wheel. He pulled out a cluster of wires, separated them, and pointed out the colors with a finger.

I couldn't help popping my head up every few seconds to check for lights, but otherwise I watched, fascinated. It puffed me up, this older homie taking the time on me, teaching me a skill.

"All right, *homes*, you tap these together and…"

The car hummed to life. Luis gave a little whoop, sat up and reversed the car out of the driveway.

"That's it, that is the way you do it. That last time was fucked up. That never happens. That never happens, *ese*. This is how it's done."

He whooped again and I laughed with him; we were predators taking down a beast.

Out of the neighborhood, back on a major street, Luis continued to teach me. He explained the different tools; told me how they worked, and what to do.

"Make sure you always check. Don't unlock a door that's not locked, you know."

He didn't tell me where we were heading. It was late, after one in the morning when we rumbled over a set of train tracks on the far side of San Bernardino and nosed up to a warehouse. There were no lights on the building nearby on the street. Luis parked in a shadow in front of the garage and said, "Let's do it. Come on."

He banged on a side door. I stood back, not sure where we were. A light came through the crack under the door but there was no sounds until we heard a click and the deadbolt released.

I followed Luis into a small garage, low-ceilinged and shallow. It smelled of dust with a sharp tang of gasoline. A little Honda took up most of the space, its hood open, the engine missing. A man leaned back on a wheeled office chair. His long hair flowed back past his shoulders. He scratched at his face with dirty hands as he mean-mugged me.

"Who's the kid?"

"He's cool, don't worry about him."

"Yeah?" He talked to Luis but kept glaring at me. "What you got for me?"

"Take a look."

Back outside, the man walked around the Cadillac. He said, "Shit. You got it nice."

"That's right, *homes*." Luis grinned over at me, stretched his hands out and said, "That's the way I do it."

The two stepped into the garage and closed the door with me outside. It was late. I was in a strange neighborhood. The night grew cold, but it was nothing. I leaned against the wall, let it block the wind. I rubbed my hands together and shoved them deep in my pockets. I didn't know how long I'd be out there, but Luis knew and that was all I needed. As far as I could tell, this homie had it figured out.

"Come on, Brad." The two had stepped out and I followed them around the side of the garage to a little truck. The man drove us back across town. I was squeezed in the back seat, shivering from the wind pouring through the windows. He dropped us off outside Luis' car.

The man left us and Luis was feeling good, laughing at nothing, happy with himself.

"Shit, *homes*," he said, "that's how it's supposed to work."

Ten minutes later he dropped me off outside my mom's apartment. It was an easy climb to the second floor and I crawled like Spider Man onto the balcony where I slid open my bedroom door. I crept in, the apartment quiet, and collapsed into bed. No one noticed; or if they did, no one cared.

I WAS PLAYING DICE AT BIG WHEEZ'S HOUSE, BUT feeling itchy. I was always restless, always wanted to keep moving, and I was thinking about finding Luis. I wanted to head out, smoke, drink a little. And Luis was cool. He hadn't shared any of the money he got for the Cadillac with me, but every few days over the last couple weeks he'd show up and drive me around. He bought me beer and gave me weed. He'd check in while we cruised, ask if I needed anything, buy me cheeseburgers. He got a me a t-shirt once.

My brother, however, had changed. He was there with me, sitting on the ratty couch talking to Big Wheez and some of the others, but he kept backing off farther and farther from the gang life. He had a job at the mall and seemed like he was chilling there more than anywhere else. I didn't like that. And every time I'd go off with Luis he'd say something about it, so I had stopped telling him. I glanced at him now and thought about doing it again: just get up and go.

But before I could move, Big Wheez waved me to him.

"Hey, Brad, get over here."

They were all sitting around the couch: Big Wheez, my brother, Rocco and Miguel. I hadn't done anything wrong that I could think of, but to have the older homies stare like that made me sweat. Big Wheez gestured to his brother, Little Weasel, "Give my boy here a chair."

Weasel moved and I sunk next to my big homie.

Big Wheez flicked his chin towards my brother. "Eric told me you been hanging with Luis."

"Me and Luis, we was just chilling."

"We know he's into stealing cars and shit."

I shrugged and started to shut down. It didn't matter that these were my friends; I knew an interrogation when I heard it.

"We're just chilling."

"We think you should cool it with this *vato*. Don't be hanging out with him like that."

"Luis?"

"We got no beef with him, but he's not in Los Dukes. He's not Sureño, understand? And you're still a little homie."

"All right."

"We're looking out for you."

I understood it. He didn't like me stealing cars and making money for Luis instead of them. And I wasn't going to argue, not with Big Wheez. I was hoping to get jumped into the set soon.

But I also figured there was more to it than money. I tried to make eye contact with Eric but he slouched next to Big Wheez as if bored. Still, I knew this was coming more from him than anyone. Eric was treating me like a child, like he was a worried mother. I didn't know what happened, but somewhere my brother had lost his edge.

I HEARD A SOFT KNOCK FROM THE BALCONY. I HAD been in bed almost sleeping, but dragged myself up to peer out the window. Luis grinned back at me from the darkness. "Hey, *ese*, you want to roll?"

Big Wheez had given me a lecture on this only a few hours earlier, and his warning passed through my thoughts for about a half second.

"Let's do it," I said.

Minutes later, after I had thrown on a shirt and jumped from the balcony, we were in another rusted-out car, cruising through empty streets.

"I got something special planned tonight."

"That's cool."

We stopped for a burger, smoked a bit, had some drink, then drove until it was late, well after midnight. We slowed up by a sporty Nissan, a brand new 300z, then Luis sped ahead. He finally parked in a shadow a half-mile away.

We crept back through the lawns and alleys. When we approached the car Luis put the screwdriver in my hand.

"You got this one."

I swallowed a rush of pride and said, "That's right."

I shoved the screwdriver in the lock, wiggled it like Luis had showed me, then yanked down. It popped on the first try and I grinned like an idiot.

"That's what I'm talking about."

I opened the door and started to climb towards the passenger seat but Luis laid his hand on my shoulder.

"Naw, Brad, you got this one, hear me."

"That's right."

He slid over to the passenger seat and I sat behind the wheel. He directed me, explained how this kind of car could be started with a screwdriver. Without hesitating, I popped it in and twisted until the engine turned over.

"Nice work, kid."

I laughed, feeling lit up inside. Luis nodded forward, telling me to drive. I was fifteen. I didn't have a permit and if I did, no one would have bothered to teach me. But Luis didn't know that. The car jerked forward onto the street.

"Whoa! Slow down."

"Yeah, yeah. I got it."

I braked too hard at the stop sign. The car spoke Please fasten your seatbelt in a woman's voice.

I said, "What the hell was that?"

"Turn signal! Shit."

"I got it."

"Lot of new cars have that. Pull down this way."

I drove down a wide street, a major road. It was late, but the few other cars on the road streaked past us.

"Speed up a little."

"Yeah, yeah."

"Watch the - fuck! Pull here. Here!"

I turned us too fast into a gas station and braked so both our heads lurched forward.

"Not bad, kid," Luis laughed. "But, shit, where did you learn to drive?"

"I didn't."

"You serious?"

"Yeah."

"Well damn. That was pretty good then."

"That's right."

"Looks like we got to teach you, huh."

"Yeah, yeah."

"But that was good back there. You got the touch."

An unfamiliar warmth spread into my cheeks. I was learning something and had someone looking out for me. A bright hum rumbled through me as Luis drove me back to the apartment.

"That's how you do it," I muttered. "That's right."

WOBBLY ON MY LEGS, MY HEAD FOGGY FROM SLEEP, I stumbled to the window and opened the blinds to see Luis. He wore sunglasses though it was one in the morning and I couldn't help but smile. I opened the window a crack and said, "Give me a minute."

I rubbed my eyes. I was groggy, but Luis had been gone for a few weeks so I was ready for an adventure. I was eager to find a nice car parked in the wrong place at the wrong time.

Within minutes, we were cruising through the night. Luis has his own car now, purchased legally. He rattled off about the engine and suspension and sound system and it was good to hear him, good to be in the car, good to be outside. With a hot breeze blowing through the windows and Kid Frost on the radio, my world was full.

"Where've you been, *homes*?" It had been about three weeks since we stole the Nissan. "It's been some time."

"Ah, you know." He rolled his hand in a small circle. "Family business."

I didn't know, but he didn't explain so I let it go. We were slowing outside a Jack in the Box. Luis sent me in to get burgers and let me keep the change. We ate as we made circles around a grocery store, Luis chewing loudly as he leaned out the window to peer at something. I didn't know what he was looking for, but I was vibrating with energy. I wanted to feel that fat clunk again when I twisted the screwdriver, feel the lock give way and hop behind the wheel.

Third time around, he pulled into the parking lot. Luis tossed the empty burger wrappers in the back seat, and climbed out. I quickly followed.

The city was quiet. There was no one in the street and only a few other cars parked around us. Lights glowed through the windows of the grocery store, but the place looked deserted.

Luis nodded towards a low-rider on the other side of the lot. "This way, *homes*."

"What about your car?"

"We'll get a ride back, it's cool."

He moved with a strange rhythm: back straight, elbows locked, almost at a trot. I stooped down and followed a few steps behind. I felt uneasy. We were exposed, anyone from the grocery store could look out and see us, but Luis didn't seem worried so I tried not to think about it.

Luis whistled as we drew close to his mark.

"Oh yeah, yeah, yeah. Look at that shit. Check out those wheels, kid."

They were gold Daytons, the wheels every big baller wanted, and even in the darkness they looked like sunbursts.

"Check that out." Luis' voice went low and lusty like he was checking out a girl. Without slowing a step, he windmilled his arm to throw the spark plug hard at the window.

It spiderwebbed neatly. Luis shoved his elbow into the glass and it fell inside. Another smooth movement and the door clicked open. He slid in, leaned across and unlocked the passenger side so I could join him. No alarms, no troubles, no lights in the rear view mirror. We took off free and clear.

No problem.

41

Luis puffed up. "It's stupid easy. These cars, this shit, it's easy if you know what you're doing."

I sunk into the seat, nodding, feeling good. I was in the presence of a master and learning some serious skills.

"Shit," he said. "Get you going, get you doing these solo. We can create ourselves a damn syndicate. Start doing this every night. Make us some money."

"Yup."

"You ain't afraid of money are you?"

"Naw, I'm not."

"That's right."

I felt like I had lucked into my future. I imagined myself with a fleet of cars, showing them off to Rocco and Eric. I imagined giving my mom a Cadillac, acting sly when she asked where I got it because in the fantasy she wouldn't really care.

I was quiet for a few minutes, thinking these things, until Luis pulled onto the 10, took it west towards downtown San Bernardino.

"Where we going?"

"To Fortuna. I got someone who'll help me with these wheels."

I nodded, leaned my elbow out the window. The wind swirled around us and I turned up the music. Another hot night, the city lights cast a soft glow against the clouds. In the side mirror I saw the flashing colors before Luis did and snapped my head around.

"Hey Luis, we got cops."

"It's no problem. There's always cops on the freeway."

I checked his speed; he was going with the flow of traffic, a few miles over the limit. I relaxed. He was right. Nothing to worry about. I settled back and waited for the lights to streak by.

They came up quickly, quietly, but didn't pass. Instead, they changed lanes and slowed down right behind us.

"Oh shit," I said. "Oh shit. Luis."

Luis eyed them in the rearview.

"Ain't you pulling over?"

He set his face hard and lowered his chin. My heart started thumping in my chest, understanding what he was about to do in the half-second before he stomped the gas. The car lurched, my head slapped back and Luis started overtaking, swerving through cars. I immediately leaned into the moment, no thoughts past the next second.

The cops fell back but not enough.

"They're still back there," I said.

"No shit. We gotta get off the highway."

We couldn't out-drive them, but if we could get to a neighborhood, get a block or two on them, we could lose them on foot.

"Ah fuck! Fuck!" He banged the steering wheel. "I got my gun on me." Closing in on 100, the car wobbling underneath us, he pulled the gun from his pocket and bent forward, shoving it under his seat.

We came up on Main Street, the sirens surrounding us from more cops, at least three cruisers. The lowrider whined, not meant for this speed.

"Here!" I cried, and pointed at the exit. Luis braked barely and we hurtled down the ramp. Surface streets empty, we skidded onto Main and blasted through a stop light. The cops followed a car length behind. Two blocks up at E Street, he pulled hard at the intersection. I buzzed, body shoved into the window, my head empty except for cursing and adrenaline. We squealed past a Lucky's Grocery and slammed into the far curb. The back tire popped over it and - with the sound of a gunshot - it blew out. The car shuddered, Luis lost control and we fishtailed to a hard stop against a little tree.

The engine hummed. Luis cursed. Sirens blared from every direction, but I figured I had a chance. I needed to open the door. Lights flashed on our windows but if I could get my head together and start sprinting - I was fast. I could outrun the police, but I needed a moment to clear my head. If I had a few seconds to breathe, I could grab the door handle and bolt.

I blinked and Luis was gone. His door gaped open and angry men were screaming orders just outside. I watched with horror as they dragged him kicking into the grass. Like a nightmare, I was frozen until hands tore me out of the car and threw me down onto the pavement.

A knee fell into my back. I wrenched my neck to see Luis's face slammed against the hood. Around us cops were barking so I couldn't understand, but Luis bugged his eyes out at me. He shook his head a fraction, a warning to say nothing, to keep my damn mouth shut.

Verdugo for Life
Three hours later

I CLENCHED MY fists, digging my nails into my palms, and pushed them into my forehead. The walls were tight, the ceiling too low. I didn't belong there; I'd just been along for the ride. I needed to get out, go wander some dark street, but they had caged me up again. I'd have to ask permission to take a piss for the next... I had to stop and rest my head against the door.

I wasn't driving. I gripped on to the those three words like a drowning man. It was Luis who broke the window. It was Luis who drove the car. It was Luis who sped away. Of course I didn't tell them that. I had kept my mouth shut. I had said, "You *houdas* don't know nothing," even as one of the cops spit-screamed in my ear. Still, I hadn't been driving. I was barely involved. I was pretty much an innocent bystander, so this couldn't be a big deal.

I paced for hours before collapsing on the bunk. It felt like a blink and the lights clicked up, which they did thirty minutes before chow. I took a breath, disoriented for a moment. But when I stood, it all became familiar and I eased into the routine. I found it strangely comforting. In twenty minutes a guard would clang on the doors and tell us to get ready. Then we'd stand outside our cells. We'd check each other out, looking for anything different from the night before. When ordered, we'd follow the line, ready for a breakfast of slop.

It went as expected. I stepped into the hallway when the guard called us out. Last time I stood a foot shorter than the rest and had to force my head to raise. But now I was fifteen and had come back cocky.

I spotted Palone first. It was a coincidence. Like me, he was back in the juvenile center again after being out for almost two years. On the outside, he kept himself looking sharp, but they didn't bring razors often to the juvenile inmates, so he looked greasy in the fluorescent light and had a patchy beard. He gave me a grin and shook his head as a way of saying, 'what can you do?'

I grinned back and puffed out my chest. I was seen and known. I had homies here. I'd be all right.

I followed the line to breakfast in the multi-purpose room. There was little chatter first thing in the morning. A guard handed me a tray and I walked to the table. They expected us to take the first chair, but I held back to let the inmate behind me pass. I wanted to sit closer to Palone.

He gave me a nod. "There's my boy, Strain. What they got you in here for?"

I told him some of the story of last night.

"GTA? Whoo," he said. "You'll get some time for that."

I took a mouthful of mush and shook my head. "Naw, *ese*, I wasn't driving."

"I don't think that matters."

Heat started to spread through my chest. I felt it rising into my cheeks but shook it off. I told myself Palone didn't know nothing. Repeated it quietly a few times. The fool didn't know a thing about the law. It calmed me down.

"Hey, this is my little homie, Strain," Palone introduced me to the table. They nodded at me, inmates named Sinner and Casper. One homie named Loco didn't speak. He was older, had to be close to eighteen. He shaved his head bald and his face smooth, so I figured he must have been a tier-tender who had better access to supplies. He studied me with dark, heavy-lidded eyes, and I knew without Palone telling me that he was in charge.

Palone said, "A couple years back we got in a riot with the NSR, and Strain threw down with us."

"Yeah, I was there," I said, "but I wasn't much help."

45

They laughed like I was joking.

I said, "They beat the crap out of me. It was crazy." I felt at home, comfortable, so I played it up, clowning some.

"Naw, you was down, *homes*."

"All right," I said. "All right."

After breakfast, I returned to my cell and met my roommate. He was a young paisa from Mexico with a wide face and a dusting of hair on his chin. He smiled at me and nodded but didn't speak much English. When it came time for school, he left and I was told to stay back and wait for my arraignment.

I had hours to kill and no cards, no homemade dice, nothing on hand, so I sat on the paisa's bunk and flipped through a bible. Then I paced. I did pushups. I stared out the window. I paced again. Through all of it, I wished I were anywhere else.

ON TUESDAY MORNING I TOOK A DESK TOWARDS THE back of the classroom and studied the shape of the massive Mexican kid's head in front of me. For a few minutes I wondered where his neck was, then I got bored of that and stared out the window. It was southern California. It was always sunny, every day, and the windows looked over an orange grove. An acre or two of trees separated us from the city.

I wanted to go home.

And I still expected them to release me. It made no sense for them to charge me for riding in a passenger seat. At the trial they'd see I was just in the wrong place at the wrong time. I would be home by the weekend.

I had said as much to the priest on Sunday. After church, he had sat down next to me, placed his hand on my arm, and gave me this look, like he understood something about me deeper than I did. I had to look away.

"Brad. What's going on?"

And for a dangerous moment I wanted to be honest with this man. I wanted to see if he had any answers, but the moment quickly passed.

"Nothing," I said. "Just trying to stay out of trouble."

"You're not doing a very good job of it."

"Pfft. These *houdas* have it out for me."

He nodded. "Can I come talk to you sometime?"

"Naw, Father. I won't be here long enough."

"Of course," the priest said, "But... you know there's always a 'but.'"

"Yeah, yeah. But if I'm still here then, yeah, I'll talk to you."

The old priest had thanked me for coming to Mass and moved on to another inmate. I'd been so sure they'd send me home, but now, two days later, I was still there, back in school at juvenile hall, staring out at the orange trees.

The teacher told us it was break time, releasing us into noise and movement. The different cliques gathered in different areas around the room. Whites clustered in one corner, blacks in another. Our rivals, the Northside Redland fools, were on the far side. I stood with the Sureños.

Loco was our leader; we'd say he had the keys. He was shorter but massive, all muscle. He rolled up his jumpsuit to make them more like shorts.

He stared at us stony faced as we clowned. "We need more homies," he said and the others shut up. "We're low on numbers." He looked at me. "What do you think, Strain? You want in?"

It was all I had wanted for years and I had to fight back my grin. "Yup," I said it without hesitation, but it didn't feel strong enough, so I added, "Hell ya."

My boy, Palone, grinned down at me. "That's right," he said. "The little homie is down."

Loco nodded and leaned back against the wall. I quieted, listening to the rest of them talk while raw energy coiled in my chest. I hated being locked up but I had an opportunity in front of me. To be jumped into the set, to be a part of the gang, it was everything. I just needed to not screw it up.

Break time over, the teacher walked to the front of the class. Before I started back to my seat, I glanced over at Loco, ready for anything. He lowered his head and spoke quietly.

"Strain, stab that big motherfucker with your pencil."

Again, I didn't hesitate, but said, "Yeah, yeah, Loco. You got it."

I sat at my desk and the classroom disappeared. All I saw was the big fool lowering himself into his seat. He had fifty pounds on me and

47

a few inches, but I didn't care. I wondered blankly if Loco had a beef with him, if there was some deeper motivation for this, but I didn't care much. Loco told me to do it, so it was done.

My heart thumped so I could feel it in my face. The teacher called for our attention and I gripped my pencil, the point hella sharp. The *vato* had leaned over so what passed as a neck became exposed over his jumpsuit. I spent a few seconds studying the fine hairs leading up to the base of the fool's head. I glanced at Loco.

No thought, no hesitation, I raised off the chair and brought my pencil down full weight just above his shoulder. It sunk in to the yellow paint.

He leapt up screaming. I fell back, a laugh bubbling up through my chest. He shoved his desk over as he slapped a hand against his neck but the pencil kept moving with him just out of reach. It reminded me strangely of a sparkler, the orange eraser dancing around until the big man finally swatted it off.

The whole classroom had shoved back from their desks, laughing or shouting. The fool stood over me, screaming, "What the fuck?"

The violence, the noise, the audience, it set my brain on fire. Every part of me was buzzing, but I shrugged, acting easy, relaxed.

I said, "Pfft."

The guard had run over with a second behind him, pushing people back.

The big man shouted, "He stuck me in the neck!"

The guard gripped my arm and pushed me towards the back. I barely felt it.

"Get against the wall, Strain."

"What?" I raised my hands, still grinning. "I didn't do nothing."

"The wall. Now."

I leaned against the wall and held there. They put me in cuffs. I'd spend some time in lockdown but that was nothing. As they led me out of the classroom, I caught a glance of Palone standing with the homies. They were laughing - and that was all that mattered.

I was in.

———

48

THE PAISA WAS MAKING PICTURE FRAMES OUT OF MILK cartons on his bunk. I couldn't talk to him; he didn't speak English and my Spanish was mangled, but we nodded at each other. I'm a talker; I like an audience, but I didn't hold it against him. He was young, fourteen maybe, and a good cellie.

It was my third day of lockdown and I was reading a Louis L'Amour book. I had picked one up my last time at Gilbert. The old west, a good guy fighting a bad guy, a pretty girl. I was into it.

Good guys and bad guys. I didn't think about it too much, but I figured I was a bad guy, and that was all right. I wore the black hat. I was the villain, the gangster. I ran the streets.

Except that didn't always fit. I loved my family and treated most people with respect. I helped old ladies with their groceries. Most of the trouble I got into was harmless, stupid stuff. The only one who usually got hurt was me.

I leaned my head against the wall. I figured I was just living, just doing what I had to do to survive. I didn't know if I'd make it as a true villain.

The music came on over the speaker like it did every night, and I closed the book and got down on the floor to do my push ups. I'd work out as long as the music played. It was part of being a Sureño. They were warriors. They didn't tolerate weakness, and I needed to be ready.

I rolled over to do sit ups and saw the paisa following me. After the sit-ups, I hopped up for a series of jumping jacks then burpees then high knees. The paisa followed, keeping up. Back to push ups, and I went harder, laughing now, seeing what he could do.

He kept with me until the music cut out. I rested my hands on my knees and nodded at the paisa who gave me a funny salute. It had been a good workout but now it was time to talk to the homies.

My first cellie, David, had showed me the trick. He covered the toilet with the plastic part of his pillow and plunged the bottom with his knee as he pulled down the handle. This kept the drain open. Then he leaned his head into the bowl and talked to others who had done the same in their cells. Their voices carried through the pipes.

I followed the steps and heard voices. It was like a party line so there was a lot of chatter, but underneath the bullshit I could hear Palone.

"Strain?"

"Yeah, I'm here."

"You are crazy, *ese*. You more loco than Loco."

"You know it."

"Hear that boy scream?"

"I heard it."

I heard another voice; it was Loco. "He knows now. That big fool knows."

Palone said, "Yup."

"We can get to him," Loco said. "He knows it. Knows he's not safe."

"That's right."

I was kneeling with my head in a toilet but felt a sick pride. I hadn't hesitated when it came time to act. I'd done it for my set.

"We'll talk, Strain. When you're out of lockdown we'll talk."

"That's cool." I leaned back on my heels and grinned. I'd been there for less than a week but I'd made my mark.

The paisa had been watching me, a strange look on his face. I stood up and the paisa moved to the sink. He shoved a towel down the drain and turned it on.

"What you doing?"

The paisa didn't answer but stared silently as water filled up the sink until it started splashing over onto the floor.

"What the hell, little homie?"

The water spread across the concrete. I stepped back, worried my cellie had gone crazy but not minding. Whatever this was, it was different. It was something new, a story to tell.

The water inched its way under the bunks. The paisa grabbed another towel and shoved it against the crack at the bottom of the door.

I said, "You are crazy."

The paisa laughed and waved his hand. He grabbed his sheet and blanket and tied them together to make a rope.

After a few minutes, we had about a half an inch covering the floor. The paisa took off his shoes and stepped into the water.

I had no idea what was going on, but I was grinning at all of it. He gestured me over and I stepped out of my sandals into the water. It was ice cold. The paisa shoved one end of his rope a foot or two down into the toilet and then pointed at the handle.

50

He walked to the other side of the cell near the door, the water sloshing under him. He grabbed the sheet tight and gave me a nod.

"Yes," he said.

I flushed, the suction pulled the sheet into the toilet, and the Paisa water-skied about three feet across the floor. He shouted "Woo!" and I started laughing. "Woo!" he shouted again and I had to sit down, laughing so hard I couldn't breathe.

He gestured towards me with the rope. I stood and leaned towards the door, pulling the sheet tight. It was the stupidest thing and we'd get screamed at in about five minutes, but I wiped my eyes on my sleeve, rolled my shoulders back and gave him a nod.

I COULD HEAR SOME CHATTER FROM THE TIER, BOYS clowning nearby. The door was finally open. I was out of lockdown.

It hadn't been that bad. For stabbing a fool with a pencil, I got five days of hanging with the paisa and that was it. I faced down their punishment no problem. I stood, stretching my back, feeling like I could handle anything they threw at me.

I felt invincible but needed a shower. I threw a towel around my neck and turned to my bunk to grab shampoo. When I turned back there were four guys in my cell. Palone stood closest, muscles clenched, eyes wide. The other three fidgeted behind him, one was grinning. Violent energy crackled between them.

"Are you ready for this?"

Even startled, I knew the answer to that question. "I'm ready for anything."

Palone's fist came heavy across my jaw, not holding back. I stumbled to my bunk and the others fell over me with kicks and punches. Thirteen seconds they said, but the seconds stretched closer to a minute as the blows landed. I tried to fight back but the first punch had dazed me and I was swinging blindly. I connected with nothing but air and took another kick to the ribs. An elbow knocked me to the ground, and I rolled furious on my side, humiliated to keep taking their hits without landing a single one of my own.

Hands yanked me hard by the jumpsuit, lifting me to my feet. Palone held me high, my toes barely touching the ground. My body

51

buzzed with violence, but the *vato* grinned at me, almost laughing.

"You in, Strain."

The others started cheering.

"You're in. You're Verdugo."

The rage drained out of me in a moment, leaving me dizzy.

Palone released me. He said, "Go take your shower, *homes*."

The four left me in my cell. I gathered my towel from the ground, and felt the first hints of pain under the adrenaline. I touched my finger to my cheek and winced.

I shuffled to the shower and took a long moment to stare at myself. The mirror was scratched to hell and distorted my face, but I could make out a red mark under my eye which would soon turn purple. As I gently probed at it, I began to worry.

I took the beating but hadn't dished anything out, not a single hit. I didn't know if that'd be good enough. Palone said I was in, but not Loco. Loco hadn't been there and when he heard what happened he might think differently. If that happened, there wouldn't be a second chance. I'd be out.

Shit.

The warm water streaked across my bruises and eased every muscle. I stood there as long as I was allowed, not wanting to leave. I'd gone through it. I'd been jumped in, but that wasn't the hard part. Now I had to find out if I was accepted.

Finally, I dried off, dressed up, hung my towel and moved to the multi-purpose room. As I climbed down the stairs I saw Palone and the others playing foosball with Loco. I quickly looked away.

But my homies spotted me and cheered. Someone said, "Ooh Loco, you better watch out, this youngster, he's on it." And they gave me my props, giving me the handshake and welcoming me.

Loco watched, his face grim, saying nothing. But when the others were done, he put his hand on my shoulder.

"Strain, pull over here."

He led me a few steps away. There, he grabbed my hand, stared me in the eye, and did the handshake.

This older homie, tough as hell and smart, with his dark face and bright bald head, he said, "You're Verdugo for life, Strain."

I grinned so hard the bruise under my eye hurt.

"You hear me?"

"Yeah, Loco, I hear you."

"Verdugo for life."

Loco went back to his foosball game. The others called me over. They clowned around, but I didn't say much. I watched, feeling quiet in myself. I had gone through it. I been jumped in.

I was Verdugo for life.

THE GUARD CUFFED MY HANDS IN FRONT OF ME AND gripped my arm. He said, "What happened to you, Strain?"

It had been two days since I'd been jumped in. The skin under my eye and by my mouth had turned swollen and purple, almost black. I had bruises across my back and my whole body ached to move. Still, I felt bigger, stronger, like I'd gained a few inches and fifty pounds, like I had juvenile hall figured out.

When I didn't answer the guard said, "Let me guess, you fell in the shower." He smirked as he pulled me down the hallway. The guards all knew what was going down but shrugged it off. This added to the swelling in my head, like the guards had become equals. Instead of the men in charge, we were all players in the same game.

Outside the courtroom, he stopped to take off the handcuffs. I rubbed my wrists though it had only been a few minutes. Then the guard pulled open the doors and it was time for my day in court.

Juvenile court was loose with no order I could follow. Judges had ongoing conversations with lawyers, with kids and even with parents and others in the gallery.

I craned around to see who came. My brother sat in the second row next to my mom. When my eyes met hers she folded her hands and lifted her face towards the ceiling; her way of telling me she was praying. My gaze flicked to Eric but I quickly turned away. Though I'd love for Eric to know I'd been jumped in, I didn't want Mom to worry over my bruises.

My court-appointed attorney slid into the chair next to me. She was a thin woman with a pinched face under a mess of curly hair. As small as I was, she seemed smaller, like I could flick her away if I needed to.

She leaned in close and said, "How are you doing, Brad?"

I shrugged.

"You okay in there? Everything all right?"

"It's fine. It's all good."

"Hm." With wide wet eyes she scanned my bruises. "I'm worried about you. If you need anything, you let me know, okay?"

I couldn't imagine what I could need that she could provide, but I nodded.

"All right. Well, I got a deal for you."

I sat up straighter, ready. I figured this was it; I'd be going home. I'd get to head back to Big Wheez and Rocco, and let them know I was Verdugo. I was for real.

"The prosecutor - they're looking at juvenile penitentiary."

"What?" My breath left me. It was like the woman touched me with electric cord.

"You were involved in a high speed chase."

My mind had been shocked blank, but I searched around for words. I spoke what had been rolling through my head for a week.

"I was in the passenger seat."

"That doesn't matter. But they're willing to give you six months here."

Juvenile Penitentiary was the next level. It was hardened criminals, murderers.

"Are you for real?" I wanted to shake the woman. I hadn't stolen any car. I hadn't cared about those rims. I had just been along for the ride.

"Brad?"

I didn't belong there. Not for six months. Not for six days. Not for anything. I had done nothing wrong.

"Brad? Would you like me to talk to your family about it?"

I felt my mom sitting behind me and nodded. The woman left me staring at my fingers on the desk. I wanted to tear it apart, the table and the whole room, but all I did was tap an unsteady beat.

"Your mom was upset," the woman said when she got back. "She's having a rough time."

That wasn't news. She was always having a rough time.

"Brad?"

But I didn't know what to do.

54

"It's a good deal," the woman said. "Take the six months and it keeps you out of the juvenile penitentiary."

That word. I couldn't go to the penitentiary; I wasn't ready.

"Brad?"

I nodded but it felt like a reflex, like something I had no control over.

"You want to take the deal?"

I turned around to the gallery for help, but only found empty seats where my mom and brother had been sitting.

"I need an answer."

She was staring at me with big eyes and a faint smell of perfume. I could see no way out. I nodded again.

"I think that's the right choice," the woman said. Her voice was kind and filled with pity. I hated it.

A half hour later, I was shuffling back to my cell with my head down. With every step I felt how long I'd be looking at the same walls. Six months, it didn't seem right. The same thoughts kept churning through my head: I didn't do nothing. I wasn't driving. I didn't belong here.

Alone in my cell, I brooded through the afternoon until school was out and I could join my homies in the multi-purpose room. They called my name and welcomed me with handshakes. Some of my black mood began to ease back. I was a Sureño. I had family in here. They had my back.

But then Palone asked, "You heading to trial, Strain?"

"Naw, I took a deal."

He cried out with several of the others. "What were you thinking, fool? Never take the deal."

The air escaped the room and I clenched up. I shook my head, staring down at my prison sandals. Palone was right. Homies were always saying to never take the deal. I knew that, but then I went and panicked in the courtroom. Because I messed it up I was going to lose six months of my life. For a terrible moment, I worried I might lose control and embarrass myself, but a hand on my shoulder startled me out of it.

"So you're going to be around with us for a bit, eh *ese*?"

Loco had leaned his head in, staring at me.

I swallowed. "Looks like it, yeah."

"That's cool, Strain." His tone was serious. He patted the back of my neck. "We need you here."

Loco was real. He had the keys. He was the big homie in Gilbert Hall. And when he looked at me like that, it made something inside me release. I nodded slowly. I could breathe again.

"I ain't going nowhere," I said.

"That's right."

I started to swell back up. I was Verdugo for life. I had my homies around me. Six months was a long time, but I had that place figured out. I was going to be okay.

"Strain!" A man's voice called to me from the other side of the room. "What are you doing here?"

Montoya, the gang counselor, grinned at me. I hadn't seen him since my first stint in Gilbert, but he came towards me with his arms outstretched like we were old friends.

"Brad, how are you doing?"

"Just living life, you know."

He sized me up, eyes bouncing between my bruises and my homies. He knew I was in deep.

"Can we talk a minute?"

I nodded and let the man take me a few steps away from my homies. He spoke quietly. "Hey Brad, what are you doing?"

I shrugged.

"You're hanging with the homeboys pretty hard."

"That's right."

He stared at me. "When you get out, there's this program I run on the streets. We got good guys and could use someone like you. We hang out, you know, play basketball. Have some picnics. You'd like it."

I grinned over at my homies and Palone grinned back, shaking his head. I shined on Montoya a little, gave him a grin and said, "That's cool. Yeah, I'll definitely check that out."

A few minutes later I rejoined my homies and Montoya walked out through the locked door. I watched him go, thinking he was a fool. He had nothing for me. All that he was offering? I figured I had all that right here.

Los Dukes

Six months later

THE SUN SHONE brightly through the palm trees. The Jack in the Box burger slid down and filled my stomach in a way jail food never did. My brother and my mom had both come this time - and on the correct day - to drive me home. It was good to be out.

It was good, but I didn't like sitting in the backseat of the car. And I didn't like listening to the way they talked, just as I hadn't liked it the last time they visited me in juvenile hall.

They had come about a month before my release. Eric had slouched in his chair, smiling at me but quiet. And Mom wouldn't shut up about him. I heard all about the job at the mall, talking like he should be proud of working at Pretzels and Cheese and going to night school. And he didn't seem embarrassed by it even as Mom kept talking.

It continued through the drive home. The burgers, the sunshine, the freedom, all of it messed up by my brother drifting away from me. He had already left the neighborhood, having moved in with some white boy ten miles away. But now he had stopped hanging with the crew. He had abandoned them - abandoned us.

I followed them slowly into the apartment, my shoulders heavy. Glad to be home but worried what the neighborhood would be like without Eric. Jail sucked but in there I knew who I was. I knew how I fit in. I understood the rules and knew who had my back when things went down.

It had made me fearless. I was the first to get my hands dirty. The first to start the fight. The first to volunteer for *contalas*, what we call it when we discipline other Sureños. I wasn't worried about any of it.

But now, I didn't know. I was Verdugo for life but didn't know what Big Wheez would think about that. And without Eric, I'd have to face it on my own.

I had barely made it through the apartment door before my sister squealed and threw her arms around me. I had to push her back to get a look at her. Something had changed. She had grown but it was more than that. It was like she had seen some stuff, like she wasn't a little girl anymore.

Mom made me tamales and we had a little celebration, the four of us gathered in the kitchen. We chatted about people around the neighborhood, about the new stores that had gone up. Mom told a long story about a cousin I barely knew.

All through it I felt itchy. I wanted to go out with Eric, see what his deal was and find some trouble. I wanted to sneak into the private school and knock over a desk, or sit on the roof, or just walk through the neighborhoods. It wouldn't matter as long as I was with my big brother.

At the same time, I felt shy around him. It seemed like he already had a foot out the door and I wasn't sure if I wanted to hear what he'd say. I was angry with him - and with my mom - but didn't know why or how to express it. I didn't have the words so I chewed my food and listened to them talk.

Finally, when dinner was over, I helped clean the kitchen, said a quick thank you and took off without looking at Eric. I hurried across the parking lot, enjoying the dusky light. I could turn any direction I wanted and walk wherever I wanted and there was no one to tell me where I could sit or when I could piss or what I could do.

Rocco's mom answered when I knocked. A little woman with hard eyes, she smiled and called him to the door.

With a shout, he pulled me in for a hug.

"What's up, *ese*? How was the stint?"

"Crazy. It was crazy."

He shoved me back and studied my face.

"Yeah, you look different. Something about you."

"Rocco, shit. I been doing some things in juvenile hall."

"That's right. That's right. We been doing some things over at Wheez's house."

He led me to his garage and offered me a beer. I sat with it on the weight bench and took a long drink. We talked for an hour. Rocco told me how he had been jumped in. He knew things now about how the gang life worked, about selling drugs. It burned hearing him talk. I knew some things about jail, but Rocco was part of the set. He was a Duke, and I didn't know where I stood.

Rocco sat back and put his feet up. "We gotta get the crew together. Celebrate you being out."

"Yup."

"Friday night. Right here."

"All right."

"You ready for this?"

I grinned. "You know me, Rocco. I'm ready for anything."

A SOFT GLOW SPILLED OUT FROM THE GARAGE. A BEAT pounded from the boombox. Walking the parking lot alone, I could see my homies Aaron and Rocco as I cut through an aisle of cars. Even my brother showed up. But there was no sign of Big Wheez.

My people. My clique. My set. But I was on the outside, looking in. No matter what went down in Gilbert Hall, I didn't belong, not yet - not until Big Wheez said I did.

I cracked my neck, cleared my throat, spit on the concrete, and stepped in.

Eric saw me first. "What's up, little brother?"

I threw him a nod. He had never been jumped in. He wasn't a part of it, so I was at least doing better than him. "You know me, *ese*."

Two girls smiled at me over their drink cups. I grinned back but felt uneasy. Besides my mom and sister I hadn't talked to a girl in six months.

I gulped down a beer to relax. I turned back to the girls but the heavy thump of bass from a car stereo cut under the sound of the party. It rattled in my stomach, growing louder until headlights shone into the garage. It was a '73 Monte Carlo lowrider. Big Wheez had arrived. Little Weasel, Miguel and Palone climbed out with him and a thrill shivered through me; now it was a party.

Others showed up. Most I knew from before, and a few I met in Gilbert; they had spent a few weeks or a month in there with me. They greeted me with extra respect; they had seen what I was willing to do.

Before the party could crank up, Big Wheez called Rocco outside the garage. My stomach twisted as I watched their heads turn towards each other, conferring about some business I wasn't a part of.

Miguel moved in front of me, blocking my view. He slapped my shoulder. "Heard you're Verdugo."

"That's right."

"They had you working in Gilbert."

"Yup."

"We gotta get you into our set, *homes*."

I looked over at my brother who had to have heard, but he sipped his drink with a blank look.

I said, "You know it."

"That's right, little homie." It was Big Wheez's voice. He was standing next to me; I hadn't seen him approach. "We gotta get you in."

"I did it once," I said.

Big Wheez ignored this and turned to my brother, "Pretzel and Cheese, how you been?"

Eric greeted him, friendly, but he didn't have the same swagger. He barely seemed to be there.

Some of the girls started dancing. I had another beer. And then another. I smoked a zig zag when it came my way and the world grew hazy, the music louder, the homies crazier. Energy rose around me but it came in glances. Two girls laughing in the corner, Big Wheez pointing my way, smoke puffing out Rocco's nostrils.

I hadn't had a drink in six months and started stumbling. My brother leaned in, worried, trying to talk to me but I shrugged him off. He had gone soft, had left the life behind. He had abandoned me and my family. I didn't need to hear what he was going to say.

I cracked open another can near the coolers, took a pull and everything was warm. I sensed a presence behind me, a buzz. I twisted to see my homies: Little Weasel, Miguel, Rocco. They looked grim.

"What's up?"

Violence crackled between them, and I flashed back to my cell with Palone and the others. I took a step back and Miguel said, "What's up, Brad?" but I took a swing before they could move. I landed my fist against Little Weasel and threw an elbow into the blur to my left but they shoved me back. I grabbed a chair to stop my fall then tried to launch into Miguel, but the other two grabbed my arms, stopping my momentum. They shoved me towards a group of girls.

Screaming, the girls splashed beer down my shirt as they scattered. With big hands, Big Wheez grabbed me and half drug me out to the parking lot. He threw me against a fence like I weighed nothing.

The big man faded back to let the others fall on me. I raised my fists but they came from all sides and I fell in the dirt, finally giving in, covering my head and waiting for it to stop. It was supposed to last thirteen seconds, and every moment I expected for hands to drag me up. I waited for the cheer, the smiles, Big Wheez welcoming me to the set, but they just kept kicking.

A girl cried, "He's had enough."

Then my brother's voice. "What the fuck? Stop!" But my brother was a fool, he couldn't help me, not any more. A foot landed on my face and it all went dark.

I woke up on my back. Bugs blurred through a yellow street lamp. The sounds of the party came as if through water. My brother's face stared down at me, his eyes too big.

"What the hell?" he said. "They messed you up, Brad. What the hell?"

I tried to tell him to back off, I was fine, I got it handled, I didn't need his help, but my head buzzed too hard to talk.

"We gotta bring him in."

"Naw, he's fine."

I heard the words but couldn't figure out who said them. The homie was right, though, I was fine and would've said this if I could've opened my mouth.

"Wheez, come on, he's gotta get some help."

"I'm cool," I said, but it came out as a moan.

"All right, *ese*, take the car."

Hands dragged me to the back seat. I heard music, saw lights from the street drift across my body, felt the hum of the car. The two in front didn't talk.

Then bright white and more yelling. The pain throbbed through my head and face. I had closed my eyes, rested the back of my head against a wall. My brother was shouting. I cracked my eyes. A weary nurse was asking about insurance and my mother's phone number. Eric, red faced, said he didn't know anything about that, our mom was working and who knew how long it would be before she got the message. He begged her for a doctor.

But the fool needed to chill. I was okay. If I could stand up, I'd go over to tell him that.

The next hours were blurry. Doctors shined lights into my eyes; they took an X-ray of my head; they gave me a painkiller. Eventually they rolled me into a quiet room. Eric sat next to me. Rocco had gone home. I kept blinking, trying to clear my head but the light hurt.

Then I opened my eyes and my mom was crying over me, holding my hand. "What happened?" she said. "Who did this to you?"

I rolled my head towards my brother who stared back. He said nothing. He still understood.

The lie came off my lips without any effort at all.

"It's nothing Ma. We were playing football in the yard." I knew she wouldn't believe me, but it didn't matter. "I took a bad fall and hit my head against the curb."

They told me I had a jaw fracture and a concussion. I thought of Miguel and Rocco and Little Weasel, kicking me on the ground. These were my homies. This was my set.

I was in.

MY JAW WAS SORE, BUT NOT SO BAD, AND MY HEAD HAD cleared up. I was recovering at home, and fine, all things considered. But my mom kept hovering near me, trying to keep me in.

I hadn't been outside in a week and I was desperate to go mix it up. It didn't help that her new boyfriend was sipping at a glass of water in the kitchen. The man was bland, didn't say much, but he was always in our space. He started gargling and I stood up from the couch.

"Do you need something?"

"No, Ma. I'm fine. I just need to get out of here. Clear my head a minute."

"You need your rest."

I knew she was trying to be my mom but if I didn't leave I'd start screaming. I let momentum take me to the door. "I told you, I'm fine." I said, and was in the hall before she could respond.

Outside, the heat about knocked me over but it was like I'd been released from jail. I had the freedom, finally, to go anywhere I wanted. I headed straight to Rocco's place.

I found him in the garage working at his cheap-ass weight set. He nodded at me and I grinned back, happy to see him. As far as I was concerned the beat down was in the past. It wasn't forgotten but I thought of it as a story I could tell; a test I had passed.

In fact, he and Miguel had come to visit when I was laid up. Mom had fixed us lunch, and they talked like I was part of the set now, like I belonged. It had warmed me at the time, but because I hadn't seen Big Wheez I still felt uneasy about it. I worried I screwed it up by going to the hospital. I didn't think it all through, but knew I'd feel on the outside until Big Wheez said otherwise.

Rocco wiped his face with a rag and suggested we walk to the park, see if there were enough homies there for a pick-up game. Only a few blocks but it felt like we passed everyone I knew. Little kids playing, old ladies I'd seen my whole life, they smiled, called out my name and asked after my mother.

We crossed Lugonia and passed through the gate. A little girl sketched hopscotch in chalk near a low wall which had been tagged by our sign. The park was Los Duke territory. During the day it was a place for kids and families, but at night it belonged to us.

"Brad, check this out." Rocco led me behind a line of trees. He checked around a little dramatically then pulled out a screwdriver, knelt by a light pole, and pointed at a little black box, like an electrical outlet without plugs. He unscrewed the bottom screw and flipped the cover to the side.

"I put my stash in here."

"I like that." I said it cool, but I was amazed. While I'd been doing my stint, Rocco had moved on to the next level. I knew none of these tricks and had to catch up.

"I got another place by the sprinklers. I try not to carry too much on me, you know."

He closed it up and we walked to the courts, Rocco teaching me as we went. Most of the action, he said, happened after the street lights went on, though occasionally there'd be people looking for a little weed during the day. They'd stop by the basketball court and chat up the homies, maybe ask for a twenty or something before they left. At night, however, they made the real money moving cocaine.

It was also night when the North Side Redland fools would try to press into Los Duke territory. The NSR were a black gang, part of the crips, and I had dealt with them in juvenile hall. I never thought much of them, but I'd been careful not to let any of them catch me alone. Out here, they'd sneak in the park through the the fence by the middle school, tag our sites, start fights, maybe shoot a round or two in our direction.

I nodded as Rocco explained all this, trying to file it all away to remember for later.

We got to the basketball court, but none of the homies was there. There was no one playing basketball, no one in the shelter. It was too hot, we figured, and expected we could find them chilling somewhere in the shade.

Rocco said, "You want to head over to Big Wheez's?"

I wanted more than anything to see Big Wheez, to know for sure I was part of the set, but I didn't know what I'd do if he turned me away.

"Naw," I said. "Let's just keep walking."

I SLAMMED THE SCREWDRIVER IN THE KEYHOLE THEN jerked it down, but it wouldn't pop.

Rocco paced around the van, eyes down, searching the dark pavement. "I can't find it, *homes.*"

"Keep looking. Shit."

We had come all that way into a hostile neighborhood for this van. We had found it no problem, right where the girl told us it'd be. Like she said, a party raged in the house next to it. And no one was paying attention to what was going on outside.

But when I threw the porcelain at the window it bounced off with no effect. Now it was lost in the street dirt and I couldn't get the door to pop.

"Aw, fuck it," Rocco said. "I can't see a thing here."

We were deep inside NSR territory; if the wrong car passed it could be a problem. But in the van was a box and in the box was a gun - an assault rifle if the girl knew what she was talking about. The fool who owned the van liked to show it off, she'd said. He'd bring girls back there and let them handle it. The girl had laughed about it, but Rocco and I nodded at each other. We'd made the plan without a word.

But then we'd hit bad luck.

"Hey Brad..." Rocco straightened up. "It's no good."

We'd have to run soon, but I figured I had time for one more try. I shoved the screwdriver in as deep as it would go and jerked down. Finally, the pop vibrated through my wrist.

"That's what I'm talking about. Rocco, we're good!"

I pulled open the door and Rocco climbed in. I kept my eyes on the house, listening to Rocco's rustling, barely there under the sounds of the party. My heart thumped pleasantly in my chest.

"I can't see nothing back here." Rocco crept back out the door.

"You got your lighter?"

He passed me his lighter and said, "Watch out. It's filled with shit."

I climbed in over fast food wrappers, loose papers and plastic bags. I flicked the lighter and traced its low glow along the edges, trying not to set anything on fire. The girl said to look for a box. In my mind this had meant a chest of some kind, something made out of wood. I didn't see anything like that on the first pass but on the second I found a carpet-lined container, more a bench than anything else. I lifted at the top and there it was: a long rifle, in good shape. I checked for ammo, but found nothing. I hefted the gun - it was heavier than I'd expected - then squat-walked out the side door.

"You get it?"

"Hell yeah, I got it."

We closed the door softly then started to run down the street; I held the rifle to my chest like I was in the army. The noise of the party faded behind us until everything was quiet. The cool night air made San Bernardino smell fresh.

A couple blocks away we slowed to a walk, then stopped near a house. I searched the lawn for a suitable bush.

"Here," I said, and started to push the rifle through the leaves.

"What you doing?"

"Stashing the gun."

"You can't leave it in the bushes."

"Why not?"

Rocco scratched the back of his head. "Some little kid might find it."

"What? Since when are you worried about little kids?"

Rocco grinned but said, "Fuck that, *ese*, we can't leave the rifle here."

"All right. Shit. But we can't carry it like this." It was a long way back to our neighborhood. "Hey," I said. "I'll put it down my pants."

I pulled out the waist of my dickies. It was a bit too tight but I loosened the belt a notch and lowered the gun down my pant leg, the barrel scratching into my skin the whole way down. I had to shove to get it past my knee.

"You're loco, *homes*."

"Yeah, yeah." I pulled down my shirt to cover the stock then grinned up. "No problem."

Rocco shook his head. "You can walk?"

"Yeah, yeah. Let's move."

Like a pirate, I stiff-legged my way through the neighborhood. Every step the gun dug into my leg, and stepping down curbs was almost impossible.

I lurched a few steps behind Rocco as we cut through a yard. On the far side, as we crossed under the street light, we heard a car behind us.

The tires screeched and the windows cranked down. Four faces leered out at us. Northside Redlands.

Rocco puffed up, "What's up, fools?"

They opened their doors, music pounding from the speakers. One of them said, "Why are there scraps in our neighborhood?"

I started sweating. Four on two and I was still sore form the beat down a week and a half ago. It wasn't good odds, but then, I had a rifle shoved down my pants.

"Hey!" I raised up a finger. "Hold on!"

I gave them enough attitude to make them hesitate. They watched as I tugged the gun hand over hand until it was free. Rocco stared with them, bug-eyed. I raised the barrel in their direction.

"There we go," I said. "What's up now, *ese*?"

I had no bullets but they didn't know that. They stepped backwards, hands raised, then scrambled back into their car.

"What's up now, fools?"

We laughed as they drove away, throwing signs at them from the middle of the street. But as soon as the car turned the corner we started to sprint. We skittered through back yards, leapt over the low cement walls until we got lucky and I almost stumbled over an unlocked bike. I jumped on the back pegs, held the gun with one hand and gripped Rocco's shoulder with the other. He pedaled us out.

One dark street passed another until we reached our neighborhood. Even then, we kept moving, barely slowing down until we made it to Big Wheez's.

The lights were on in the house and music thumped from the back yard. The garage was dim, but we found a couple homies hanging on the couch. They were just chilling, looking too drunk to do much of anything.

Big Wheez stepped into the garage as we walked up. I hadn't seen him since I'd been jumped in. When he grinned at me, looking pleased to see us, something in my chest that had been tight for days finally relaxed.

"There's our new homie," Big Wheez said. "Where you been?"

I shrugged and touched my cheek without thinking. "You know me, Big Wheez, just out there living."

"Just living. Yeah, yeah. What the fuck is that?"

Rocco was holding it, but I said, "SKS Rifle, Semi-automatic."

"What the hell? Where did you get it?"

"Took it from some fool over on Mentone."

He nodded. "That's right," he said. He took the gun and admired it. He wouldn't give it back but that was understood. It belonged to him now. It belonged to my set. Same as me.

FRIDAY NIGHT, WE WERE HANGING OUTSIDE THE Godfather's. Rocco and I walked through the cars; we shook hands, grinning and clowning. I nodded to some *vatos* from juvenile, other homies from the clique. I'd been rolling with the gang for a few months and had stories to tell. I had people laughing; I teased the girls. I was living life, being young.

A lowrider, Big Wheez's Monte Carlo, pulled up and he leaned out towards me. He gave a nod to Rocco, telling him to take a walk so he could talk to me alone, and that puffed me up. Just me and Big Wheez, conferring. I rested my hand on the hood.

"Listen, Brad, we're glad to have you as part of the set. You been doing good."

I liked hearing that.

"This guy Luis? He's not a bad homie. We don't have any beef with him, but listen. When he comes back, you don't kick it with him any more."

I hadn't heard from Luis, didn't know when he'd get out but figured it'd be soon. I had been looking forward to seeing him again.

Maybe Big Wheez saw what I was thinking, I didn't know, but he said, "He's not a bad homie, but you're Verdugo. Hear me? You belong to us."

He looked me in the eye, and in that moment I'd do whatever the big man said.

"That's right," I said.

"All right?"

"All right."

Big Wheez pulled away and I floated toward my homies outside Godfather's. I wanted to talk to everybody, tell my stories, have a great time, but I found a mob of people in my way. I didn't pay much attention to them at first but when I got close I saw it was a group of white boys. And they were screaming at Rocco.

A red-faced blond fool was saying, "Hey, you remember me?" He was huge, looked like a football player.

Rocco waved a hand dismissively. There were five or six of them, all a few years older, all jocks looking to intimidate my boy.

The blond fool stepped closer, getting into Rocco face, shouting, "You sold me bunk weed!"

Rocco gave him half-lidded eyes. "What you want, *ese*?"

I belonged to Los Dukes, they belonged to me, so before I had a thought in my head I had pushed my way into the circle.

The fool said, "Who the hell are you?"

I flung my head forward into his face. The crack flashed through my brain into the back of my head, but the jock fell back, blood gushing from his nose.

One of his friends pounced forward but Rocco and Miguel took him down. The other white boys all stepped back, watching as Rocco laid a kick on their friend. He spat out, "I didn't sell you no bunk weed, mother fucker," and kicked him again. "I don't do that."

The jock on the ground rolled over. He tried to get up, but I had knocked the fight out of him. I grabbed Rocco by the arm.

"Hey, *ese*, let's go."

He screamed at the jock, "I don't do that, fool."

"Let's get out of here, Rocco."

We moved, but hearing no sirens in the distance, we took our time. The crowd in the parking lot turned back to their own business as the jocks picked up their friends.

We laughed about it as we walked. My head ached for days but the low throb made me feel good. I had been there for my homies; I'd showed up for my set, and that was all that mattered.

Portland
Six months later

FOR THE FIRST time in I didn't know how long I climbed the stairs to my mom's apartment. I was out of my mind, not-seeing-right exhausted.

Most nights I'd sleep wherever I found myself, mostly at Rocco's or sometimes crashing on a couch in Big Wheez's garage. I never ate anything except what was nearby, usually fast food or something from a gas station. Finally, after killing myself like this for months, I had hit my limit. My body was wrecked like an old man; my knees hurt walking up those steps. All I wanted was to lie down somewhere safe.

The apartment was quiet. My sister was at school, my mom at work. I didn't know or care where the boyfriend was. I paced through looking at stuff, feeling it all strange and unfamiliar. The criminal part of my brain told me I should trash the place, and take anything valuable back to Big Wheez because that's what I did. I'd been a thief as long as I remembered, shoplifting for Eric and his friends when I was a little kid, so I'd feel no guilt. I may even have done it, but every time I blinked it was a struggle to open my eyes again. It had all become too much work, always searching for an unlocked door, a car parked in a shadow, a purse held a little too loose, an empty apartment, whatever. I needed a break.

I rested my hand on the wall and leaned in to my brother's old room. It had emptied out months ago when my brother left town. He had gone full legit, joined the Air Force and took off for basic training somewhere. Last time I talked to my mom she started crying as soon as I mentioned his name; she was so proud. That was two months ago. I hadn't seen much reason to come home after that.

I rummaged through the fridge, found a block of cheese and cut a piece. I chewed without thinking, without tasting it. After the second bite I figured I wasn't as hungry as I had thought and decided to take a shower.

The last shower I took had been at Big Wheez's days before, and the water had been cold and tasted like rust. Now I breathed in the steam and something in me relaxed, something that had been coiled up. This lifestyle had been punishing me. It was all shadows and running and too many drugs and a weeks-long pounding in my brain.

Still dripping, I stepped out of the bathroom with a towel around my waist and searched for a change of clothes. I heard a sound from the hallway, and found a man in the kitchen, digging through the fridge: the pasty white boy my mom had been seeing. He had a beer gut and needed a shave. The man nodded at me, unsurprised and not interested. With a shrug, he shuffled to the couch, sat down heavily and turned on the TV.

Fool seemed like a trespasser. I was still skinny, still had a baby face that couldn't grow a mustache but I knew I could him take him, no problem. He was nothing. I studied the side of his head for a long moment, then stepped into the bathroom to fix my hair.

My mom came home, and I listened to the sound of her voice mixed with his as they talked about me. She sounded nervous or upset, I couldn't tell, but I came out and let her give me a hug.

"I've been worried about you, *mijo*," she said. "Where've you been?"

"Just living, Ma."

"What does that mean?"

"Nothing. I've been chilling with Rocco."

She grumbled at this but started making me some rice and beans. I didn't say much as she talked about my sister, then my brother, how good he'd been doing, all that. After a few minutes she sat the food in front of me and watched me eat. My eyes grew heavier with each bite and I rested my head in my hand, chewing sideways. My mom said

71

something but I couldn't concentrate enough to understand.

"Do you hear me?"

"I'm tired, Ma, sorry."

"I said, Bradley, that maybe you should think about visiting your dad. Get out of the city for awhile."

I took another bite and a part of me thought that, yeah, maybe I should. I liked Portland. I had some friends there.

"Don't you think that'd be a good idea?" Mom said, and I was about to agree but she glanced over at the boyfriend with her eyebrows raised.

"Ma, I'd get in the same kind of trouble up there. It'd be no different."

"We think it'd be a good idea."

I didn't know who she meant by 'we,' but I had already put up as much of a fight as I had left in me.

"Sure," I said. "Whatever."

As I laid down in my brother's old bed I figured I'd head out for a few weeks, maybe a month, as a kind of vacation. I sunk into a deep sleep, thinking I'd be back before anyone knew I was gone.

I HAD TO SHARE THE LITTLE ROOM IN MY GRANDMA'S house with my dad, but he gave me a little time when I first got there. He stayed out and let me set my things near the bed I'd be sleeping in, though I didn't haven't much. The room was tidy and as I put my stuff down I thought of my dad as my new cellie. It was about the right size. The walls were bare except for an ancient painting of a bird. Metal awnings blocked the sun and kept the room dim even in the middle of the afternoon. Put some bars on the windows, stack the beds, and it could almost pass for Gilbert Hall.

My dad knocked - something he'd never bother to do again - and invited me to eat. When I came out of the room he grunted. "Hope you'd change for dinner."

I was wearing my California clothes: dickie shorts, white t-shirt, high socks, Dodgers hat. I said, "This is all I got, Popps."

He grunted again and my grandma came in from the kitchen. "Mr. Wonderful!" she said. "It is so good to have you back."

"Thanks, Grandma."

"But you're so skinny. Don't they have food in California?"

"Not like you make, they don't."

She patted my shoulder and reached around to put out a meatloaf covered in ketchup. She carved out a huge slice, bigger than anyone should eat, and laid it on my plate with a smile.

"This I don't like," she said, pointing at the cross tattoo on my fist. "Why would you put something like this on your body? You're so handsome, Bradley. Such a good looking boy to be doing this to yourself."

"I don't know, Grandma."

She asked about my sister, Melissa, and my mom. Eric was my dad's stepson so she asked about him politely but didn't dote on it.

We ate. The TV blared loud in the background. A painting of an old man praying hung on the wall. The air smelled like cigarette smoke and grandma and cooking. It all felt right.

My dad scraped the last of his meatloaf on his fork. He had changed since my last visit. He'd stopped drinking and his eyes were clear. He looked my way and I felt like he saw me. He said, "You're getting a job this summer."

"I don't know, Popps."

"I'm not asking. I'm telling."

I couldn't imagine myself wearing a name tag and working at some mall, but I kept my mouth shut.

After dinner we sat down in front of the television, and my dad leaned back and focused on the nightly news. He watched it sternly, like the newscaster was disappointing him. I started feeling itchy, uncomfortable being closed in the little house.

I said, "I gotta go to the bathroom."

My dad glared at me, saying *why are you telling us?* with his eyes.

Grandma nodded. "You know where it is."

The only bathroom was through my grandma's room. I walked by her dresser, letting my fingers run over the glassy wood. At its far edge, I stopped and held my breath, listening to the sound of the television for a long moment. Then I eased the top drawer open until I could see the envelope: my grandma's social security money. It was always there, always cash, and replenished every couple weeks. I fingered the bills, getting a sense of the amount before pulling out a twenty. I had done it often when I stayed here the first time. I didn't think about it enough to have a conscience; I'd just grab some money and run off with my friend, Shawn. We'd spend it on baseball cards or video games.

I closed the drawer, went to the bathroom, then shuffled back to the living room. I was ready to leave, but my dad's heavy stare stopped me.

He said, "I got some errands to run tomorrow."

He studied my face as a commercial for laundry soap ran behind his head. "I was wondering if you'd like to join me."

He turned back to the TV. My dad's voice had sounded hesitant, almost shy. It made me uneasy, like the floor had grown unsteady underneath us. He wasn't angry. It wasn't a punishment. He was just looking to hang out. It was something that had never happened before and I stared for a moment at the side of his head. I rubbed the back of my neck, confused, but finally I nodded with my whole body.

"Sure, Popps. Yeah."

I didn't understand what was going on, but I sat down on the couch. It felt like too much work to leave the house. I didn't feel like searching out some trouble. Instead, I decided to stay in with my dad and grandma and watch TV.

Grandma got up to pop some popcorn. I slouched down and shoved my hands into my pockets. The twenty dollar bill rustled against my fingers. For a moment, I felt a twinge of guilt.

WE SAT NEXT TO EACH OTHER ON THE BENCH OUTSIDE the bakery, me with a donut, Popps with a cigarette. He rarely spoke, but I felt his presence. He was often ornery, but he kept showing up. Almost every Saturday around one o'clock for the last two months, he'd grab his jacket and I would know to meet him at the truck. We'd run to Ace Hardware or the post office. He'd browse at a couple stores. We'd end it with a donut and a smoke.

My dad crushed the ash under his foot, I wiped frosting off my face, then we walked back to the parking lot. Chewing had kept me quiet, but I started talking now as he drove us home, offering opinions about the Raiders upcoming season. Dad rarely said anything back. He maybe wasn't even listening, I didn't know, but he never told me to stop. I told him a little about school. I had been showing up almost every day. I talked about girls, how I thought they were nicer in Portland than California. I told him about Shawn's baseball season, and my new friend TJ. I kept going until my dad pulled up to the garage.

Outside the truck, I told him I was heading over to Shawn's house and he nodded. I hopped on my bike. It was a cool day in the late spring. It had rained earlier and everything smelled good. The trees were starting to turn green.

I felt mellow. I missed my homies in San Bernardino, but not enough that I'd want to head back. Here, I had a bed every night. I had a sweet old lady calling me Mr. Wonderful. I got donuts.

I hadn't changed; I was still a thief. I'd steal car ornaments and shoplift at the mall. I still took the occasional cash from my grandma's dresser. I never thought much about any of it, but still, I felt calmer. I didn't feel the same need to create havoc. I didn't mind spending nights with my dad watching TV.

At Shawn's house, I walked in without knocking and his mom told me he was in the basement. The kitchen smelled like grilled cheese and cigarettes. A Mariners game was playing in the living room. I ducked down the back stairs as a phone started to ring behind me. Shawn's head poked over the back of the couch. Before I could say hello, his mom called my name. The call was for me.

I hurried up, and pushed the phone to my ear.

"Brad, you gotta get home," my dad growled. "It's your grandmother."

I sprinted out, and pedaled furiously down the sidewalk. My lungs burned after half a block, but it wasn't far. I skidded around the last corner in time to watch the ambulance pull away. My dad was standing by his truck; hand on the door.

When I caught my breath, I asked, "What happened?"

He shook his head, stony-faced and silent.

DAD MUTTERED, "I'M GONNA GRAB COFFEE," AND turned towards the cafeteria so I had to take the elevator by myself. It was a lonely walk down the hallway; nurses bustled past me and members of other people's families stood close, leaning into each other. I didn't like hospitals much, but I breathed the antiseptic smells, ignored the beeping machines and found my grandma's room, no problem.

My grandma who was always happy to see me, who called me sweet names and fed me even when I wasn't hungry, she looked like the life had been sucked out of her. Barely a week had passed and skin hung loose to her face and black spots marked her skin. Death had her in its grip and I hated it. I hated the way her hand curled around the bed sheet. I hated hearing her moan through the pain medication. I hated knowing I'd done nothing for her but show up and steal her money.

Her eyes found mine and her face twisted into something close to a smile. "Mr. Wonderful," she said, but the cancer in her lungs made her voice sound like a shoe dragging through dirt. "Mr. Wonderful... It's going to be all right." She'd seen my tears and was trying to comfort me. "Everything is going to be okay."

I leaned in for a hug but got snagged on one of her tubes and she groaned. I stumbled backwards and stood awkwardly, shifting my weight from foot to foot.

"Mr. Wonderful," she said.

I wiped my face on my sleeve.

She swatted at me weakly. "You should go now."

I didn't know where my dad was and didn't know what to do, so I retreated to the doorway. I stopped to blow her a kiss, but she had shut her eyes. "Love you, Grandma," I said, but couldn't tell if she heard me. It was all wrong. It all felt wrong.

She died the next day.

I STOOD BY THE FRONT DOOR. IT WAS A SATURDAY afternoon, one o'clock. A couple weeks had passed since the funeral and my dad was slouched on the couch. He took a deep drag from a cigarette. Smoke drifted from his nostrils.

It was too much weight. I felt it, those last looks from my grandma, the empty house, the cold sandwiches we ate every night. A pressure was building inside me.

The TV was off. He snuffed out one cigarette and lit another. It sounded like a dog panting when he coughed. I figured a ride in the truck would help us both.

I said, "Hey, Popps?"

He shook his head with a grunt.

There'd be no errands that day. There'd be no donut. I went to the bathroom and stopped at the dresser. There was a last twenty dollar bill in the envelope and I felt no guilt - or anything else - as I shoved it in my pocket.

WE STOLE SOME POT FROM SHAWN'S MOM AND smoked it in the basement, but it didn't mellow me out. I had the itch. I needed to move, get outside. I couldn't sit around, not with the wood panelling and carpeting, the hard couches, not with the baseball game on TV. It was all too slow and Shawn's mom would be home soon. She'd start making dinner and I couldn't handle the smell of cooking meat.

I nodded at TJ who was taking up half the couch. He had a violence in him and wanted to throw down against the world. I loved that, hanging with this bruising white boy.

By the time I stood up, TJ already had started lurching toward the stairs. Shawn trailed after us, shrugging, not into it. He had short hair, compact muscles, clear eyes. He was a jock. He liked to get high sometimes but he liked being on the baseball team more.

We wandered off into the neighborhood. The houses were cramped and old with dirt smeared along the sides. Brown weeds broke through the cracks on the sidewalk. It was mid-summer but nothing felt alive. We crossed a busier street, mist touching our faces. I was talking nonsense, the pot working in me making me not able to keep my mouth shut.

Shawn had his shoulders up; he pulled his flannel closer to his neck and said we should head back to the basement, but I couldn't imagine that. I couldn't sit in that basement for another second, not when there was a world outside to mess with. I needed to burn something, steal something, kill something, anything.

Down a quiet side street, I saw a garage not fully closed, the door up about three feet. The mist turned to drizzle; it was two in the afternoon but no one around; no kids outside. The houses all looked deserted, the windows mirrored by gray clouds. The road dead ended in a tangle of weeds and a barbed wire fence.

I walked up the driveway like I owned it then squatted to peer under the garage door. My knee rubbed onto the concrete. TJ stood next to me, too big for the job, a giant target for anyone driving by.

"Let's check this out."

Shawn shook his head. "Naw. I think I'm going to bail."

I glared back at him, not getting it. Here was something to hit up against, something that would help get my mind right for a few minutes, but Shawn was already backing away.

He raised his hands, "This ain't my scene."

I waved him off, releasing the fool to go watch his baseball games, but adding him to the list. I knew I wouldn't do that. I'd never abandon my homies, but for some reason they kept doing it to me. I didn't understand it. First Eric, then my dad, then my grandma.

There was something about that list which didn't make sense, but I hurried into the garage because I didn't know how to deal with it. I didn't how to deal with the old woman's eyes smiling at me, calling me Mr. Wonderful one night and then she was gone. I couldn't handle her last words, telling me to get out of the room, or the look on her face. It chewed at me. I didn't know how to deal with how my dad had changed, but I didn't have to when I was inside a stranger's garage, feeling that thrill of being somewhere I didn't belong. The stakes were high enough and it was almost enough to smooth away the itch.

Against the back wall I found a chest fridge and pulled at it, the magnet resisting me at first before it gave away. I grinned at what I saw. TJ, taking up too much space behind me, kicked at something on the floor.

I called him over. "You gotta check this shit out, *homes*."

He stood next to me staring down into it like a treasure chest. The fridge was full to the top with beer and hard liquor - big bottles of the good stuff. We started slapping at each other, laughing almost to tears, trying to figure out how the hell we were going to get it all home.

WE CAME DOWN THE STAIRWAY IN THE MAX STATION on our way to the mall. I was The Gaffler, the baby-faced thief. Tony and TJ would stand back as I took whatever I could and the clerks wouldn't suspect me even in my Sureño blue. It was Portland, the suburbs; they didn't know what to make of us.

TJ had introduced me to Tony. He was Sureño out of LA, an 18th Streeter. Dark skinned, almost Brazilian by color. He always wore a blue hat, flat brim, with his Jheri-curled hair spraying out the back. He replaced Shawn easy. He was small like me with crazy in his eyes.

I was on fire. It had been two months since Grandma died and I still slept at Popp's house, in Popp's room - we left her room empty - but I stayed out as late as I could. My dad tried stopping me at first. I got home late after missing school and he grabbed me by the collar and we went at it. He was stronger but I was younger, arm on arm, grunting and quiet in the living room. Both of us pulling our punches but not much if we could get an elbow to the throat or the gut. I kept my eyes shut or down at the ground, okay with the fight but not able to look the man in the eyes, not able to handle what I saw there. I fought in the moment, not thinking but feeling like I was fighting for my life until I broke away. I stumbled out the door, and stayed away as long as I could.

There was nothing at home, not any more, so I'd sneak in at three in the morning and sleep as late as my dad would let me.

But mostly I kept away, like I was doing now, cutting though the MAX station on the way to the mall. As long as I was moving I was okay. When the world eased into a blur around me I could handle it, so I was glad when Tony, TJ and I walked down the stairs to see the smear of red.

They were XIV fools. XIV were a smaller set of Norteños. When Sureños run into Norteños in the street, it was immediate, on-sight violence. The fools wore their red gang colors just like Tony and I were wearing blue.

We stepped onto the platform, the people jostling around us a blur, walking home from work in their button-down shirts. They were faceless spectators, barely there, as these gang-banging Norteño fools started throwing their signs in front of us. They shouted the slang, calling us scraps and stars.

We half circled them, banging back at them. Behind us, the stairs led away from the landing otherwise we were surrounded by a mesh fence, like a cage. The air barely moved and smelled of exhaust and garbage. I told them to go fuck themselves and felt the normal people scatter around us.

TJ wasn't wearing blue, so they didn't know he was with us. When he stepped into our line, the XIV fools' eyes went so wide we could see white all around. They shut up and tried to step back, but there was nowhere for them to go.

I saw a fight already won. The feeling of power and violence smushed all the rest of the it, my grandma, my dad, all of it into nothing.

One flashed a gun under his shirt but we just laughed. Tony shouted, "You ain't got no *curette*." And he was right. The fool had nothing but a finger in his pants. Tony stepped close to one with a heavy gold chain and said, "So what do you got, fool?"

And it was on, three on two, barely a fight and it went fast. One of them got a hand around Tony's neck but TJ picked him up and tossed him like nothing over the railing to fall down onto the stairs. I laid into the other fool, full of a fire that burned everything else. I lost myself in it until Tony gripped my arm screaming at me.

I blinked at him. He looked scared, eyes as wide as those fools we fought. "We gotta get out of here, *ese*, we gotta move."

I heard the yelling around us. I saw the people. They came out of the blur staring at us, mouths open, shielding their kids. With it, I saw the gum on the concrete, the sun streaking through the grate, a fast-food cup trampled in the corner.

A man shouted from somewhere. Someone whistled but I didn't know why. All of this in a second and in the next I shoved my hands through the Norteño's pockets searching for cash, figuring I should get something for my trouble. And then we ran.

We sprinted back the way we came. It was a multilevel MAX station filled with people and we had to go up before we could go down. I ran for my life like I had many times before and again the world retreated to nothing. I had no other sense but the next moment.

Lungs burning, I had to slow to a trot across the bridge. I heard men yelling over sirens: an ambulance and cops. On the far side, I started sprinting again out of the MAX station into the neighborhood. Tony split off in a different direction, but TJ and I stayed together, following an alley behind a row of houses. We heard more sirens now, even closer.

I thought nothing, but if I ran fast enough I'd get away from all the shit. Near an empty lot filled with weeds and a rusted out car, I saw a cop leap out of his cruiser. He swore at me to stop but I knew if I could keep going to the next house, then the next alley, I could make it.

I hurled myself forward, but my legs were heavy, and the cop gained on me easily until he gripped my arm. I ripped away but another cop had come and he yanked me to a stop. They shoved me against a wall, pushing me into it until my hands were spread and my cheek rubbed into the concrete. They slammed TJ next to me.

The cop shouted, "Get on your knees!" but TJ told them to fuck off. The cop swung his baton at his knees and he crumpled.

Then the cop turned to me. "Get on your knees!"

I knelt down before he finished talking.

Still, I didn't feel it. It was all a blur. Handcuffs, dented speaker, one for processing, interview rooms where I kept my mouth shut. It passed while I floated above it.

But eventually, when a mushy-faced attorney rubbed my back and explained the situation, I had to wake up. My dad stared dead-eyed across the table. I had no drugs in my system. I sat on a hard chair and had to face the consequences of my actions: Eighteen months in the juvenile penitentiary.

Portland, Oregon
1991

Alternative Learning

Eighteen months later

POPPS BARKED AT me to close the window. I did it with a shrug, no worries. The man had picked me up from the juvenile penitentiary. He had given me a hug in the parking lot. He was driving me home. I could follow his rules in the truck.

"Brad, listen..." We rumbled over a lonely two-lane road. "This has gotta be it."

"It will be."

"You gotta change your ways, Son."

"Yup." I nodded with my whole body.

He idled at a stop sign. There were no cars coming from any direction; farmland on all sides. He turned his body towards mine, lowered his head and said, "You need to make some changes, you hear me? You gotta have a plan."

"Yessir."

"Go to school. Or get your GED."

"Yup."

Satisfied with my answers, he started to drive again. It was about the most words I'd ever heard my dad say in one go and it came from a place I didn't recognize. He was trying to be a father to me, but I was no child - not any more.

As the telephone poles rolled past, Popps went silent and I thought back to the day they took me to MacLaren juvenile penitentiary. Tony had been there with me. We were sealed in a room, all cinderblock except for a little window showing a sliver of hallway. We chewed peanut butter and jelly sandwiches as an inmate took a leak in a toilet four feet away.

A shiver hollowed out my stomach as I waited to be cellie-chained and shackled, but I was talking big to Tony. He'd been looking at me with wide eyes, not able to hide his fear. Even though his whole family was connected and he'd known nothing but the gang life, this was his first time incarcerated.

Popps grumbled something from the driver's seat bringing me back to the truck. We were driving into the outskirts of Portland. He rubbed hard at the back of his neck and grew quiet again.

In the silent truck, I remembered the sounds of the chains. They rattled down the hall like a wraith from a horror movie before the guards banged open the door. They called names; their voices bored, their eyes empty. They'd taken Tony first and he shuffled out with his head down. The door slammed shut, leaving me alone with strangers.

It repeated a few minutes later. Chains rattled, the door opened, and they called my name. It gave me bubble guts when I followed them to the next room. This one also had a little window and a toilet. I had to take a shit four feet away from everyone. The others clowned at me about what I was doing, but that was all right. Their laughter broke some of the tension.

A half an hour later, they stood us against the wall, and I rested my forehead against the cinderblock as they shackled my wrists to my ankles. As a guard used the cellie-chain to connect me to the others in line, I tried to sink into myself. They turned and ordered us to step forward. I followed each command, trying not to feel any of it, but when I moved my left leg, pain shot through me.

"Hey, officer, my ankle chains are too tight."

He said, "Keep moving."

They chained us into two rows in the back of a van. After a few minutes, it backed up, pushing me into the inmate next to me, though I could barely move. I tried again to disconnect from the shit, but I couldn't. It was too real. It made me want to cry out, but I couldn't do that either. Tony was there, a few inmates up on the opposite side.

86

He looked at me and I could see he was scared.

I swallowed down my own stuff and grinned over at him. "Hey, *ese*," I said. "How you like my jewelry? Looking good, huh?"

"Yeah, yeah." He had given me a weak smile. "Yeah, you looking sharp, Strain. You looking sharp."

I didn't know how to tell Popps any of this. Maybe I still had a baby face, but I was no child, not any more. At MacLaren, they had looked to me, Tony and others, ready to follow. And I had tried to lead. I tried to organize the Sureños and get some things going. It didn't fly - there weren't enough of us there - but I had learned some things. I had earned a reputation. They had started calling me Loco. I had grown up.

All these things were in my head as Popps parked next to the garage, and as I followed him into the house. I stood for a moment just inside the door. The air was thick with dust but it smelled right. I missed my grandma, but the Price Is Right was on, and a rare beam of sun streamed through a window. It was as close to a home as I had.

Dad disappeared into his bedroom. I grabbed the phone and tapped in a number. They had released Tony two weeks earlier and he told me to call when I was free.

I listened to the ring, ready for whatever was coming next.

I ROLLED OUT OF BED, THEN IMMEDIATELY WISHED I hadn't. I had gotten messed up the night before with Tony and his family. They lived on the far side of Portland, the only Hispanics in a black neighborhood. His uncle Chavo had offered me up some mushrooms; told me to pour hot sauce on them to help the taste.

I'd been in the penitentiary and had no tolerance for getting high so the drug had hit me hard. For hours I couldn't move from the couch. Finally, I stood, but only long enough to empty my guts into a garbage bag. After wiping my face with the back of my hand, I told Tony I needed to leave.

I had made it home and passed out. Now it was almost noon and everything hurt.

"Get moving, Brad. You got that picnic." My dad's voice was gruff but almost shy. He sounded like he had before grandma died, like he was making an effort.

"Yeah, yeah. Thanks, Popps."

In the bathroom, I splashed water on my face, trying to clear my head, but it didn't help. I returned to my grandma's room, where I'd been sleeping, and winced as I pulled on a shirt. I owned nothing - no posters, no luggage, few clothes - so her room looked exactly like it did when she was alive. I leaned against the dresser - it still had some of her old clothes in it - and had a rare moment of regret. The world wasn't solid underneath me. It was the mushrooms and the hangover, but it was something more too.

I didn't have time to recover. From the kitchen, my dad yelled, "Come on," and I had to trail after him to the truck. He didn't say much, thank God, as he drove us through Portland. But when we crossed into Vancouver, Washington a few minutes later, he cleared his throat.

"I got some errands to run tomorrow."

We stopped at a stoplight. I stared out the window, but couldn't get my eyes to focus on anything.

"Want to come with?"

"Sure, Popps." The words gave me a headache.

A half block later, he pulled next to a park and idled. A young woman ran up to the car. I barely recognized her; she was too old to be my sister. I climbed out as my dad called her Punk'n from the driver's seat. He gave her a half hug through the window before driving away.

"Hey Brad," she said. "You're tall."

We walked into the park together. The fresh air helped but my balance still wasn't as steady as I would have liked. And I was nervous. My mom and sister had recently moved to Vancouver, Washington, a suburb of Portland. This would be the first time I'd spent time with them in almost two years.

I saw them before they saw me. Mom and her boyfriend were under a tree by a winding river. She was laughing about something and looked so happy it made me uncomfortable. I didn't feel like I belonged to this family any more.

My sister said, "We're getting ready for a picnic."

"Yeah," I said. "I can see that."

We took a few more steps closer and I saw a man who had been hidden by a tree. His back was perfectly straight and his dark hair closely shaved. I had to stop for a moment and look again: it was my brother, Eric. Some part of me wanted to sprint over, grab him in a big hug, but I was no child, not any more.

"*Mijo!*" my mom called. She gave me a hug and called me her *corazon*, her *nene*. Eric pulled me close and used a lower voice than I remembered to tell me he was glad to see me. My sister hugged me again. The boyfriend said his name was James and shook my hand. His eyes lowered before the introduction was over. He was bigger than me, but seemed thin, like a blank piece of paper.

We sat around the picnic table. Mom passed around some chicken, but I couldn't stop looking at Eric. This man with the stern gaze, standing, sipping a soda but with his shoulders back like the park belonged to him; this was my brother.

They asked polite questions. They told me they missed me. We ate good food and drank until my head cleared up. It was a perfect day: sunny and warm but not hot. After lunch, Eric brought out a football and said, "Play some catch with me, homeboy." He said the last word with a smirk.

We drifted into the field and started throwing the ball. We talked then about the penitentiary, about San Bernardino, and about the old crew, Aaron and Rocco and Weasel.

Bellies full, sun high, we didn't play long. He tucked the ball under his arm and stepped close. The rest of the family was just out of earshot. I could see my mom cleaning up, James sipping at a beer.

"Hey, Brad, listen. We missed you."

"Yeah, me too."

"No, listen to me. It was hard for us."

"Yeah, yeah." I figured it was a little harder for me than for them, but only said, "Me too."

"What are you doing now? Where's your life headed?"

"I don't know yet."

"But you gonna quit that gang shit, right?"

With his straight back he had seemed to gain three inches and I had to crane up to look him in the eye. The sun shone right behind his head, casting his face in shadow, but I could feel more than see the serious way he was looking at me. "Yeah, *ese*," I said. I probably still had mushrooms floating in my system but I wasn't thinking about that. This was my big brother. Every word he said meant something. "Yeah, I'm done with that shit. I'm gonna get some schooling. Like you did. Get my diploma."

"You serious?"

He stared right at me and I was dead serious. I swore I'd stay clean. I swore I'd get my degree and go to college. I was lying to myself as hard as I was lying to him, but in that moment I meant every single word.

FOOL'S NAME WAS YANZI, BUT IT DIDN'T MATTER. HE stood over me in shop class and said, "Hey *ese*, where you say you're from?"

He was from an XIV crew; they called themselves Brown Pride or BP, and they had been messing with me since I got there. I hadn't been to a regular high school for a year and a half, and the first day I maybe talked too much, acted too proud of coming from southern California. Now it had been over a month but they wouldn't leave it alone. They'd stop me in the hall, in the bathroom, after class, always asking, "Where you from? Where's that you said you were from, Strain?"

But none of them had touched me, so I ignored the fool and went back to my project, making a toolbox out of sheetmetal. Mike sat next to me, working on his. He and I had been friends since my first day. He was Hispanic, from East Los and wore the Sureño blue. He said he'd been jumped in by the Avenues and I had heard of them - they were a solid set. He was big, not huge, but built, and had a low simmer to him, like he'd stay calm no matter what.

The teacher barked instructions over the sound of a band saw. Mike was talking music when this Yanzi fool walked by and shoved me with his shoulder. I didn't see it coming and twisted off my stool; I had to clutch the table so not to fall on the floor.

Slow and quiet, I straightened up, sat down and went back to the project. I acted like nothing happened, but inside I clenched up. No way some BP fool was going to mess with me. Not with my homie Mike sitting there.

In MacLaren Penitentiary, they had kept us in four person cells called lodges. First day I walked into mine with another inmate, Ryan, who was part of a white power gang which had made the national news for killing a young Nigerian man. Without warning, Ryan had grabbed a white boy off the bottom bunk, threw him to the floor and said, "I don't sleep on the top bunk." His fingers had left red marks on the kid's neck. The kid didn't do a thing but mutter, "What the hell? I didn't do nothing," as he moved his stuff. After that, the other inmates had smelled the kid's weakness and made him pay for it.

I would never let that happen: not in prison, not in high school. But I was patient. I did my project and listened to the teacher. I watched Yanzi mishandle a staple gun - not staring, just waiting.

At the end of class, Mike and I went to our lockers next to the door to grab our backpacks. Mike turned to leave, but I gripped the lock in my hand and turned back. Yanzi was leaning at a table talking to some other BP fools and I cut straight to him, no thought, no hesitation. He saw me a couple steps away, and turned his head towards me as I swung full strength with the sharp edge of the lock in my hand and crushed it against his cheek. He flew back. His skin split open. Blood sprayed. I fell on him as he hit the ground and laid into his face.

Hands grabbed me, pulled me off. I screamed, "Fuck this fool."

The teacher barked like a cop, "Strain!"

"I'll kick his ass."

"Strain, get out of here. Go to the principal's office. Now."

I struggled to free myself, make the fool pay.

"Strain!"

The teacher's voice got through enough and it was like I woke from a dream. I looked down at Yanzi at my feet, heard the other kids shouting around me. I had blood on my shirt. "Out!" he said, and I ducked off, hurried down the hallway. I started to run, searching for the nearest exit, but didn't get far.

"Hey kid!"

"Huh?"

"Were you in that fight?"

As a reflex I said, "I don't know what you're talking about," but I had Yanzi's blood on my hands. They took me to the principal and the principal called the cops as I slouched in the plastic seat. The adrenaline seeped out of me as I waited, and I sunk inside myself. I didn't think about what would happen next or the promises I made to my brother. I barely thought of what had just happened, except that the BP fool got what he deserved.

At the police station, the cops asked me questions but I didn't know what they were talking about. I didn't know there had been a fight. Shoot, I barely knew there was a high school. I put on my prison face, ready for whatever, and disappeared to where they couldn't touch me.

I had braced myself for a jail cell, but I was led instead out to a waiting room. There, I found my mom talking to a cop. She was leaning forward, eyes red, cheeks wet, acting like they were on the same side.

"He keeps getting in trouble. We just don't know what to do with him. We just don't know what to do."

Still riled up from the day, I shouted, "Mom!" Both heads jerked towards me. Mom's eyes were red. I said, "What are you doing?"

"You shouldn't talk to your mother that way."

I shook my head and stared at the door.

The cop said, "You need to start listening to your mother, Son. You need to change your life around."

It was always the same thing, but this cop knew nothing. My mom knew nothing. I did what had to be done.

"Come on, Ma," I said. "Let's go."

I HAD MOVED OUT OF MY GRANDMOTHER'S BEDROOM and into my mom's living room. Most mornings I rolled against the wall and slept through my mom or sister or James moving around, but today I needed to get up early. After three weeks of sitting around, I had my first day at the Alternative Learning Center, the ALC. We called it the Assholes Last Chance. It was my only option after busting that fool's face. I expected it would be like a little prison with red-faced men in uniform screaming at us to get in line. It didn't sound like my scene, but when I was with my family, I was always serious about straightening up my life, so I had told my mom I'd give it a try.

I swung my feet from the daybed and rubbed my eyes; it seemed a lot of work to stand up. Dust floated in a sunbeam and I dazed out, watching it.

"Bradley, it's time to go."

"Yeah, Ma, give me a minute."

I closed the door on the little bathroom. There, I pulled on my tan dickies, my white shirt. I set my blue hat just right and tucked the blue bandana in a back pocket. As an extra I dug something out of the bottom of my bag. Earlier, I had taken a two ball from an old pool table and shoved it inside a sock. Its weight stretched the fabric towards the ground. I got the idea from my time at MacLaren's where a couple bars of soap and a sock made a useful weapon.

A minute later, I followed Mom to the car. It was sunny but cold with traces of snow still lingering from winter. Mom was quiet as she drove, but broke her silence after she parked in the lot.

"Bradley, this is it. You understand?"

"Yeah, Ma, I know."

"You need to keep your head down and do the work. This is your last chance."

Assholes Last Chance, I thought. It made me grin.

"You have to take this seriously."

"I do, Ma. I swear."

Four squat trailers sat across the field behind the traditional Evergreen High School. Mom and I followed the sign that said 'office' where a woman opened the door. She wore a flowery blouse over skinny arms and looked for a moment like she wanted to give me a hug.

"Mr. Strain," she said, "we are so glad you are here. You don't need to worry about a thing. This is a place tailor-made for you and your needs. The kinds of things that caused you trouble in your last school simply don't happen here."

Her voice was syrupy and her eyes misted up behind pink-tinted glasses. It was so different than what I had expected, I almost laughed.

"Thank you," she said to my mom. "We'll take good care of him from here."

My mom gave me a last glare and left. The woman took me back to a trailer, knocking gently on the door.

Inside a group of teenagers swiveled their heads to stare at me. I didn't know any of them but they all looked familiar. Their grins, their humor, the way they dressed; it was a classroom full of people like me. I sat towards the back and they had me laughing in seconds. The teacher softly pleaded for us to settle down. She asked us politely to listen. While she talked, I met JBone and Donald.

JBone was a white boy. He wore overalls with one strap hanging loose; it made him look like Marky Mark. Donald was black. When he took off his hat, his hair poofed out like a mushroom. He grinned at all my jokes. Two solid homies, they made me feel at home before class was over.

After we were dismissed, half the kids gathered in the field and started smoking before the next period. Donald passed a pipe filled with dope. I took a long pull, grinning, almost giggling. The ALC was filled with the troublemakers, the throw-away kids. These were my people.

I exhaled and asked JBone, "Tell me serious, is this place for real?"

JBone snorted smoke out his nose. "You know it, brother. You know it."

NONE OF US HAD A CAR. MIKE HAD ACCESS TO HIS dad's lowrider, but we had to sneak it out after the man fell asleep and it was too early for that. So we were walking, not sure where we were going but I was feeling good. It was a nice night; it had been bright and sunny during the day, but it had turned cool so I had my jacket on.

When we found ourselves outside a Safeway, I said, "Let's get something to drink."

My two homies shrugged. Mike was solid, out of East Los, smart, ambitious and fearless. And the fool who looked like Marky Mark, he went by JBone and had something crazy in his eyes I understood. He wasn't Hispanic, but he was up for anything.

"I got no cash," Mike said and I looked at him like he was crazy. Then both of them shrugged again and I didn't understand it. Maybe these guys weren't as down as I thought. My old homie Rocco wouldn't shrug. And Miguel would've been in and out already.

"What the hell? Ain't you thirsty?"

They looked at each other like they didn't understand what I was asking.

"Shit," I said. "All right. Wait here."

I shoved at the door and cruised in. With each step, energy built in my chest, pulsing out. In the back, I didn't bother to look around, but grabbed the first forty I saw. I tried to shove it down my pants, but it wouldn't fit. I tried to hide it in my coat while holding the neck but that was no good. Ten seconds had passed and I'd had enough. Clerks at these places never stopped anyone and I needed to prove myself. Like I had done with Aaron and the set in Gilbert hall and Big Wheez and just about every other homie I'd known, I needed to show Mike and JBone that I could be crazier than anyone they'd ever met.

I grabbed a second forty, one in each hand, and headed to the front door. I walked calmly, smiling at them through the window. I lifted the bottles up, an early celebration before I scored.

A woman's voice called out, but I ignored her. A middle aged man, dressed in khaki pants and a blue polo trotted at me from the right. He waved his hands, telling me to stop. Then a third man, heavyset, face covered in zits, stepped in front of the door, blocking my way.

I put the beer down, a countertop right there, smiling as I did, knowing Mike and JBone were going to get a show. I pulled the end of the sock from my pocket like a magician until the two ball tumbled down my leg, its weight stretching the cotton. I started swinging it, swirling in a tight circle like a gladiator, my smile turning into a laugh. I said, "You better back up. You don't want none of this."

The sock gave off a little whistle as it whirred above my head. I could feel my homies eyes on me; I started to imagine the story I'd tell, but a flash to my right stopped me.

A man shouted, "Vancouver PD, drop it!"

He was short, with wide shoulders and hair shaved close to his scalp. His voice had the tone of a cop. He flashed his badge and I saw the holster under his jacket.

"Drop the weapon!"

It landed like a punch. I froze and my sock went limp. Sickness filled my gut as I raised my hands and backed up. Sirens blared outside. He twisted my arms behind my back. But even as pain seared through my shoulders, I made a point to grin out the window at my new homies, JBone and Mike.

"WHERE YOU BEEN, BRAD?" HIS VOICE WAS HEAVY gravel so he somehow sounded even bigger on the phone.

"You know me, Big Wheez. Kicking it with my homies in Portland."

"You did some time up there, huh?"

I nodded into the phone, imagining him on the other end. I pictured the slow grin, the slant of the big man's head when he talked to you, always letting you know he was in control. There was no one like Big Wheez around Portland. Not yet.

"Yeah, I did some time."

"They treat you all right?"

"It was all right. I met some people."

"Yeah," he said. "I heard you were jacking some XIV motherfuckers."

"Ey, I don't know nothing about that."

"Naw, but you're the real deal, huh?"

"I'm just living, Big Wheez. I'm just living my life."

"Naw, man, I heard you're real. Rocco's been talking. Heard they call you Loco now?"

I had a hard time talking for a few moments. Tony had started calling me Loco at MacLaren and now it had spread so my big homie knew my name. People were talking about me. I had a reputation. It confirmed I was on the right path.

He said, "We could use you back here, Loco."

"You know how it is. I got my family up here."

"Heard about your brother."

"Yeah?"

"That's a good man."

"We're all proud of him."

"The Air Force? That's real good. "

I didn't like talking about Eric, so I said, "Big Wheez, I wanted to ask you about something."

"Here it is."

"I'd like to start my own set in Vancouver."

"You do, huh?"

I did. After my arrest in the Safeway, I only spent six hours in custody. A week later at court they gave me a good attorney. She explained to the judge that I hadn't actually stolen anything because I never left the store. Said my actions were self-defense. Told them I backed down immediately when the cop identified himself. I strutted out of that courtroom, felt untouchable. I was ready for the next step.

"This area is wide open, Big Wheez. Lots of opportunities."

"Who you got up there?"

"Some XIV fools call themselves Brown Pride. We'll take care of them no problem."

"Who're your homies?"

"I got a solid crew. Mike, he's out of East Los, was part of the Avenues down there. He was out with Peewee."

"Peewee's solid. Who else?"

I had a white boy and Donald, who was half-black. This wouldn't fly with Big Wheez or the Sureños. They kept to their own race, I knew that, but I was living in the Pacific Northwest. There weren't Hispanics up here like in Southern California. And D and JBone, they were down. They'd be good homies, but I didn't know how to explain any of this to Big Wheez.

"I got a few others we have to jump in."

"That's right. That's right. All right, Loco. Let me get with Peewee and we'll talk."

Sureños were organized; they had a hierarchy. My big homie, Big Wheez, would talk with Mike's big homie, Peewee, and they'd connect with a bigger boss, a homie running the show - usually from prison. If the big boss said yes, they'd give us the okay and put us on the books. Then we'd have to jump our members in and they'd get put on the list. After that, we'd be registered. We'd have to pay our dues but we'd get supplies and protection.

Of course, it could go the other way. If our big homies didn't think we'd represent, or had some reason not to trust us, then we could get green-lighted. This meant they would mark us for other sets to come in and take us out.

Big Wheez said, "This was smart coming to me. You're doing good out there."

Again I swelled up and had a hard time getting my breath to speak. I had done it right, was moving up, getting noticed. I was doing exactly what I needed. I had the Sureños behind me and nothing in my way but some Brown Pride fools led by a chickenshit named Jack Hall.

After I hung up, I sat grinning for a moment. They had no idea what was coming.

Los Tiny Dukes
Two days later

MIKE PULLED INTO the alley. It was a quiet neighborhood in the middle of the night, no lights inside, no one outside. I directed him to park behind a squat house next to an old truck.

"Wait here," I said.

From the back seat, JBone coughed. "What we doing here, Loco?"

"You'll see. I'll be right out."

I found the spare key under the flower pot and eased the back door open. Inside, everything was quiet. Light glowed from the microwave, otherwise it was dark. The smell of cigarette smoke lingered under something damp I didn't recognize. But the place was clean and well ordered, exactly as I expected.

The man's bedroom door was open. I could see his form in the bed and found the rumble of his snores strangely comforting. I moved quietly past it, but needed a moment when I stepped into my grandma's room. I remembered her smiling face, her calling me 'Mr. Wonderful,' the brown envelope in the dresser. The forty I drank had taken the edge off; but it didn't go far enough. I had to swallow against the hollow ache in my chest before I could move again.

I opened the closet door and started digging around on the floor. Behind a box, under an old blanket, I found Popp's two 45s; they'd been hidden in the same spot for years. I shoved each in a pocket and stood quietly, barely breathing. The buzz cranked up as I eased the closet door shut. My dad slept fifteen feet away and I felt the thrill of it; the high stakes pushed away the crazy swirling in my head. I snuck back into the hall, listening for changes in his breathing, then out the door. The lock clicked behind me. After tucking the key under the pot, I climbed next to Mike.

"This is what I was doing, JBone."

I handed a pistol back to him as we pulled onto a main road. Music pounded underneath us as JBone messed with the safety, handled the ammo, loaded it. He leaned forward between me and Mike and aimed at the windshield, at the cars in front of us, at the houses rumbling by.

Back in Vancouver I pointed to another alley and told Mike to stop. I hurried around to the trunk and grabbed the shotgun; we had sawed it off weeks before and the weight sat comfortable in my hands. I was a predator, a warrior, a monster. I eased back in the car. We had a few blocks left to go.

"I guess we're not tagging tonight," JBone said. For the past three nights we'd been spraying our new name around the neighborhood. I had come from Los Dukes in San Bernardino so I figured, since we were younger and smaller, my new set should be Los Tiny Dukes. Mike had liked it all right so we started tagging LTD over any place the BP fools claimed territory.

Now I was ready to throw down. I had shown up, ready to be a gangster, and this fool Jack Hall and the BP were done; they just didn't know it yet.

"Naw, man," I said. "We're not tagging tonight. Pull down this way. We're going to pay a visit. Turn off the lights here."

Mike stopped in front of Jack Hall's house. We had driven by it many times over the past couple weeks. The place was dark from the outside, no signs of life.

"Should we go for the windows or what, Loc?" Mike asked. He knew what we were doing without me saying.

I wanted to scare this *vato*. I wanted to piss him off. I wanted to start a war. I said, "Naw, *ese*," and I climbed out of the window. My feet dangled on the passenger seat and the shotgun rested against the roof.

Hall had his car parked in the driveway, a sweet lowrider, polished new; he drove it around like he owned the neighborhood. I turned the shotgun towards it and let loose. The gun slammed into my shoulder, and his rear window exploded, the blast echoed up and down the quiet street. I pumped it and shot again. His side mirror shattered with a boom.

There was a series of pops underneath me as the 45s went off. Six more times I pulled the trigger, smelling the gun powder, watching the fool's car twist and fold. After my last shell was spent, I sunk down, my ears ringing.

I said, "Let's go."

Mike peeled off through the dark alley.

JBone screamed, "Hell yeah! It's on."

"That's right," Mike said. "We're showing them. They ain't going to get us out of here."

We pulled onto a Main Street and cruised with the spare traffic. I sat back and listened to my homies celebrate. A buzz crackled through my fingers, out of my skin. I thought about the chaos, the coming war; I imagined Jack Hall stepping out of his house and seeing what we did. It loosed something in my chest and I started to laugh. I banged the dash, the windows, shouting until my throat hurt.

TONY LIVED IN A CRIP NEIGHBORHOOD AND IT SEEMED like everyone on the street - and a few in the windows - stopped to watch Mike and me cruise through in his dad's Monte Carlo. Their eyes followed us - our music thumping - all the way until we stopped.

My mind buzzed as we climbed out of the car, on full alert for someone to say something. Two men at the corner started mean-mugging us, and my body tightened, ready to throw down with any one of these fools - or all of them. But as soon as Tony stepped out his front door the tension drained away. His family was known and we were under their protection.

Tony seemed oblivious to the people watching us. He eyed the car and whistled.

I grinned. "You like our ride, *ese*?"

"Yeah, yeah, Loco, where did you get it?"

Mike's dad passed out early and we snuck it out of the garage, but that was more than I wanted to explain. I said, "You know me, fool."

100

Tony grinned and led us into his house. It was crowded and noisy, felt like they had a party going on all day. A couple younger sisters chased their cousins. Older homies argued around a table in the kitchen. We sat on the couch and Tony offered us weed and drink.

Tony said, "What you been doing, Loco?"

"Just chilling. Just kicking it with my boy, Mike."

Mike gave Tony a friendly lift of his head.

Tony said, "You two homies stirring some shit up?"

I leaned back, hands behind my head. "We started a set."

"No shit?"

"No shit. We talked to Big Wheez. Mike talked to Peewee. It's legit."

"You serious?"

I shrugged. "Do I look like I'm fucking around?"

I told him about Jack Hall, skinny as a street sign, his Jheri-curl poking under his hat. Others stopped to listen and I told them about shooting up the car. I played it for laughs and got a good response from the room.

"Damn, Loco, you are crazy."

"That's right. And I need to talk to Chavo, see if we can make a connection. We want to start selling."

Tony nodded, looking like he knew what was up. "My uncle, he likes you." As he said this, the front door opened like they had timed it. Tony laughed. "Aw shit, there he is."

Chavo grinned as he worked through the room. After he met Mike, Tony slapped his hand on his uncle's shoulder. "Chavo, you got to hear this crazy mother fucker. Loco, tell him what you been doing."

I was happy to tell the story again. Chavo laughed at the right parts. He said "We should call you Crazy-Loco. C Loco. You been working."

"That's why I need to talk to you. We got some business together."

"We do, huh? Well, let's get to it."

Mike hung at the couch as I followed Chavo down a back stairway into the basement. It looked like an office, with a corner desk and a rolling chair. Wood panelling went halfway up. A framed Jordan poster hung on the wall. He had stacked a pile of rims on the floor and a couple cardboard boxes had been shoved in the corner, but mostly he kept the place clean. He invited me to sit on the weight bench.

I started in immediately. "Big Wheez can't set me up right away so I

101

thought you and I could have an arrangement."

"Hold on there, homie." He opened his beer and rolled the chair closer to me.

I said, "I'd like to push a little coke, you know."

"Yeah, yeah, I hear you, Loco." A girl's laughter came muffled through the ceiling. "But I don't know. Tony told me stories about MacLarens." He shook his head. "And the MAX station."

I didn't like his tone of voice. This was a key part of my plan; I didn't know what I'd do if he turned me down. I slumped on the bench.

"I'm a businessman, you understand? I'm not into that gang shit. I don't want headaches, Loco. I just want to sell my product."

"I will sell your product."

"I don't know if you're ready."

"I don't..." I rubbed hard at my face. "What's this about, Chavo? I never ratted on anyone. You can trust me. Ask Tony."

"I know that, Loco. I trust you. And I like you. But... shit."

"You know me."

"Yeah..." He took a heavy gulp of beer. "How about this? We start you out small. I'll get you a quarter of coke."

An ounce of cocaine was about the size of a golf ball. A quarter ounce would fill a plastic baggie about two fingers high.

He said, "You work through that. Bring me back my cash and we'll see what's up."

I said, "I was kind of thinking I'd buy it from you clean."

"Nah, this is better. You bring me my money and we'll go from there."

"What's my cut?"

He grinned. "Bring me my money, Loco, and we'll go from there."

I wanted to bolt up, pace the room, curse, but I kept still. I didn't want to answer to another big homie, but I needed money. And to get money I needed his drugs. I had bigger dreams than Chavo knew. I wanted to lower the thunder, be a legend, scatter the fools like dice.

"All right," I said. "Let's do it."

We shook hands. It didn't go as I'd wanted but I got what I needed. Los Tiny Dukes were in business.

———

"HOW DO WE SELL THIS SHIT?" I WAS MORE THINKING out loud but JBone was there, my road dog, walking with me. We weren't far from my mom's place. And we weren't going nowhere, but I liked to move. It helped me think.

It had only been a couple days, but I was impatient. Coke sold itself, so it should have been no problem. Do it right and customers would come find me. But I couldn't figure how to break into it. Before, with Big Wheez, I'd just do what I was asked, go where the boss told me. But now I was the big homie, and I couldn't move any of it.

JBone wasn't much help; he was a smiley white boy, up for whatever, but not much on ideas. He just grunted. "I don't know, dude. I don't know."

"We gotta know some fools who need a hookup, right?"

JBone didn't get a chance to answer. Three sharp bursts from a pistol came from behind us; it sounded like firecrackers behind a window. We spun to see a car hurtling our direction, the driver a blur through the windshield, but clear enough: weak face, red hat, skinny arm gripping the pistol. Jack Hall. I shoved JBone back into a bush as more pops burst from the gun.

I covered my head. Another pop then the tires screeched around a corner and the engine faded. The street became dead quiet around us. I poked my head out of the bushes.

JBone sat up, muttered, "Ah, fuck."

I saw no cars, nothing around.

"Ah, fuck."

"Check it out," I said. "I think we're clear."

JBone stood up next to me. Eyes wide, clutching at his shirt, he said, "Ah fuck!"

"It's cool, *ese*."

We stepped onto the sidewalk. There were no headlights, no car sounds, no sirens. I glanced behind us. On a fence about chest high, several good chunks had been gouged out of the wood. Bullet holes.

"Check it out," I nudged JBone. "Don't know how the fool missed us."

"Ah, fuck!"

Something between a laugh and a scream gathered in my chest and I let it go. It was on. Jack Hall had taken his shot. Adrenaline was coursing through my body like a drug and I needed to move. "Fool missed us, JBone, come on."

I led him across the street at a trot.

"That was crazy, Loco."

"Yeah, yeah, yeah." We turned down an alleyway and slowed to a walk. JBone kept muttering curses under his breath but I said, "We got to celebrate."

"What are you talking about?"

"That fool messed up and we got to celebrate."

We cut through back yards in case Jack Hall decided to swing back, then jumped a fence near the Safeway parking lot. I headed straight for the front door.

"Ain't you banned from this place?"

I grinned. "They didn't mean it."

"Loco..." JBone shook his head and started to laugh. "You are crazy."

I was on a streak. They couldn't throw me in jail; they couldn't shoot me; I felt invincible. I wanted to scream again, rage against the police, the BP, the whole world.

JBone and I pushed through the door and we moved straight to the liquor. I grabbed a bottle of Thunderbird because it was smaller and I was feeling manic not stupid. We walked out with the liquor barely hidden in our coats. The checkout lady pretended not to notice.

A block behind the store, we stopped at a little park and settled on a picnic bench. I couldn't stop laughing, but JBone had gone quiet.

He didn't see the bigger picture. In less than ten days I had organized a set, got a coke connection and started a war. I imagined calling Big Wheez, hearing his heavy laugh when I told him.

All I needed now was some customers, which was crazy. The product should sell itself.

AFTER MOM DROPPED ME AT THE ALC, I ALWAYS FACED the choice to go to class or not. Today I had nothing else going on and figured it was usually a good time, so I slouched into the back row. I clowned through the first couple hours then went out to the smoking area with JBone during break.

We lit up, and talked about nothing. I shuffled in the grass, damp from a recent rain, until my shoes soaked through. I liked the smell of mud and wet pavement; it had never smelled like that in San Bernardino.

Three stoners from the high school crossed the field towards us, and I figured I'd try something Tony taught me. I had a baggie of coke in my shorts that I'd been hustling around. I sprinkled some of powder on top of the weed and ran the flame over it so it melted down to saturate the dope. Tony had called it a primo.

The stoners joined the circle, eyes dreamy and distant. They had their own gang colors: flannel jackets unbuttoned over old t-shirts. I offered them a hit of the primo and they each took a deep drag.

I watched without much feeling, my mind elsewhere. I didn't like this part, hustling to find a market. I wanted to mix it up, throw down with the other gangs, make a riot, create some mayhem. But I knew none of that could happen without a cash flow.

In the end, my efforts came to nothing. A distant bell rang across the field and the stoners nodded at us and took off. I shrugged back to class.

A couple more days passed and I still couldn't find customers. I didn't know what to do so I headed back to school. Usually I hung in back with JBone and clowned, acted like an idiot, but that day I kept to myself, sulking. For one morning, my failure made me a model student.

At break I barely noticed the same three stoners coming across the field, but they called to me before they got close. "Hey man, we've been looking for you."

"Yeah?"

"Where did you get that weed?"

"You like that? That wasn't just weed. That had a little coke in it."

"No shit?"

"No shit."

I pulled the powder from my pocket and showed them how to burn it on top. These white boys watched like it was a magic trick.

I looked at them, a thrill spreading in my chest. "You want to get hooked up with this?"

They checked in with each other, a grin and a nod.

"How much you want?"

"We'll take - what do you got?" They each pulled out a wad of bills and started counting.

I made the sale. They smoked and talked about a party that weekend. I tried to get an invite but it didn't come. After the bell rang, I watched them walk back to Evergreen High. It was a start.

At break the next day, I found the stoners waiting for me. Eyes wide, they asked for more. Told me others were asking about me and wondered if that was cool. I said, "Yeah, yeah, send them my way."

Over the next week, they kept showing up, bringing others with them, all kinds of kids both from the high school and the ALC. One girl said, "Hey Brad, I didn't know you had coke."

I'd done nothing but telegraph that information for over a week, but I shrugged.

It was crazy who started showing up at break. Kids I wouldn't have imagined: jocks, preppie kids, some driving up in nice cars. It got so I had to hand off some to Mike and JBone. They'd sell it and get the cash back to me.

Once it started, I dumped those first four bags within a week. I called Chavo, laughing at my success.

"Hey *homes*, I got your money."

"You got my money? You serious?"

I was dead serious and part of me wanted to say something smart to remind the man he hadn't believed I could do it, but I didn't want to hurt our bond. I had much bigger plans.

THAT MORNING, MOM HAD DROPPED ME OFF AT school, but I waved at her and then walked a different way. I took a bus, kicked it around town, found a homie and smoked a little weed. Not a great day, but it didn't matter because tonight I'd be with Chavo. I spent most of the day thinking about it, working through how I'd handle him, what I'd say when we met.

Now, it was midafternoon and I was almost home. I trotted across a busy road, raising my hand to slow a pickup truck before it ran me down. I still had time to kill, so figured I'd lay low for a few hours, maybe take a nap. But on the sidewalk outside my mom's apartment

I had to stop as it took me a few seconds to understand what I was seeing.

Popp's truck was parked hard against the curb, one tire riding up on it. He could be here for a hundred things, none of them good.

It took another minute to decide what to do. Finally, I climbed the stairs like a boxer, fists up, fast feet. My stomach clenched up and my body with it, every part of me bracing for a fight. My dad had tried to shape me up with his fists and belt my whole life, but the last few years I had been fighting back. He was bigger than me but I was younger and knew how to take a punch.

At the landing, the apartment door opened before I reached for it. My dad started yelling instantly, "Get your ass inside now, Brad!"

I stepped in to the kitchen and stood still, with my back straight, and my eyes on the wall. His face was bright red as he screamed, "Where are the goddam pistols, Brad?"

It took me a moment. I had kind of forgotten about the guns, or at least forgotten where I got them. Thinking about Jack Hall made me grin.

"Is this a joke?" He gripped my shoulder and shoved his face into mine. "Do you think this is funny?"

"I don't know what you're talking about."

"Brad. You don't want to mess around with me. Did you sell my guns?"

"Naw, Popps, I didn't sell nothing."

"Where are they at right now?"

Mom was crying in the living room, pleading for us to calm down. The fear in her voice got to me.

"All right. All right," I said. "I'll grab them."

On the ceiling of the hallway closet was a panel to an attic space. I pushed it open and pulled down a Nike shoebox. Inside, the pistols rested against each other. I tried not to look at Mom as I handed them to my dad.

"How long have you had these?"

"Awhile, I don't know." I knew exactly, almost down to the minute. "I don't remember."

He clutched the guns to his chest. The muscles in his jaw tightened.

"I just wanted to check them out. Do some target practice out in the woods. I didn't mean no harm."

Popp's voice lowered to a growl. "Did you bring them to school?"

I had kept them in my bag for awhile and brought them to school more than once. "Naw, Popps, I didn't bring them to school. Why you tripping? Nothing happened. Why are you flipping out on me?"

He spoke to my mom but pointed a trembling finger towards me. "You better do something about him."

"Keith, leave him alone." Mom dabbed a tissue to her eyes. "I'll handle it."

"You better ground him for a long time."

"I will. Keith. It's done." She patted his arm.

I raised up my hands. "I didn't mean nothing by it. I swear."

"Keith..." my mom said.

He pointed his finger again and said, "You need to change up your life, boy." He breathed heavy, his jaw clenched tight. I could see in his face that he wanted to grab at me, but didn't want to fight in front of my mom. Finally, he twisted around and left, slamming the door behind him.

Mom couldn't look at me. I studied her for a long moment, the back of her head lowered towards the floor.

"I never even used them, Ma. I didn't think he'd care."

She shook her head and shuddered. I felt an echo, a small whisper, a moment of something like regret.

It passed quickly.

I grabbed a couple things from my bag, a little cash - I had to take the bus to Chavo's - and a clean shirt. I took my time so as not to run into my dad in the parking lot.

"Good-bye, Ma," I said.

She didn't answer but sunk into a chair. She rested her head in her hand.

I left.

"HEY LOCO, HAVE A SEAT, HAVE A SEAT."

I sat down on the weight bench, Chavo on his rolling chair, and leaned forward, elbows on my knees, feeling this moment. The look in the man's eyes as he greeted me upstairs, the tough ass coke dealer was showing me respect.

"So... you sold some shit."

"It was easy, Chavo." The words slid out smooth and satisfying. "I did it just like you said; I dropped it on some dope and the white boys couldn't get enough."

"That's right."

"They lined up for that shit. I sold my bindles in a week."

"You did good."

My chest puffed up, sitting with this man in his basement, knowing he was smart. He knew what he was doing and he was working with me.

"Now you just got to keep your customers."

"That's right."

"Keep it steady. "

"Yeah, yeah."

"Don't get crazy, now, you understand me?"

"Come on, you know me."

"I do know you, Loco. That's the trouble."

"Come on." I gave him a back handed wave. For the moment, in that basement, I heard what Chavo was saying, and was with him. "I'm not into that crazy shit. I'm a businessman. I'mma keep it cool," I said, and, at least until I got back onto the street, I meant every word.

"This gang war shit, that's not good for anyone."

I nodded. "Yeah, yeah. I made my point. Now it's just about making some profit. Keeping it steady, keeping customers."

"That's right."

"But you know." I gave him a slow grin like I'd seen from Big Wheez; like I knew what I was doing and wasn't trying to hide it. "It'd be better if I had more product. If I could buy it from you, you know. So I don't have to keep coming out here."

"You sure you ready?"

"I'm ready for anything."

"All right." He slapped his knees with both hands. "Let's do this."

He gestured me over to a workbench. From a low shelf he brought out a brown-papered brick and set it down. He unwrapped the paper to expose white powder, still holding its shape. With three sharp stabs from a pick he pierced it, and put the chunk on a triple beam scale. He trimmed it to an ounce and packaged it up.

I swaggered upstairs with eight thousand dollars worth of coke in my pocket. I flung open the door, and the music was pounding; homies were drinking, tripping, dancing. Mike slouched in a chair, smoking, talking up Tony's sister. I leapt into the party with a shout, and we went all night. The world blurred into sweat and laughter. It wasn't until dawn that we finally stumbled outside.

The street lights were blinking off as we waited at the corner. When the bus arrived, I slid my dollar in the machine and worked my way through a strange mix of early commuters and people like us, young men with empty eyes coming down from their highs. Exhausted, I collapsed onto a plastic seat. The road rumbled underneath us, the sound relaxing, but I refused to close my eyes. I had an ounce of coke in my pocket, and a ninety minute ride to get it home.

Battleground
Three weeks later

WE PARKED OUTSIDE the McDonald's, under the soft yellow glow of its sign. Mike had bought himself a car, and we'd been doing the loop, cruising up and down on a Friday night like teenagers did.

Another car stopped next to us. Our clique was growing. The four of us, me, Mike, D and JBone, made up the core crew, but others hung with us now, homies just looking to have a good time.

It was happening; I could feel it. I had been mixing it up wherever I went and people were talking; my reputation was spreading like smoke in a basement. Horror stories were floating around about this gangster, Loco. He was crazy, fearless, violent. I'd see it in their eyes when they met me. Their eyebrows would shoot up as they tried to make sense of my baby face. Because I looked innocent and small, some would make the mistake of dismissing me, thinking I was nothing. I spent most of my time trying to prove them wrong.

I leaned back on the hood, the engine still hot under my palms. Lights from the strip mall came hazy through the mist. I started telling my homies the story about the rifle, how I shoved it down my pants. They laughed with me, finding it hilarious. These were my people; they showed me respect, but still I felt itchy. I wanted to mess with somebody, show them I was real. I always needed chaos; without it I didn't know who I was.

And chaos always showed up. That night it was a lowrider rumbling through the traffic. Its windows were open and its subwoofers threw out a bass line I could feel in my gut. The body had been sanded down to gray metal, but I recognized it, no problem. The driver had skinny shoulders, and a wisp of Jheri-curl poking underneath his red hat. It was Jack Hall.

I tuned out my homies clowning behind me and watched hungrily. His back bumper scraped the pavement as he turned into the parking lot across the street. BP *vatos* gathered around the car. Hall had installed hydraulic switches, and he pumped it up and sunk it down. Someone shoved a cigarette pack underneath to see how low it would go and hooted like a fool.

The thrill of violence pushed out every other thought and feeling. I started towards them, a foot into the grass, shoe pushing into the dirt, but JBone stopped me with a hand on my shoulder.

"Hold up, Loc."

I whipped around, worried he'd gone soft, that he wasn't ready to throw down. But JBone's eyes were wide and angry. He wanted this one, even more than me. I stepped aside and let my boy lead the way across the street.

JBone stutter-stepped through a break in traffic, white boy grabbing at his waistband, pulling up his sagged pants until he was next to the car. The BP fools reacted to his momentum by flinching back to give him space around the door.

"Hey, Jack Hall, get the fuck out of the car."

He squinted out the window. "Who the hell are you?"

"We're Los Tiny Dukes, fool." JBone banged at him, flashing our signs.

"Fuck you, scraps."

"Get out of the car."

"What you think you're going to do?"

"You're about to see." JBone spit, then went still, rooting himself in the concrete. Jack Hall's homies stayed back, waiting for their big homie to act. Finally, he cracked his door enough for JBone to pounce. He ripped it open, pulled Jack from the seat and pounded his face, two hard blows so he crumpled. A few seconds and the fight was over but JBone didn't stop. He slammed Jack's head against the door.

Too late, the BP crew started to react. A big fool lunged, but Mike and I were on him with a riot of elbows and fists before he could get to JBone. The others fell on us; I took a fist hard to my head and my face slammed on the concrete. I took a few hard kicks in the ribs until one of my homies pulled me up.

The sound of sirens made us all scatter. Mike, JBone and I stuck together; we ran behind the store, and down a dark alley. I was bruised up and limping but laughing with every step. I said, "You beat the hell out of him."

JBone nodded, still intense, still feeling it. "Fuck that dude."

I slapped him on the back. "Yeah *ese*, you're my boy."

Mike trailed behind us. He had been quiet through the whole thing, but now he said, "You guys are crazy."

"Come on, Mike, that's the end of BP right there. They're done." I grabbed him around the shoulders and laughed until he shrugged into a smile. "They're done."

He shook his head and said it again.

"You guys are crazy."

REBECCA REYES. BECKY. SHE WAS HISPANIC; HAD DARK skin, bright eyes, and big hair. She was small; her bones seemed too thin, like a bird's. She lived in a nice house near the park. Her dad was a long-haul trucker and her mom was off visiting family. It was Friday night, so she threw a party.

A bald Mexican dude got there the same time I did. His name was Cisco. He was a mean-mugging bad-ass from L.A., and he was huge, had a hundred pounds on me. He'd driven up in a wide truck, bass thumping out the back. He climbed out, barely acknowledged me with a nod.

We opened the door together and the party poured out: music, laughter, smoke. I felt good; I'd bought myself a new pair of Cortez, and strutted around, hoping everyone noticed. I smoked some primos, drank a beer. It was a smaller crew, just the clique and a few others. It was low stress with no business. Homies danced and I drifted, grinning, hugging, telling stories to make the girls laugh.

After an hour, I went looking for Becky. She was cool, always smiling at me. She had a laugh which could keep a party rolling. I liked how she'd grab my arm when she talked. I liked the way she did her eye makeup. I liked the smell of her perfume, all of it.

I asked another of the girls where Becky was at, and she nodded to the garage. Then she raised her eyebrows, worried, like there might be some trouble going down. I nodded, the drugs affecting me, clouding me, but hurried out the door.

The garage smelled of dust and oil. A couple naked bulbs cast a dim light. There were no cars or any sign of Becky. Instead, I saw Cisco in a shadow, leaning over something against the far wall.

"Cisco," I called. "What's up, *ese?*"

He turned towards me slowly, stumbling a little. When he lifted his head, I saw his eyes were droopy and sullen. Behind him, dwarfed by his size, I could see Becky now, trying to pull away.

"What?" he said. He yanked her into his body. "What?"

I grinned, acting calmer than I felt, and stepped in a little closer. "Hey *homes*, you don't have to be like that. It's all right. What you doing?"

"You need to go, Strain." Even slurred, his words had a sharp edge. "I'm trying to get something going here."

Becky glared at me, begging me with her eyes not to leave.

"I can see that," I said. "But why don't you get back into the party. Your homeboy Mike wants to talk to you quick."

He had turned away from me, and started grabbing at her, pulling on her clothes. She struggled, but carefully so as not to provoke him.

"Come on, Cisco, let's talk. I was going to ask if you want to join Los Tiny Dukes."

He shook his head. "Why would I want to join that shit."

I didn't like that, but let it slide. "Mike wants to talk to you about it."

"I'm already Sureño." He turned, glaring down at me, and finally let Becky go. Breathing in my face, he repeated. "I'm already Sureño."

"I hear that." I kept grinning up at him. Adrenaline buzzed through me. He was a mountain who could lay me out with one punch, but I was hoping it wouldn't come to that. "But why don't you head inside. Mike's got some business."

114

"I'm with the girl." He jabbed a thumb behind him.

"Our girl seems a little stressed out."

We stared at each other. I braced up, ready for him to take me down. But he blinked slowly and muttered, "Aw fuck, Loco." He let Becky inch away. "Ah, fuck it."

With that, he stumbled drunk and high back in the house. I breathed, almost laughing, surprised I was still standing.

"Thank you," Becky wrapped her arms around me. Her tears dampened my neck. "Thank you, thank you, thank you."

"No problem. He's drunk."

"He's an asshole."

"That too, yeah."

She kissed my cheek as she let me go.

I said, "I'll keep an eye out for you, okay?" and walked her back to the party. In the corner of my vision, for the rest of the night, I could see her smile.

RAIN POUNDED DOWN, THE THICKEST DROPS LIKE A sheet just outside the porch. Music thumped so I felt it under my legs as I leaned next to the front door, smoking a primo. I was in the right location, where anyone could find me, buy from me. Homies streamed past on their way into the house and on their way out. I slouched back, and said hey to everyone. The railing was loose underneath me and damp, but it was good being out there. All afternoon, whenever I looked outside, rain had pissed against the window. It had kept me caged, but now I was out, ready to mix it up. Mike liked the money, D liked the drugs, but me, I liked being known. I liked being seen. I grinned like a madman, the heart of the party. When a homie saw me for the first time and their eyes grew wide, that was more my drug than anything.

During a quiet moment, I was distracted by headlights appearing around a far corner. As the car grew closer I could see it was a lowrider. I watched, already grinning, as it streaked into a wide puddle which had collected several blocks of rain. Water gushed from under its front bumper and past its tires.

I bobbed my head to the music, loving the show these fools were giving me. The car stopped in a half-foot of water. Fitted with hydraulics, it lifted up and inched forward until I could see four heads behind the windshield: busters rolling up like they were something big. I guessed it was a rival set, probably Norteños from XIV.

Everyone on the porch had stopped to watch as waves lapped back against the lowrider's grill. We screamed out advice, growing louder as the engine started to sputter. When it died, I threw my head back and laughed until tears came. Next to me JBone folded over; he couldn't breathe.

I yelled, "You ain't driving no boat, fool." The others homies howled. I shouted, "You need a rope?"

A window rolled down and a head popped out, looking like a turtle coming out of his shell. He cried out, "This is XIV, fool."

"And we're Los Tiny Dukes." I grabbed the rock they'd been using to prop the door open - it fit perfectly in my hand - and hurled it at them. It fell short but the splash hit the window.

"We're gonna kick your ass."

"You going to have to get out of your car first."

More laughter. JBone had a grin bigger than his face. I picked up a beer bottle to throw but stopped when the barrel came out of a back window. The rest of the gun followed. I stumbled back too fast to identify it, but it was huge. The shots burst out and rolled on top of each other as the homie sprayed bullets into the air.

Laughter turned to screams, but in a way it was all the same to me. I was mixing it up with real bangers. Shit was going down and I'd get another story to tell. Still, I was in no hurry to die, so I jumped off the side of the deck and landed in an inch of mud. It squished up around my Cortez sneakers as I scurried around back. More shots popped from the direction I was running on the other side of the house. I tried to change directions, cut back, but slipped and fell hard to my knees.

I crab walked back around the corner, then stood up and started to run. But I only made it a few steps before taking a fist square in the mouth. My feet kept moving but my head stayed still and I landed on my back.

An XIV member named Torez stared down at me. He grabbed my shirt, yanked me up and threw me against the house.

JBone lurched out of a shadow and tackled him. Torez had size, but

JBone caught him surprised and sent him stumbling into the mud. I fell on him, with JBone beside me, the thrill of flesh against my fist until the rifle cracked again. It sounded too close. JBone and I scrambled back into the shadows. The party was over.

"Aw shit, Loco, I think I lost some teeth."

A few blocks away, we stopped under a street light. JBone grinned at me. He had a two-tooth gap in his top row. If it wasn't for the blood and bruises, he'd look like a little kid.

He spoke with a lisp, said, "Some fool caught me with a beer bottle."

We hooked up with a homie who lived nearby and he drove us to the hospital. I waited with JBone, hassling the nurse until he was seen.

I fidgeted in the waiting room, thinking about him tackling Torez for me. Big Wheez would never understand why I was hanging with a white boy, but that didn't matter. I knew JBone had my back. I'd clown hard on him for his fake front teeth after that, but I did it with respect. That white boy was solid.

WE SAT AROUND THE KITCHEN TABLE AT DONALD'S house. It smelled of smoke and something else that was too sweet, like rotting fruit. His dad didn't live there but his mom was upstairs; we could hear her footsteps creaking above us. Mike rested his head in his hands. JBone leaned back and blew smoke towards the ceiling. Donald had half his body inside the fridge, digging for something.

Mike muttered into his arms. It was hard to hear him but he was talking about making a run to Chavo to get more coke.

D said, "Why don't we rock it up? It's what people are doing, they want to smoke it."

Donald was solid; he'd throw down when he had to, but he was usually relaxed. He'd been part of the crew from the ALC, but he was black which was a problem. Mike and I were already thinking about jumping in JBone. D might push Big Wheez too far.

I shook my head. "What are you talking about? They already smoke it."

"Nah, Loco, that's in the primos. There's a lot of neighborhoods out there they like it rocked up."

117

It made me uneasy. Big Wheez never rocked it up. And he stuck in his own neighborhood, and sold to his own people.

D pulled out a can of beer and popped it open. "Lots of money out there if you want it."

Mike lifted his head. His eyes brightened. "You know how to do it?"

"Shit, you serious? Yeah."

We heard footsteps clomping on the stairs then after a moment Donald's mom appeared. She was probably in her thirties but seemed older with leathery skin and a low scratchy voice. "What kind of trouble you boys getting into?" She smiled through red, cracked lips.

D said, "Loco has some coke we'd like to rock up."

He put it out just like that to his mother. I stared back and forth between them, not sure if I heard right. Then I said, "Hello, Mrs. Brandt."

She cocked her head at this, and gave a flirty grin which made her look younger. She said to D, "What are you talking about?"

He said, "We want you to teach us to make crack."

She laughed. "You boys don't want no part of that shit."

I had no idea what was going down, but I was never one to let a crazy moment pass without diving in head first. I tossed a few packets of coke on the table and said, "You have no idea."

Her laugh quickly turned into a cough.

I said, "You know how to rock this up?"

"I did it for Donald's dad for years."

"Well, let's see then."

She shrugged. Again, she grinned at me and this time I noticed her eyes were glassy and unfocused. "All right." She waved a finger. "But I'll only show you once."

JBone put on music and we made a party of it. It was a strange time, a funhouse mirror. It was five people in hell playing a perverse game of make-believe: baking in the kitchen with Mom. It was a nightmare version of family, but I clung to it.

And in the end, we had a batch of crack cocaine.

"What happened?" I pointed at the pan. "You used up all my coke."

Donald's mom laughed, a throaty sound, phlegmy. "Aw, honey, you know how much that'll sell for?"

She gave a number.

Mike said to Donald. "You can sell this for that price?"

"Yeah, man, that's what I been saying. Just let me in."

D had access to the neighborhoods. And he had a house we could cook in. With him in the set, we would be able to move some serious product. Mike nodded, ready to jump him in that second. And in the smoky haze, a mom there acting nice to us, it felt enough like family - these were my brothers - it made sense.

What Big Wheez didn't know wouldn't hurt him.

NOT EVEN NINE O'CLOCK AT NIGHT AND WE WERE drunk, high, and stupid, hanging three tables deep in our park, well past the reach of the street lights. And the park did belong to us: Los Tiny Dukes had claimed it. We ran out the BP fools first and then the XIV then West Side Piru and any others who tried to get close. It had only been a couple months and LTD had become a force; people whispered about us, telling each other the things we did. Some of it was exaggerated or made up, but that didn't matter. I thought I was becoming a legend.

The primos and crack filled our pockets with cash. My homies were buying cars, chains, new clothes. We strutted around like kings. It was all good, happening like I'd imagined, but there was still something which needed to be done.

With the boombox thumping next to me, my fried brain picked at a familiar problem - what to do with Donald and JBone. They weren't Hispanics. Big Wheez wouldn't like it; he wouldn't understand that rolling in the Northwest was different than in Cali. He could even call me out, green light me.

I grunted, done with it. It was too much thinking. I was never good at working out consequences, and I should have done it already, weeks ago. It was time to act.

I grabbed Mike's shoulder and led him a few steps outside the circle. Behind us, the sound of girls mushed with the low voice of Donald muttering nonsense.

I said, "Hey, *ese*, you been jumped in down in East Los."

"You know it."

"And I'm Verdugo."

"That's right."

"We're both part of a set. We're Sureño."

"Yup."

"But these fools ain't. They running our drugs. Donald's bringing in cash. JBone is down for anything."

"That's right. That's right."

"About time we put them in."

Mike raised his head, looked at me serious, and gave me the nod. He was hardcore from The Avenues but he understood. I pushed any last thoughts of Big Wheez away because I couldn't do anything about it.

Nothing else needed to be said so we bounced back to the music, to the red glow of cigarettes, to JBone's panting laughter.

I said, "Ain't that right, D?"

"What?"

I hit him closed-fisted aiming for the jaw, hard, not keeping anything back, and Donald sprawled back onto the grass. Two hard kicks then I pulled him up before he got his head together. I said, "You got thirteen seconds, fool."

Donald swung at me without taking a breath and it knocked me back, but Mike shoved him down. I came at him with a kick to the ribs.

JBone grabbed my shoulder, "Whoa, Loco! What the hell?"

I shrugged off his hand and said, "Now it's your turn, fool. Thirteen seconds."

JBone raised his hands but I tagged him before he could move, twice hard in the face. I was grinning as I did it, a thrill in my chest pulsing through me as I punched him again. JBone fell on the ground, then took a good kick. A red rage ran through me and it all felt right.

"Easy, Loco." Mike gripped my arm. "Thirteen seconds." He pulled me back, holding me until the violence in my brain cooled to a low burn. I blinked and noticed the girls had scattered. I heard the traffic, the music, felt the humid air.

Mike helped JBone to his feet. "What the hell?"

"You just been jumped in, fool."

"What the hell?"

"You're jumped in. Now you're part of Los Tiny Dukes. You a

Sureño for life."

I threw my arm around JBone, and the four of us, brown, black and white, hugged and laughed and took long gulps of beer. It didn't take long before the girls drifted back, wide-eyed and ready to dance.

I PARKED MY DAD'S TRUCK OUTSIDE AND BROUGHT my boy TJ into Mike's garage to meet the homies. After the assault at the MAX station a few years back, TJ had gone to a different juvenile facility than Tony and I had. We hadn't seen much of each other since we got out, so I was eager to introduce this giant white boy around. He nodded at each of them then sunk into the leather couch that'd steal the change out of his pockets. I squatted on an upturned five gallon bucket under the Easy E poster. I felt comfortable, closed in, safe.

Daylight squeezed through the cracks of the garage door. The music thumped gently in the corner. A month had passed since we jumped in Donald and JBone, and I had more stories to tell of LTD. I dropped them on TJ, watching his eyes widen, the slow smile creep across his face. He laughed and told me I was crazy, just like I wanted.

I had tried the same with my old friend, Shawn, the night before. I'd spent the night at my dad's place then hung out in his basement, just like we'd done when we were kids. I told him my stories, but he wasn't into it. Shawn was getting ready to graduate high school. He had a baseball game coming up. He was worried about playoffs. He kept shaking his head, asking why I was doing those things.

So when TJ showed up, we left Shawn behind and went looking for trouble. Next day with my homies in Mike's garage we were still hoping to find it.

"Hey Brad," JBone said. "Let me borrow your dad's truck. I need to help someone move."

"Sure." I tossed him the keys.

"All right. Be back in a bit."

A new kid, Brett, had been hanging with us. He was fifteen years old and looked up at JBone like a little brother. "Can I come with?"

"Yeah, yeah, come on."

They left. TJ and I hung back with Mike. I said, "Hey, *ese*, we're taking a road trip, me and my boy TJ, heading to Texas. You okay here when I'm gone?"

Mike chewed on a cigarette, looked up at me like he didn't speak English.

I said, "You got this while I'm gone?"

He nodded slowly, like I wasn't making sense. Finally, he said, "Yeah, Loco. We got this."

"Make sure D gets his coke."

"Yeah, yeah." He gulped down his drink. "How long you gone for?"

"Shit, I don't know." I looked at TJ, making sure he was watching all this. "What you think? A week?"

TJ nodded, puffed smoke out his nose.

"Yeah, Loco," Mike spoke like I being stupid. "Yeah, I think we'll be all right."

Mike was like that, acting like he did all the organizing, all the work, but I let it go. I leaned back against the wall and told TJ about facing down some XIV fools behind a Handy Andys. This big *vato* wanted to throw down on me but I took out my two ball in the sock. When he looked down at it, I brought it across his face. TJ laughed just like I wanted.

The door opened, and light flooded the garage, blinding us. It had been less than an hour since they left, but JBone and Brett came panting inside. They slammed the door behind them. When my eyes readjusted I saw JBone was sweating and Brett had a purple bruise on his cheek.

"Ah shit, Loco, we fucked up."

I leapt up. "Where's the truck?"

"I wrecked it, *homes*. I wrecked it."

"Naw, you didn't."

"Yeah. Shit, it's... You know how Clint has that Mustang? We were heading back to his place and started racing down Fulton, just messing around, and... fuck."

I swore with him. My heart started to pound where I could feel it behind my eyes. I didn't exactly have permission from my dad to take his truck. TJ and I had snuck over to his garage and found the key hidden under the bumper.

JBone scratched the back of his head. "Steering wheel froze up on me. I couldn't make the turn."

122

"Just down Fulton?"

"Three blocks over. Wrapped it around a tree."

We all squeezed into Mike's lowrider and drove to check it out. We found the scene just like JBone had said. The hood of my dad's truck was crumpled around the trunk of a tree. The left wheel was twisted the wrong way. The emergency lights were blinking weakly at us. A small crowd had gathered; the cops would be there soon.

I said, "Anyone see you?"

"Yup."

There was no hiding it. My dad's stolen truck would be found totaled in my mom's neighborhood. They'd traced it to me easy.

TJ took off as soon as we got back to the garage, our road trip forgotten. I figured the cops would come looking for me soon. It made me jumpy and paranoid, but there was nothing to be done.

IT WAS JBONE'S IDEA; THE HOMIE HAD GROWN UP IN Oregon and had the equipment, so the Los Tiny Dukes packed up our stuff and went camping in Battleground State Park. We found our site, set up a few tents, tossed around some sleeping bags and opened a cooler. The stars came out and I sat by the fire with Becky next to me. I gazed up at the moon thinking if my homies from southern California could see me now, they'd lose it. I couldn't imagine Big Wheez resting his ass on a rock or Rocco sleeping on the ground.

I took a long pull of beer, then leaned into Becky. I opened my mouth to say something smooth, but startled at the sound of a dog. It was close, just beyond the first row of trees. One bark then a few more even closer. I grinned at my homie, JBone. I figured he knew about camping, he'd explain the noise away. But JBone had leapt up and was stumbling back from the fire.

"Oh shit," he said.

A moment later I heard the voice of a cop. "Clark County Sheriff!" He sounded closer than made sense. "Everyone on the ground!"

I jumped from the log and darted past the fire into the trees. A path cut off into the woods and I sprinted along it until it disappeared into underbrush.

A dog barked behind me, too close and getting closer. Feeling its breath on my ankles, I high kneed it, kicking my feet out until it grabbed my pant leg, teeth scraping into my skin. I tripped then tumbled down a ridge. I thought as I spun that it was a lucky fall. I'd stand up at the bottom and keep running. But then I slammed against a tree, and the dog had me pinned before I could roll away. A German Shepherd - biggest I'd ever seen - snarled, drool dripping into my mouth.

The cop shouted, "Don't move! She'll bite!"

But the dog and I were eye to eye so I didn't need any warning. I wasn't about to move for anything.

The cop called off the dog, cuffed me, and led me out of the woods. I told them nothing on the walk to the cruiser. I told them nothing in the interview room. I told them nothing at all until I saw my lawyer in the holding cell. When she asked, I told her that I stole the truck. I told her I crashed it. I told her I did it by myself and my homies knew nothing about it.

They released JBone the next day. I got thirty days in a juvenile center, but didn't mind. With how crazy things had been, I figured I could use the break.

Homies
One month later

I KEPT MOVING, listening to the phone ring on the other end; it had a long cord so I could move the length of Mike's garage, the smoky haze swirling behind me. I'd only been out for a few days, but I was ready for this.

Finally, I heard Big Wheez's low drawl and I pointed at the boombox, miming for Mike to turn it down. Wheez and I talked about the neighborhood a few minutes, then he said, "You got some things in motion up there, eh Loco?"

"It's crazy, Wheez. Every day something's happening. But we been moving some serious shit."

While I spent thirty days in a juvenile center reading Louis L'amour books, my homies had kept things rolling on the streets.

I said, "My boy, D, we been rocking it up and he's got some hookups. Those fools can't get enough of it."

"They smoking it, huh?"

The question seemed to have an edge. Crack was associated with black neighborhoods and I worried I'd said too much. I closed my eyes and tried to focus. I needed to turn the conversation into safer territory.

"Yeah, yeah. And we took out the Brown Pride. My boy JBone took down their big homie Jack Hall. They're done. Shit, it's crazy. We're pushing into the XIV neighborhoods now, mixing it up."

"You doing good."

I warmed to the words, imagining the look on Big Wheez's face. His head cocked, the slow smile. I grinned over the phone.

"We got a park up here. We got some territory."

"You got some good homies with you?"

"Yeah, yeah, we jumped in D and JBone."

"Who are these *vatos*?"

He needed details. Sureños kept careful records of who belonged to each set. So I told him about Donald and JBone, gave him full names and addresses. I told him how solid they were. And of course I left out a couple important facts.

It made me uneasy, but I wanted that next level: the drugs and the guns; chaos going out, money coming in. More than that, I needed to impress Big Wheez, show him what I could do.

"That all sounds fine, Loco. All right, we got Miguel and Rocco going to head up there in a couple of days."

I nodded with my whole body, slapped Mike on the shoulder.

"Now you're talking."

"They'll bring you a kilo and a few pieces."

The good news just kept coming. I was getting the supplies, the backing of Big Wheez and Los Dukes, and my childhood buddies were coming up. It couldn't get better.

"They'll have some stuff for you but listen, homie. This shit ain't free, you understand?"

"Come on Big Wheez, you know me."

"This ain't a gift. You got to pay your dues. We splitting the coke sixty-forty, you get me?"

I felt like I just won the lottery and barely listened. "Yeah, yeah, I get you."

"And you're paying for the guns too. We'll work something out."

"It's all good."

"All right, Loco. You sure you ready for this?"

"Come on, Wheez," I gestured to Mike to turn the music back up until I could feel the beat under my skin. I said, "I'm ready for anything."

THE CALL CAME IN THE MORNING, TELLING ME
Rocco and Miguel were heading up 15 towards Vancouver. I fidgeted
around the apartment all morning and started staring out at the parking lot way before there was any chance they'd be there.

I'd spent the last fews days talking about nothing but my California homies. I made them out like celebrities to my crew. I kept saying
things like, "These *vatos*, they real. Understand me?" I had paced the
garage and told JBone to be cool. Said it a half dozen times.

I was stressing because D and JBone were a problem I didn't know
how to solve. I only hoped if I could show off the production, Rocco
would get it. If he and Miguel could see what we were laying down,
the money we were bringing in, it'd be okay.

But I was stressing. I kept arguing with them in my head. This
wasn't southern California; I was only working with what I had. I
imagined Rocco hearing this; I could see him nodding. We'd known
each other for years. I'd get him to understand.

Right on time, a Monte Carlo - not a lowrider but gleaming white
and slick as hell - pulled into the parking lot. I hurried outside, grinning like a fool. I leaned against a tree like I was patient, like take your
time, but when they climbed out - Rocco and Miguel with their Locs,
their Cortez shoes, with flat-brimmed Dodgers hats over shaved heads,
they looked straight California - I leapt forward to give them a huge
hug.

I hadn't seen these homies for years and they'd grown up. Miguel
had become a heavyweight, like bodyguard big. Rocco looked like he'd
been living hard. They had changed, but it didn't matter. Seeing them
was like coming home.

I brought them upstairs. They hugged my mom and sister, and
shook hands with her boyfriend. Since he was a white boy, I took it as
a good sign.

Mom made enchiladas and had us sit at the table. We talked about
San Berardino, the neighborhood, my mom's old friends. We clowned
and ate and had a great time.

After dinner, Mom and James went to their room, my sister left,
and we turned on the Nintendo. Three bad-ass gangsters, we were

still teenage kids. We played Tecmo Bowl. We stayed up late, drank soda, blew on the game cartridge, ate chips. We'd pick one of two plays and send Bo Jackson up the middle. When we grew tired of that, we moved to the porch.

"Cold up here, homie."

"Yeah, yeah," I said. "It gets worse."

Rocco and Miguel took the chairs, I leaned on the rail, smoke puffing between us. "So Big Wheez said you into some serious shit."

I grinned like an idiot and said, "It's crazy, Rocco."

"But Los Tiny Dukes? That's what you come up with?"

"Hey, that's a cool-ass name."

"Yeah?"

I nodded. "You bring some supplies with you?"

Miguel had been quiet, but he spoke up, excited. "Hell yeah we did. Big Wheez must like you, Strain."

I loved hearing that.

"We got an SKS and a couple Barettas. A thirty-eight."

"Oh yeah. That's how you get started. Where'd you hide the coke?"

Rocco gave me a wink. "You'll see tomorrow."

With his bald head and mustache, the hint of a goatee, he looked like he'd grown up. I couldn't help it. I grabbed him by the neck and rubbed his head.

He shoved me back. "Stop that, fool."

"I can't believe you're up here."

Miguel turned his eyes on me. "Where your homies at?"

"You got homies?" Rocco laughed. "Nah, can't believe that."

"I got a few. They're solid."

"Yeah?"

"One of them is a Sureño out of East Los."

Rocco lost the grin and looked impressed. Everything felt all right. I said, "From the Avenues."

"You *sedio*? That's real shit."

"You know it."

"Who are these others?"

I gave Rocco a wink. "You'll see tomorrow."

MIKE GRINNED AT US FROM THE DOOR. I STEPPED aside and said, "These are my homeboys from Verdugo."

He shook their hands, and welcomed us in. He introduced them to his mom and sisters; his dad was at work. Rocco and Miguel were respectful. Everyone was smiling. Everyone was Hispanic. It was all good.

After a few minutes, we excused ourselves and went downstairs, which was as close to a home as I had. Sometimes I pulled down the daybed in my mom's living room, but more often Mike would let me sleep on this couch in his garage. I showed Rocco and Miguel around with pride, telling them how things went down.

Eventually we locked the door to the house and I said, "Mike, show them our product. Fire some of that shit up."

I turned on the music - the bass rattled a set of keys on the table - while Mike packed a bowl. I soaked in the look on their faces as Mike melted powder on top: Rocco grinning, Miguel nodding. They each took a hit.

"That's good weed, Brad."

"We got some good shit up here. The coke's not as good as down in Cali though."

"That's right. That's right."

Mike grinned. "My Big Homie, Peewee, told me you guys were coming up here. What you got for us?"

"Oh, you know." Rocco looked at me. "Can we bring shit out here?"

"Yeah, yeah. Let me just..." I pressed the button. Gray light spilled on our faces as the garage door crawled into the ceiling.

Rocco stepped out and backed the car to the edge of the garage, then Miguel grabbed an army green duffle bag and the spare tire out of the trunk. He tossed them on the bed as the garage closed behind us.

"That's it?"

"Oh yeah."

Grins all around, giddy as they pulled the guns out of the bag and tossed them on the bed. Assault rifles, pistols, ammo clips, boxes of bullets. Even a kit for cleaning.

It felt real, all of it. Rocco bringing this stuff out. Wheez trusting me, telling me I was doing good. And it felt like power, holding the weapons, feeling the hard plastic and metal, all of it sinking into the mattress. I thought I was a warrior; I thought I was a man.

Mike said, "What's up with the tire?"

"Check this out." Rocco let the air loose and said, "You got a little crowbar?"

Mike did. Rocco used it to pry the rubber back and, after a moment, he pulled out a small brick wrapped in brown paper. He tossed it down, then pulled out another and another, seven in all, until there was a kilo of coke sitting on the bed. It'd make us about fifty thousand dollars after we rocked it up.

Mike turned the music up. We gripped each other's arms and laughed at nothing. All that product, sitting in an unmade bed next to guns and ammo, we were going to own this town.

Rocco slit open a package and we each took a snort off the knife. It burned my nose then dripped into the back of my throat. My eyes grew wide. I had no fear.

They'd get it. Miguel and Rocco, they'd understand. We would go meet D and JBone and it was going to work out. I'd been stupid for being worried about it. Rocco was my oldest friend and Miguel was easy. I couldn't remember why I'd been so stressed.

"Shit homies, let's get moving. We gotta get you to meet the others."

I felt Mike staring at me, looking grim, but I didn't care. I was doing it. They'd meet Donald and they'd see. They'd get it. No worries. No problem.

I KNOCKED ON THE SIDE DOOR. IT WAS A GRAY DAY but the coke made me feel good about this. I knew my homies would like Donald. They'd see past his mushroom hair and black skin and get that he brought in cash. He had a whole neighborhood locked down for the brown. He was solid.

But it all went wrong from the moment Donald opened the door. Rocco's mouth dropped open then he drew back, his eyes hard. He lowered his head, and sunk into a stony silence. Miguel, next to him, froze for a long second. He betrayed no emotion, but didn't shake D's hand when he put it out there. Instead, he just gave him the smallest head nod and muttered, "What's up?"

All that before we made it through the door. Donald handled it right. He welcomed them inside and offered chairs, but the bad feeling only grew worse. When he turned his back, Rocco gave me a look like he was going to spit on the carpet.

I kept trying, faking it, pushing too hard. "Woo!" I said, my voice crazy loud. "Hey D, you got some forties, right?"

He said sure and climbed the stairs to get them.

As soon as he was gone, Rocco said, "What the hell, Strain?"

It was like my chest and stomach disconnected from my body and started to float. I shook my head hard, like a dog drying off.

"Come on, Rocco, it's not like that. This isn't California, *homes*. Hispanics are few and far up here. My boy, D - he's solid."

He looked at me with disgust. "That fool's Sureño?"

"He's solid, Rocco."

My brain swirled around for more to say, but I gave up when D came back downstairs. He brought four bottles of Old English with him.

Rocco gave him a hard stare. "So where you from?"

D passed Rocco a beer, said, "West side."

"West side of what?"

"Vancouver."

It was like I was watching a murder in slow motion. I wanted to leave, take Rocco and Miguel somewhere else, back to Mike's and have things be good and easy again, but I couldn't bring myself to move.

I said, "My boy has the West Side locked down."

Miguel stared at him through half-lidded eyes. Rocco said, "And you're Sureño?"

Donald grinned like this was all right, like my homies weren't about to beat him down. He said, "Yeah. Loco and Mike jumped me in. It was crazy."

I said, "D's tight. He got a good hit in. Knocked me back hard."

Rocco's eyes drilled into me, making my stomach twist up, but I just kept nodding at Donald. I said, "Hey, let's play some pool."

Rocco shrugged into it, and for a moment it felt like a miracle. After a few beers, some weed and a game of pool, they started to relax.

131

Miguel even smiled once as D told a story. They listened when he told about the business he was doing, the amount of weight he was moving.

It gave me hope and I was stupid enough to push my luck.

I said, "Hey let's go to the park. Get some shit going, see the *chicas*."

"*Chicas*?"

"Yeah, Rocco."

He lowered his head to stare up at me. "These girls Hispanic?"

They mostly were, depending on who showed up, but I was never one to sweat the details. I nodded and they followed me up the stairs and out the door.

AN HOUR LATER, WE HAD THE MUSIC GOING AND MY homies were dancing with two Hispanic girls from the clique. The park was dark and cool. Becky sat near me on the picnic table. Rocco and Miguel hadn't looked at Donald or talked to him since we got there, but that was all right. I thought they were coming around. I figured they just needed a nudge.

"Hey Rocco," I said, "you ever try acid?"

"Naw. We don't have that shit."

We each took some hits. I gave Rocco a few to make sure he'd feel it, hoping to loosen him up. Then I hurried over to the Becky's house to call up JBone.

I barely had to say a thing before he shouted, "Hell yeah, Loco! I'll be right there."

His tone gave me a flash of panic. I wanted to tell him to play it cool, maybe not sag his pants, but JBone had already hung up.

Back at the park, Rocco greeted me with a friendly nod. Miguel was staring up at the sky; a sliver of the moon and stars were visible behind wispy clouds. These were things you rarely saw in San Bernardino.

It wasn't long before we heard JBone across the park, calling out in his white-boy voice. I winced as he strutted up, hand grabbing his pants, stupid-ass grin on his face. I saw him through my homies' eyes and wanted to hit him myself.

He stood too close to Rocco and spoke too loud. "Holy shit, dude, is it good to meet you."

The earth softened underneath me. Rocco went cold, nodded once then shook his head. Miguel crossed his arms. JBone kept looking from one to the other.

Desperate, I turned up the music and breathed a little when they got back to dancing. Rocco melted into a girl. He closed his eyes and I hoped that would be enough. But the slow song ended and Kid Frost came on.

Rocco sat down, glared at JBone, and shook his head. "What makes you Sureño?"

I clenched up. Even in the shadows I saw Rocco's dark face turn red but JBone didn't seem to notice.

"Brad came up here and showed us the way you guys were doing it down in Cali, you know? And we're down with you guys. We're down with the brown." Thinking he was saying the right thing, JBone nodded at his own words. I felt something coming, and panic rose into my throat as the fool twisted to grab his beer. When his back turned, Rocco tore the blue bandana out his pocket.

"You don't know nothing about this." He didn't say it loud, but didn't have to. "You don't know about the blue. You don't know what this stands for."

"Yeah I do." JBone slowly set his beer down. "I'm Sureño, fool."

"I think you're shit," Rocco said.

It was like I was back with Luis speeding into a high speed chase. I was trapped. It was bad, about to get worse, and all I could do was watch.

Rocco said, "What you want to do about it."

JBone bobbed back a half step then busted Rocco in the face with a sharp jab. It sent his sunglasses off the top of his head.

Rocco growled, "You're going to choke on this rag, motherfucker!" He snatched JBone by his neck. JBone was swinging but didn't connect. Rocco pushed him back so he tripped over the sidewalk and Rocco jumped on top of him.

On my other side, I heard Miguel spit at Donald, "What about you, fool?"

My boy, D, launched himself at Miguel but Miguel took a side step and threw him down. Mouth open like a fool, I could only watch as Miguel beat down Donald on one side and Rocco beat down JBone on the other. Seconds rolled by like this, with me standing there, frozen.

Finally, Mike called my name and it woke me up. I leaned down and gripped at Rocco's shoulder. With some effort, I was able to pull him off.

"Come on, Rocco," I said. "Let's chill out, brother."

Rocco twisted under my hand and slammed his fist hard into my mouth. He grunted as I stumbled back.

"Rocco!" I tasted blood. "What's the matter with you?"

Mike was trying to pull Miguel off D.

"Chill out!" I screamed. "Both of you. Shit. Chill the fuck out."

Punching must have drained the fight out of him because Rocco's shoulders slumped. JBone scuttled backwards until he could stand up.

I shook my head. "JBone, D, just get out of here. We'll meet up later."

JBone helped Donald up. The two threw a couple last curses before limping out of the park, but no one listened to them. The girls had run off during the fight which left Rocco, Miguel, Mike and me by ourselves.

It had all gone wrong, worse than I could have imagined. I slumped down on the bench. I felt scarred, burned up inside.

"What the hell, Rocco?"

He had started pacing back and forth, his fists gripping air, his eyes blinking too fast.

"I'm tripping, *homes*. I'm fucking tripping."

"You gotta calm down. It's going to be all right."

"Naw, it's not going to be all right." Rocco shook his head. It was a cool night but he was sweating into his shirt. "It's not going to be all right, Brad. It's not going to be all right."

I FOUGHT IT AS LONG AS I COULD, BUT FINALLY blinked awake. A throbbing pressure inside my head squeezed outward. My mouth had no moisture and tasted like sand and blood. I rubbed hard at my face.

Dirt on the narrow window filtered out most of the light, but enough morning sun managed to fill Mike's garage so I could see my homies. Miguel was asleep on the floor. Rocco, on the couch, had his head thrown back, his mouth open. He breathed loudly.

A hazy weight in my gut told me that something was wrong, then my memory filled in the details. The whole thing made me sick, almost queasy. I was in a bad spot. If Rocco said the wrong thing to Big Wheez, we could get green-lighted. Then it wouldn't matter how far we were from Cali, the Sureños would come for us and take us down.

I wouldn't think Rocco would do that to me; we had too much history. But then I wouldn't have thought Rocco would punch me in the mouth. Nothing was making any sense.

"That acid, *ese*. Shit," Rocco looked up at me with bloodshot eyes. "I don't want nothing to do with that again."

"Yeah, yeah," I said and we laughed a little together. Miguel smacked his lips and asked for water.

"Shit. I need a smoke."

Rocco started moving, and Miguel followed him big and silent, like a bodyguard. They opened the side door and blinked into the gray morning. I saw an opportunity. Me and Rocco, we went way back. If I could just talk to him, make him understand, I could maybe fix this. I nodded at Mike, signaling him to stay back, and followed them outside.

The three of us leaned on the Monte Carlo. We took deep pulls on our cigarettes, and let the nicotine clear our heads.

"That acid..." Rocco said, "Shit."

"Yup. That got crazy." I tried to laugh but it hurt my head. "You punched me, Rocco."

"Yeah."

"You straight up hit me on the mouth."

Rocco nodded

"Hurt like hell. I'm still swolled up."

"I got you good."

"Yeah, you did."

It was easier for a moment, just the three of us. We knew each other forever. We were more brothers than friends.

"I don't like that Donald." Miguel said it low as if I would agree with him, but I shook my head.

"Naw, *homes*." I wanted to grab the both of them, and make them see sense. "Donald is…"

Rocco wouldn't let me finish. "What the hell is going on up here, Strain?"

"My boy, D, he's…"

This was my chance to explain, to make it all okay, but my head was pounding and when I tried to speak the words wouldn't come.

Rocco lowered his head and glared at me, "You gotta come back home."

"I got shit going on up here. I got things happening."

"Los Dukes could use you. Things are getting crazy."

I hated this barrier between us. I wanted it to be like it was the day before. I wanted them to understand.

"I want to, but hell… I got…. Shit. Donald is solid, Rocco." The words started gushing out of me. "My boy is solid. He's got neighborhoods locked down. He is bringing in cash. We'll move this kilo easy 'cause of D. Yeah, he's not Hispanic, but… We're doing it for blue." I found myself shouting at them and it felt good. This pressure that had been building up for weeks was finding a release. "We are Sureño. We are doing it for the blue. We're doing it for brown. That's… And D and JBone, they get it. They get it… it's different up there. It's… Shit."

I winced; my head pounded hard at each word. Finally, I waved a hand at them, wishing I could say more, but feeling empty. A cold drop of rain landed on my forearm. I brushed it away.

Rocco shrugged. "All right, Brad, all right." He tossed his butt on the pavement. Miguel smoked the last of his cigarette in silence.

"We gotta move."

That hadn't been the plan, but I nodded. I leaned back against the car and closed my eyes.

"It's different up here, Rocco."

"It's cool. It's cool. But you gotta come home soon."

"I want to."

"Naw, *ese*." He laid a hand on my shoulder and leaned in, unsmiling. "You need to come home. You got me?"

We hugged. I had lead in my guts, but I said, "Yeah, Rocco, I got you."

MIKE WAS SKETCHED OUT. HE DIDN'T CARE MUCH for the gangster life - all he cared about was the business - but he knew if our big homies got pissed, he'd have to care. He knew if they green-lighted us, sent a *cantala* to discipline us, we'd have a serious problem.

The situation was messed up, but when Mike reached behind the dry wall and brought out a brick, it made it feel better. No matter how bad things had gone, we still got the supplies we needed. Mike unwrapped the coke, and measured out a couple ounces to rock up at D's. We stored the drugs at Mike's but processed it at Donald's. Mike's family had no idea, and Donald's didn't care.

As we cruised through the city, rain beat down on the car so loud we couldn't hear each other to talk. It gave me time to think. Rocco and I went way back. Big Wheez had set us up to makes some serious money. We had guns. We had connections. It shouldn't be a problem. I nodded at the thought: no problem, no problem, no problem.

By the time we got to D's house, I was feeling good, optimistic even, but then we found him pacing his kitchen like he'd been caged up.

"Damn, Loco," he kept saying. He couldn't stop moving. "Your homies are crazy."

I shrugged, acting more casual then I felt. "That's how we do it in the Sureños."

"Nah, but that was fucked up."

The block of coke sat on the table, still half-wrapped in dirty plastic. Music thudded through the ceiling from a room upstairs.

I said, "Listen, D, this is who we work for. That's Sureño."

"Not sure if I want to be a Sureño anymore."

Heat rose in my throat, prickled at my skin; the tension of the last three days swelled back into my chest. "Listen homie," I said. "You're in. You understand? You're in it."

Mike said, "Chill out, Loco."

I started shouting, "Naw, Donald, you are Sureño. You been jumped in, fool." I became aware I had a pistol tucked under my shirt. I had volunteered to do *cantalas* in juvenile hall; I'd been laying down gang discipline since I was fifteen. If I had to, I'd do it again right there in my homie's kitchen. "You don't leave Sureños, understand?"

Mike raised his hands. "Whoa, whoa, chill out," he was saying, but

I barely heard him. I slit open the package of coke, just enough for the powder to bulge out.

"They provided this shit, you understand? We work for them. You got it? You're in it for life."

Donald sunk into a chair. He didn't look at me, but said, "I get it."

I took my first breath since I started talking.

"I get it, Loco. It's fucked up, is all I'm saying."

Mike said, "Yeah, it was, D." He looked at me steady. "Yeah, it was fucked up, but let's get working here."

We started the work. The rain pelting against the windows, the smell of the gas stove, the music thumping above us, it all made me quiet. I kept picturing Rocco, red-faced, jumping on JBone and I wondered if he was right. These fools were soft. They weren't Sureños; they had no idea. They were black and white. They knew nothing about the blue.

I took another hit of coke and it cranked up my temper. Big Wheez would be right to be pissed. My Cali homies were right; this was stupid as hell, working with these fools.

All these thoughts were like poison in my head, and I grew sicker with them with each minute, but then JBone came dripping into the kitchen. He grinned like an idiot, too eager, his pants hanging down to his knees.

I said, "Where you been?"

He mimicked my voice, said, "You know me, fool," and made a crude joke which made me laugh.

He got to work and I leaned back to watch them. JBone's presence had eased the edge off my mood but didn't fix anything. These were my homies. This was LTD. I knew they were solid, but as the first batch of crack came out, I couldn't shake the feeling that it was all messed up. I kept thinking of Big Wheez, imagined him sitting with me, watching, telling me I had done it all wrong.

Loco
Two weeks later

B ECKY LIVED IN a small house just off the park with low ceilings and plaster walls. An arch separated the living room from a dining area; it had a couple bedrooms in back. It was her party so she had pop garbage on the boombox: Whitney Houston mixed up with Bobby Brown. Forties and empty pizza boxes covered the table. Members of Los Tiny Dukes held down every corner of the room.

Becky and her friends swayed in the middle of everyone, shaking their hips. They were trying to get heads turned their direction, but most of the homies were focused on the coffee table, smoking crack or primos or weed.

The party grew louder, crazier, but I slouched in my own corner, not talking, barely high, watching the crowd. I hadn't heard anything from Big Wheez or Rocco, but I couldn't shake it. I liked my LTD crew; they were my family, but shit. I sat back watching JBone nod along to BoysIIMen and just didn't know.

I couldn't shake my mood, but every few minutes I'd look up and notice Becky and forget my troubles. She had long brown hair, dark skin, smoky eyes, tight pants. Her hair was puffed up and she kept smiling and then looking away then smiling again.

Finally, she peeled off from the other girls, and glided towards me, timing her steps with the music. She was a little off beat, but I liked it. She leaned in and I smelled something sweet through the smoke. She pulled me towards her and I half stood, crouching awkwardly as I reached up and kissed her. Fireworks went off in my head. Then she pulled me after her, still dancing offbeat, and I tried not to step on her heels as I followed her back to her bedroom.

She closed the door and the air smelled less of smoke and more of her. The floor was clean except for clothes pushing out of a crack in the closet. A table under a mirror was filled with girl stuff I didn't understand: a scarf, a spray can, little bottles. She sat next to me on the bed. Our thighs touched. The music hummed through the door, but everything was muted. There was just me and this girl. Then she kissed me again and everything disappeared.

Eventually we rejoined the party. I walked down the hall feeling light, my problems forgotten. I stepped back with my homies trying to hide a smile, but JBone cried out, "Dude, your neck!"

The party turned and they all started laughing. I could sense Becky watching from the other side of the room.

JBone said, "Your girl's a vampire!"

I touched my fingers to my neck and found it warm and sore. Moments later, I stared at myself in the bathroom mirror. A bruise bigger than my hand spread from my jaw to my shoulder. It was the biggest hickey I'd ever seen.

I returned to the living room with my hands raised, and offered a half shrug. I was more proud than embarrassed, but Becky fled into the garage. For the next hour, I waited for her, swiveling my head to the door whenever someone moved. The party shifted around me but I didn't care about any of it. Finally, she stepped back in the living room and raised her eyes to mine. Her nose crinkled when she smiled and the world was all right.

THE TRUCK'S REAR LIGHTS REFLECTED THE GLOW from the street. We had seen it on the way to a house party and it was still there on our way back. It was late, after midnight, and the truck sat in the back of an otherwise empty parking lot. An easy mark.

Brett asked, "Should we jack it?" and it was like he was speaking my thoughts because damn right we needed to jack it. I felt stupid walking. Mike and JBone had already bought cars; they cruised around in style but it was October in Vancouver and I was still on foot. It didn't make sense.

But nothing was making sense. Nothing came easy. Nothing felt right, like I was off-balance, like something bad was about to happen. The feeling never stopped, even after Big Wheez called, finally asking about some business. He didn't say nothing about Rocco and Miguel so I hung up not knowing where I stood.

Becky was exciting but complicated. We'd seen each other a lot in the weeks since she gave me the hickey, but I couldn't seem to say the right thing around her. I could never figure out what she wanted.

Nothing was like it was supposed to be. But jacking a truck? That was something I understood.

I grinned down at Brett. He was a little homie, barely fifteen, small boned, and pale. He always wore the same old jean jacket and acted hella-grateful to be near us.

A familiar thrill started buzzing through me as soon I started explaining to Brett how to do it. I slammed the screwdriver in the lock and showed him how to twist it, pushing down until it popped just when I said it would. Brett's eyes went wide, grinning when I pulled open the door. For a moment - with the kid looking at me like I knew something - the world made sense. I slid to the passenger seat and told him to get in.

"Aw shit, Loco, I don't know how to drive a stick."

"That's all right. You're gonna learn."

I had a hard flashback to hunching in a Cadillac with Luis, the older homie showing me the tricks. Yeah, that situation had ended badly, but I figured I had this under control. Brett looked up to me like I was Big Wheez, and I'd be like a big brother to him, but better. Unlike my own big brother, I'd stick around.

I talked him through it. Screwdriver in the lock, pull down as you twist. He tried a few times, cursing, then like a miracle the engine turned over and started to hum.

"That's how it's done."

Brett shouted in triumph.

"Let's drive. The pedal on the left side there, that's the clutch."

He leaned back and stared down at his feet.

"Put it in reverse now."

After a few tries he was able to force the shifter to the R. The truck jerked back a foot and died.

"Naw, shit, clutch first." I restarted the engine. "Pedal on the left. There you go. Now ease it out."

The tires squealed, we lurched backward and the truck died.

I laughed, started it again, said, "No problem. Take it easy. Let's go forward."

The car jumped forward, almost stalled, jumped forward again and stopped.

"Damn homie. You got to take it easy."

"I thought I was."

"You know we're trying to steal this car, right?"

Brett looked lost, "I don't..."

I laughed again, but it had been a couple minutes and it was getting stupid hanging out in that parking lot. We needed to move. I said, "Give it another..."

He punched it and the engine went dead. But no problem. Five minutes later we were cruising through our neighborhood, free and clear, with me behind the wheel.

WE WERE TANGLED INTO EACH OTHER ON THE COUCH, talking about nothing, acting goofy. Some gameshow was on tv. I was seventeen and full of talk, but truth was that Becky was my first girl. Things were going well between us and it made me feel better about everything. Big Wheez, rival gangs, the cops, all my worries faded as we watched white people win cash and prizes.

Becky's mom called from the kitchen. "You're staying for dinner," she said, and it wasn't a question. She was a short woman, big-hipped with sad eyes. She was cool with us being together as long as Becky stayed close to home.

She said, "It's nothing fancy."

"It smells good," I said. "Thank you."

We gathered around the table. I'd done drugs off of it more than once, but I didn't think much about that; I was happy to be there, eating chicken and rice. The sun streaked through a side window so the light was warm but faded as we ate. The food filled me, slowed everything down and Becky's mom's voice was low and warm. When we were done, Becky said, "Thanks, Ma."

And being funny I said, "Thanks, Ma," but it felt right coming out of my mouth. Becky rubbed my arm as I took a drink of milk.

I stood and grabbed my plate and the half-empty pot. I was feeling warm and comfortable, clearing the table like a regular family. But as I headed into the kitchen, the low rumble of a big truck started rattling the glasses.

Becky shouted, "Daddy's home!"

Her mom said, "He's early."

They both stopped what they were doing, smiled, and watched the door. They seemed happy, like there'd be no problem. But I'd never met the man and immediately felt uneasy. I lowered the pot gently into the sink and waited.

After a moment, the man lurched into the house, a heavy duffle bag over his shoulder putting him off balance. He was thick, big-bellied with a bald head and wide face. He looked tired, like he hadn't showered for a couple days. He gave his wife and daughter a kiss then stepped back to glare at me. He studied my white t-shirt, my flat-brimmed blue hat, the blue bandana, Cortez shoes and locs.

I was still small and skinny, shallow-faced from the coke, but I tried smiling. I looked the man in the eye and offered my hand. "Nice to meet you, sir."

He gripped my hand and held it, his face darkening.

"No," he said.

"Daddy."

"Not this boy. No."

I had braced myself, knew it was coming; still it landed like a hammer to my chest.

Her mom said, "Why don't you sit down and have some chicken."

"This one," he stabbed his thumb at me, "needs to get his ass out of here."

The comfortable feeling I'd had moments before burned into something bitter and sick. I raised my hands and started backing towards the door.

"And I better not see you back here again, you hear me?"

Becky followed me outside, but I had already sunk into myself and couldn't hear what she was saying. On the front step, the man yelled, "We don't have a problem now, but we will if you come back. You hear me?"

Becky said she'd call in a few days when her dad went back on the road, but I only had enough energy to shrug. She left me in the driveway. The garage door banged shut behind her.

I climbed into the truck and sat stunned for a moment before twisting the screwdriver to start it. I backed into the street and drove towards Mike's garage. Above me the clouds had turned purple, almost black, threatening rain.

BRETT FORGOT TO SIGNAL AND TOOK THE CORNER too hard, but he was getting it. We were on the edge of Vancouver, making a drop. Usually I'd act the Big Homie and send someone else but Becky hadn't called me and everything felt wrong. I needed to move.

I chewed on a handful of fries. I'd bought the kid a cheeseburger, thinking back to how Luis had done the same for me. I had the money now, but hadn't been using it. It had been about a week and we were still driving the truck we had stolen together. My other homies had cars and chains, but that part of the gangster life didn't interest me. I bought some clothes, shoes, got myself a Jheri-curl - but that was it.

"Hey Loco, how's this four wheeler shit work?" Brett pointed at button on the dash. He hit the switch and a light turned on. He said, "Now we're four wheeling?"

"That's right."

"Check this out," the kid said, and he pulled hard at the wheel. The tires screeched onto a dirt track over a wide undeveloped space. The truck leapt and fell underneath us.

"What the hell, fool?"

"We're four wheeling!"

The truck lurched hard left and my head banged against the window. I grabbed the handle on the ceiling, shouting, "Easy, motherfucker."

"What's the problem? Let's see what this can do."

It took effort but I shifted my tone. I didn't know where we were, Brett barely knew how to drive, and I had things to do - but I had to be Loco. I was never the guy to say no. I shouted, "Fuck yeah. Gun it."

We picked up speed down a small hill then came up over a crest too fast. My stomach dropped; the ground fell away for a moment then exploded towards us. The front of the car crumpled into the earth and my face slammed into the dash.

Pain flashed through my face. Blood gushed out of my nose. I knew immediately it was broken.

Cursing, I pushed the door open. Heat rose from my chest behind my eyes. The engine clicked with the crickets as I stumbled around, trying to find the kid to beat the hell out of him. I almost stepped on him cowering in the dirt, holding his wrist to his chest. I screamed, every word hurting my face. Rocco had been right, all this was shit, these homies, the whole place. Vancouver was weak, soft; I didn't belong here with these fools.

I grabbed the kid, pulled him up, blood dripping into my mouth, off my chin. I started telling Brett he was a piece of crap, but heard my father's voice come out of me.

It freaked me out enough to stop. I took a heavy breath and let him go. He fell back hard on a patch of weeds.

I pulled off my own shirt to wipe my face then returned to the truck. It was almost funny how much blood streaked down the plastic into the cracks of the glove compartment. I pushed my shirt through it but only smeared it around - and more kept dripping from my face onto the seat. I cursed again, thinking I'd need to come back with a bucket of water and bleach, but knowing I wasn't going to bother.

I squatted back against the door, my head ringing, my nose throbbing. I didn't know what I was doing there. I couldn't remember the last time I felt good about anything. I thought briefly about my brother, how he had gotten out. He'd moved down to a base in Texas, I'd heard. I wanted to get out of there, start driving, find him and start over. I looked down at my hands; they were sticky with my blood. Anywhere had to be better than this. For a wild moment I figured I'd do it, leave as soon as I got home, but I knew it was bullshit. Texas was impossibly far away.

On the other side of the truck, Brett kept telling me he was sorry, but I was too tired to do anything but shake my head. Eventually I stood up and we stumbled across the field. I held my shirt against my nose. Bett hugged his wrist to his chest. Leaving a stolen truck behind us covered with my fingerprints and blood, we started the long walk home.

I SAT BACK IN THE LEATHER, FEET UP. THE COUCH tried to pull me in, put me to sleep, but I didn't want to do that.

I grunted. "We gotta get out there, mix it up."

Mike had his head bent over a notebook. He chewed on a pen.

"We gotta go do something."

He said, "Yeah, yeah, yeah."

"John's got a party going. Let's do it."

"Nah, I gotta figure this shit out, *homes*."

"What the hell?"

Mike didn't answer, just made a mark on the paper, smearing blue ink around like it meant something. My brain was buzzing so hard I winced. "What the hell?"

"Checking how much we owe Big Wheez."

"What the fuck?"

"We gotta do this shit, Loc."

"We're doing good though, right?"

"Yeah, yeah."

We were doing more than good. Money poured in; rival gangs had been pushed back. My reputation had spread, but none of that touched the itch.

"Shit. What's Donald doing?"

"D left a couple hours ago to crash."

"Right," I said. Donald had been going hard into his own supply. "What about JBone?"

"I don't know."

I could find JBone, but he'd chilled out too. Becky wasn't calling and Brett screwed up. No one was around. With nothing to settle me down, I didn't know how to function. Life only made sense when things were crazy and I was Loco.

"Fuck it, Mike, let's get out of here."

"In a bit."

The coke churned up my brain so I needed to mix it up, rage against someone, throw down, but for the next hour all I could do was pace. Finally Mike closed his notebook too slowly and slid it to the far side of the desk. He rubbed his face and sighed first, but we were moving. We got in his car and cruised Vancouver. Cold night, November, a threat of snow, it all felt wrong. Wrong state, wrong weather, wrong life.

We stopped outside an apartment complex in a dark neighborhood at the boundary of Los Tiny Duke territory. I stopped for a moment in the parking lot and looked up. I could hear the thump of the bass through gray windows, and it dulled the edge.

The party was loud and got louder after we joined. Homies kept turning the music up over the shouting then shouted louder over the music. Arguments turned into shove fights, beer spilling on the carpet. Girls pleaded for everyone to cool it. It was chaos falling into violence. It was perfect.

A cloud of smoke hung from the ceiling in the kitchen. But there - homies three deep from the table, no room to move - I spotted my sister, Melissa. She was smoking a blunt, maybe a primo. I had heard she had a problem. And I could see it in her eyes, half-lidded, looking up at me unfocused. Her skin was sweaty and sad.

I didn't know what to do about that. I felt responsible for her, but detached, like she was on the other side of a glass wall. I stared at her for too long even as the shouting around me got louder and fools started shoving. I watched her leap up, start moving and only then I heard people yelling about the cops.

I scrambled too late. Officers were at the door so I pushed against the crowd, moving to a back bedroom, hoping to find a window or some other way out. The voices came loud, barking orders from the hallway. I fell into a closet, and worked my way through some winter coats, zippers scratching into my skin. I leaned against the back wall, brain buzzing so it hurt.

Moments later, a cop shined his light in my eyes, too bright, and I twisted my head down. There was a smirk in the man's voice when he said, "Brad Strain. We've been looking for you."

Suspenders

Eleven hours later

A THICK FOLDER laid closed on the table. Steam rose from a paper cup. Behind me, I heard whispers of attorneys and parents talking to their kids. I could sense the anxiety in the room, but I had gone deep into myself so it couldn't touch me.

Last night, I had stared at the floor and told the cops what they needed to know. I was driving the truck. I had done it alone. I had no idea why my blood was on the passenger seat.

This morning I had to come to court, but it was no problem. I was seventeen. I'd do another month in a juvenile center, nothing I couldn't handle. Better me, I figured, than Brett. I'd done it before. The judge started speaking to my attorney about the case. No problem. I just wanted to get it over with.

"Mr. Strain," the judge found my eyes with his. "We are done with you here. We'll let the folks across the street deal with you."

I jerked like the man had slapped my face. Behind me, my mom gasped. Across the street meant county jail. He wanted to charge me as an adult.

"Your honor!" My mom spoke from the gallery. "Please don't send my son to the county jail. He's a child."

"He's about to turn eighteen, ma'am."

"Please your honor. Don't give him... we're trying not to give him an adult record."

My attorney spoke, her voice breathy and thin. "Your honor, we would like to keep him in the juvenile system."

The judge raised an eyebrow then paged through my file. He shook his head at what he read. "It's too late for that. He's had plenty of chances."

He looked up, ready to say something else, but a clerk entered from a back door and leaned over the bench. The judge raised his hand and swiveled away. I gaped forward, staring at the back of the man's head; his bald spot made a perfect circle. Sweat beaded on my face, and made my shirt stick to the back of the chair. I didn't know if I could handle adult jail.

My heart started ramming against my ribs. My hands weren't cuffed. I could run. Maybe I'd get out of there if I surprised them and got lucky.

No, even stressed as I was, I knew that was stupid. I wouldn't make it out and had no place to go if I did. Still, older homies loved to tell stories about the things they'd seen in adult jail and I knew I wasn't ready for that. I twisted back to look at my mom. She had her eyes closed in prayer.

I had no options. I had no idea what else to do so I closed my eyes like she was doing. I prayed harder than I had ever done anything. *Dear Jesus*, I said, *get me out of this. I'm not ready for this shit.* But that felt wrong, so I said, *Sorry for swearing, Lord, but please. I am not ready for this. I am not ready for this. Please God. Please Jesus. Please Lord.* I folded my hands, squeezing so it hurt.

The judge cleared his throat. "Mr. Strain, we're going to do one favor for you. We'll let you off on bail to your mom, under her recognizance. Mrs. Strain you need to keep him under control."

My eyes went wide. I wanted to shout out loud. It was a miracle. The heavens had opened and God had given me a gift. The judge kept talking but I prayed, *Thank you, Jesus!* Then in the next moment, I gloated. This fool judge didn't even know what he'd done. He didn't know who he had just let loose. Then I thanked God again, all of it making sense in my head as I walked out of the courtroom, free.

In the hall, my mom gripped my arm, wiped her eyes with a tissue, and said to the attorney, "Now what?"

149

My attorney eyed me. "Well, you're looking at sixty to ninety days, maybe, in county jail." The woman nodded as she spoke. "One option, if you want to show good faith, is to do some community service."

"Yeah, yeah, yeah," I said. "What's that?"

"Call a church," she said.

It all landed hard: the prayer, the miracle, and this lady talking about church. Something was going on, something big. I had God watching out for me and I was all about that.

I kept nodding, grinning as my mom and the attorney talked. I figured I'd lay low for some time. I'd still have to keep my customers happy, keep Donald supplied, but I'd back off from some of the heavier gangster stuff. Instead, I'd head down to the church and see what else God would do for me.

DAVE TOOK OFF HIS CORDUROY GOLFER'S HAT AND tucked it into a back pocket. He held the door open then followed me into the sanctuary. I had been in there before to sweep the floor and restock the pencils but this was different.

The silence was thick with the faint smell of incense. Sun glowed through the stained glass windows, so Dave didn't turn on the light. He asked if I would follow him; said it looking down like he was shy. Then he walked me to the chapel, off the side of the main sanctuary. He held a candle between his fingers and asked me if I knew about them. Did I know about the saints, about Mary? Did I know how to pray?

I had worked with him for ten full days. I helped him put colored lights around the church, and carry a heavy wooden stable out of the basement. I helped him salt the sidewalk and mop the entryway. He showed me how to start the snow blower and pointed down the driveway.

Every day, Dave wore red suspenders over a white shirt and a cross around his neck connected by a black shoestring. He did everything quietly and with a smile. He asked me questions and listened when I talked about whatever was in my head. He rested his hands on his belly and told me I was doing a great job. And now he was asking if I knew how to pray.

150

I said, "Yeah, yeah, my mom took me here when I was little."

"This church?" he said. "St. James?"

"Yup."

He nodded at this. "That's wonderful," he said, and he ran his hand through his hair, a white tuff on a bald head. "You know why I brought you in here, Brad?"

Now I was the one nodding. I already knew what he was going to say.

"I think you're lost," he said.

I'd ignored the speech many times before from all kinds of people, but I was feeling different. Adult jail was hanging over me like a hammer.

"You need to change your life around."

I nodded again.

He breathed deep, and lit the candle. "I thought maybe you and I could say a prayer together here."

Remembering what happened last time I prayed, I was all in, eager for another miracle. Dave closed his eyes. He had told me he had a daughter about my age but in the moment he seemed like an old man. I folded my hands next to him.

He prayed for my soul, prayed for my actions, prayed for Jesus to claim me, prayed for Mary to hear us.

And I prayed for the attorney to do her damn job and for the judge to be cool.

He said, "Amen."

I said, "Amen."

We sat for a moment in silence. I heard a low groan, probably the boiler starting up. I heard the traffic muffled outside. I heard the wind rattling a loose window. It was almost a holy moment, but only one thing was going through my mind: *Please Lord, don't let them send me to jail.*

I PULLED ON THE PHONE CORD AND LEANED BACK, making the Jordan poster crinkle behind my head. I was in Mike's garage, listening to Big Wheez rant. Today, his voice had no humor in it, no slow smile. I wasn't going to hear a 'Good job, homie.' Or, 'I hear

151

you're doing good work up there.' None of that.

"Where's my money, Strain?"

"It's no problem. I been caught up with the cops. I got some troubles but it's no problem. I'll get you your money."

"You think I'm playing with you?"

"Naw, Big Wheez."

"I'm not playing with you. This is money, homie. I'm not your fucking Santa Claus. You understand me?"

"I understand. Let me send you what we got."

"I'm not keeping track of that shit. You gotta pay your debts in full."

"Shit. If I don't lay low for a bit, you won't ever get your money."

"I don't like to hear that, Strain."

"Come on, Big Wheez, you know me."

It felt like a knife was twisting hard in my gut. I'd been trying to push the feeling away, but it just kept growing worse. It was bad when I felt this way. This was when I got crazy and did something stupid. But I couldn't get crazy talking to Big Wheez.

"I'm going to get you your money. A couple weeks is all."

"This was a damn mistake."

"Just hold up a moment."

"A damn mistake."

"You'll get your money." I cringed at the whine in my voice.

"Damn right I'll get my money. Damn right. But you fucked up. Rocco told me, Strain. He told me about the homies you running with."

The twisting cut lower into my guts, but I couldn't do anything. I had no moves to make.

"You got a white boy up there and a black. A fucking joke."

I squeezed my eyes shut.

He said, "We got some history, you and me."

"Yeah, yeah, we do. You know me, Wheez."

"So you got some time, Strain. But I'm not playing."

With that, the phone went dead and I found myself sitting on the floor. At some point I had slid down the wall without noticing. Mike sat a few feet from me, folded over his desk, staring at his notebook. Slowly, I climbed back to my feet, feeling dizzy, and put the phone in its cradle on the wall.

I felt lost, just like Dave kept saying at the church. I was still working with him, almost every day for the past month. And as I started thinking about him with my head resting against the wall, I figured a prayer couldn't hurt. Conscious of Mike next to me, I whispered to God, and asked him to rescue me. Deliver me from evil. Deliver me from Big Wheez... or whatever.

I opened my eyes and turned to Mike. "We're fucked."

He swiveled in his chair.

"Big Wheez is pissed."

"You gotta calm yourself, Loco."

I'd started pacing. I was ready to freak out, stab a fool with a pencil, take down some red-tatted busters in a MAX station, do something crazy.

"Calm down, Loco, it's cool."

"Naw, *ese*. You're not hearing me. We're fucked. Big Wheez, he's coming down on us. We're gonna get green lighted."

"Brad, listen. We're cool. We got the money."

I shook my head.

"I'm telling you we got it. We're good."

"Naw, Mike. We're fucked."

"I gotta grab a drop from Donald but he's got it ready. We can send Wheez a package tomorrow."

I stopped moving and stared at him stupidly. His words were slow to break through, but when they finally did, I said, "All of it?"

"Yeah."

"Well... shit," I sunk to the couch. More confused than anything, I muttered a half-hearted, "Well, that's all right then."

Mike swiveled back to his notebook, leaving me light-headed and hopped up with unused adrenaline. I stared at the wall and thought hard about what just happened. A strange laugh bubbled up through my chest. I had God figured out. If I prayed hard enough then he would take care of things. He'd get me out of jail. He'd pay off drug dealers. It all made sense.

———

DAVE'S DAUGHTER SAT SMIRKING AT ME FROM THE kitchen table. She had a clever look in her eyes, fourteen, fifteen years old, acting the little sister as soon as I sat down, teasing me about my clothes.

Dave's wife had made pork chops. She reminded me of my grandma, squeezing my shoulder, asking if I wanted seconds, pretending not to hear me say, "No thanks."

I ate too much food and had more heaped on my plate, but before I could offer to help clean up, Dave said, "Brad, come on outside with me. I want to show you something." He pulled me with him, not waiting for me to thank his wife properly, his stubby legs almost at a trot to the driveway. There, he pointed at an ugly-ass car parked next to his double-wide. It was a white Datsun station wagon at least ten years old. Rust covered the bottom edge and spread up the bumpers.

Dave looked at me, his eyes glassy, his mouth drawn tight. He laid an arm on my shoulder and said, "Brad, I been real impressed with your work at the church."

I had been working hard all winter. I'd been doing it mostly to impress God, but also because a part of me liked it. The work helped with the stress, and I'd been stressing hard.

Big Wheez kept calling every couple weeks. We'd paid him off, but he wasn't done with me. Last time we talked, he said, "I'mma have my homeboys drop another load off with you."

"Hey, hold off right now. I'm in trouble."

"Listen, Loco," he gave my name a hard edge, "you're Sureño. You started a set, now you gotta run that shit. You in it for life. You got dues to pay."

"I know, I know." I pressed my hand against my stomach. It felt like it was being squeezed flat. "But things are tight. Just hold off a bit and let me get shit together."

He hadn't liked this, kept telling me I was a mistake. Finally, he growled, "Stop fucking with me, Strain," and the phone went dead.

After that conversation, I'd gone to see Dave. He had me mop the floor for bingo night. In that hour - bent over, slopping gray water, smelling bleach - I didn't think about Big Wheez. When I was done, I had stood just inside the kitchen and admired my work. I could see the fluorescent lights reflected in the floor. It had felt good.

154

Now, outside his home, Dave said, "These past few months, Brad... you've been working hard. I been proud of you and I wanted..." He stopped and took off his hat. He rubbed his head like a genie would pop out, then gestured again towards the Datsun. He said, "I want you to stay on the path you're on. So... shoot. Here's something for your hard work."

He reached into a pocket and bought out a set of keys connected to a plastic fob. He put them in my hand. I gripped them harder than I needed to, not sure what to say.

"It's not much to look at, I know, but it's got solid... it's in good shape underneath. She's got a new battery and decent tires. It needs some more work to get her humming but she'll get you home today and I can help you out with the repairs it needs, you understand? Take your time with it, and she'll be a good car."

I could see how much it meant to him, and his warmth was catching. It spread through my chest. On the other hand, I was an eighteen-year-old kid and this car was hella-ugly. I couldn't imagine what JBone would say if I tried picking him up in that thing. Or Rocco. My homies would never stop laughing.

He said, "I'll follow you home today. It'll get you there, but like I said, she needs some work."

I told him how much I appreciated it, and climbed in. The door creaked open and shut. It smelled like old people and exhaust. The front seat had lost it's give and I sunk towards the floor.

The next day I would head to trial, but I felt all right about that as I backed out. The car rumbled underneath me; it needed a muffler and smelled strongly of gas. The radio was on an oldie station and I figured I'd might as well leave it there. I drove to my mom's place, pleased but hoping the whole way that none of my homies would see it was me behind the wheel.

MY NEW SHIRT BUTTONED DOWN IN FRONT AND WAS tucked into my new slacks. It scratched at my neck and waist, but I looked slick, like an upstanding young man. I was ready to face the judge.

I had been trying to change. How much of it was genuine and how much of it was fear of adult jail, I still don't know, but my mom was fully committed to it. She set aside an entire day for me. She took me through the mall, helped me try on shirts, bought me lunch at the food court. And now she sat behind me at the trial, rooting for me. My dad was there too.

I felt good. My attorney had met my eye and told me straight that I had a good chance of going home. It was my first offense as an adult, so with the community service I had done, the judge could let me walk. My attorney hadn't promised it; she'd put other possibilities out there, but I didn't listen to any of those. I was going to walk out there the same as I walked in. I had the Lord on my side. I spent the last three months cleaning his church. As I far as I understood it, he owed me.

And after this, the Lord and me, we'd be cool. I had learned religion now. Do the work, get the reward. I figured I'd back off from the gang stuff. I wouldn't quit, but I'd take it easier. More Brad, less Loco. I'd straighten up just enough to watch the blessings roll in. No problem.

The judge was a red-faced man with sweaty hair. He stared down at me, holding his glasses against the side of his head. Adult court was more formal, and the room was quiet except for my attorney talking. She detailed my community service. She said it was my first offense. She argued I should get off with time served. I sat back, eyes closed briefly, ready to offer a sincere thank you to the Lord.

The judge breathed a half chuckle. My eyes flicked open in time to watch the man shake his head.

"No," he said. "I don't think so."

My breath caught in my chest. I heard my attorney's voice rise; she said, "Your honor, it's his first offense."

And again that laugh, and the man said to me, "Mr. Strain, I just can't let your juvenile record go." Even as he talked, I started to sink into myself, so when the judge said it would be 120 days, it came from far away.

My 'thank you' to Jesus was souring in my head. I had been lied to. My attorney, my mom, Dave, God, all of them were full of shit. I had done the work. I had showed up for school. I had shoveled snow. I had cleaned out toilets. All because they said it would help. I had done my part, but it had gone to hell. I had done the work, but this - the judge, the trial, my attorney - all of it was bullshit.

A fire in my guts, a heavy heat, pushed up so I couldn't breathe. I was aware of my mom crying behind me, heard her panted breaths, but I didn't care. She lied to me. They all lied to me. I couldn't look at my dad. I kept my head down as a guard led me out and shackled me for transfer.

The cuffs pinched my wrists as they led me to adult jail where'd I stay for four months. I had done the work, but it had all led to this. Brad Strain had been a fool to believe.

No more. The heavy door closed behind me and I sunk in, bracing myself for all of it. I'd be stripped down, ordered around. I'd have no privacy, no darkness. I steeled myself, ready to beat down, to attack. I'd act hella-crazy until they all backed off. I was Loco and Loco was the only thing I understood.

Angel

Eight months later

HIS EMPTY FORTY thudded against the carpet at his feet. Ty Angel said, "Let's go find some trouble."

My other homies, Mike and JBone, waved him off but I was as eager as a little kid. "Do you really?" I said. "You really want to?"

"Yeah, let's roll."

Tyler was a rich kid, and he drove a classic low-rider, a '63 Impala. I knew he was just slumming it with the homeboys, but it didn't matter. This fool from the suburbs offered me the release I needed.

With money on my books and Sureño connections, the 120 days in adult jail hadn't been nearly as bad as I'd feared. I'd done my time no problem, but after getting out, the cops wouldn't leave me alone. They kept picking me up for violating probation, mostly for fighting. At the gas station, behind the mall, the cops would find me and I'd do fifteen days, then thirty, then forty-five.

And things weren't going right in Los Tiny Dukes. We were surrendering area without pushing back. Donald had been dipping too hard into the crack so that he was rail thin with hollow cheeks. He was no longer there even when he was. Mike was still bringing in the money, working with Chavo, but the money wasn't enough for me.

The gang, the ghost, the legend of Loco was fading but then there was Ty Angel. He'd showed up at a house party a few weeks before where we made a bond immediately. And now we climbed in his baby blue Impala, and cruised towards Westside Piru's territory on the hunt. It didn't take us long before we found the Frenn Brothers in the back of the arcade. They had their backs to us, focused on a game.

There were a few seconds of violence followed by silence. The screens flashed different colors onto Ty Angel's face, blue then red then pink, making him look alien. The air was thick with the smell of hot electronics now mixed with blood. The brothers laid on the ground at our feet, their bodies at odd angles. They were moaning, moving slow, one of them had his foot up against the Street Fighter game they'd been playing, the game still going on without him. His character got punched in the face until he lost. KO'd in real life and on the screen.

I grabbed Ty to pull him out the back door, but he was rooted in place, staring at me. For a half a second I saw it all in his eyes. Hate, rage, ready to throw down with whoever we could find. He was starving for violence; he was a menace to society. The movie had just come out and the rich white boy wanted to live it. We were the bad guys, the beasts, and when we slammed open the back door of the arcade, blood on our shoes, I certainly wasn't thinking of Dave. I'd given up on prayer at the trial. I'd learned it was all bullshit, and this was all there was: power and violence.

Laughing, Ty and I sprinted through the back hall and scurried into the alleyway. We found his car where we'd left it, and tore into the night, looking for more trouble.

TY BUSTED THE DISPLAY CASES WHILE I RIPPED OPEN the register, both of us moving nonstop, jacked with adrenaline. Sweat dampened my hat, streaked down past my eyes. I had a bandana over my nose that kept creeping down so I tugged at it after stuffing a final handful of watches in the duffle bag. We sprinted outside, not thinking past the next step, and threw the bags in the trunk. I fell on top of them and closed the lid over me. Angel drove, the idiot fish-tailing out of the parking lot.

I rearranged the bags so I could settle deeper in the trunk. He whooped from the driver's seat, banging on something loud enough for me to hear. The car hummed smooth so I figured we were cruising the highway away from town.

I screamed out, "That's how you do it!" and he shouted back, "That's right, Loco!" Ty Angel was a fool, red faced and 'roided up, but none of that mattered. Who it was never mattered. I showed this white boy how it was done. I showed him I was Loco and no one could match me for crazy.

Five minutes out, red and white lights flashed under the lid of the trunk where the wind whistled through. I released a string of curses and kicked at the side of the car.

"Oh shit," Ty Angel screamed back me. "Lights behind us, Loco."

"I know."

"What do I do?"

I jerked around in the trunk, feeling through the duffle bag until I found the gun. No bullets, no clip, but it was something. I shouted, "Pull over, fool!"

The car slowed, pushing my back into something metal like a crowbar. Another moment and gravel rumbled underneath us. Holding my breath, I gripped the gun with one hand and the lid of the trunk with another. It was no kind of plan, but I was ready to throw it open and stab the gun towards the cop. After that I didn't think about what would happen.

"Fuck Loco! I cut my hand in the pawn shop."

I thought I heard a door close but I shouted out, "Put a bandana over it."

A male voice came muffled through the metal; it spoke without urgency. There were no shouted commands, no sirens from approaching backup. The driver's door opened and the car shuddered underneath me. I figured the cop asked Ty to step out, which was confirmed when I heard the sound footsteps came around the back of the car. From there, I could hear the cop clearly.

"You know why I pulled you over?"

I held the pistol to my chest, ready.

Ty said, "No sir."

"You were driving down the wrong side of the highway."

I had to swallow a curse. I started thinking that if things turned bad, I should take down my idiot partner instead of the cop. Then, in a moment I lost all my options when Ty sat down on the lid of the trunk, locking me in. I wanted to knock the white boy's head off, but I kept quiet and listened as the cop directed him through a sobriety test.

With my knees folded to my chest, I squeezed the pistol like a baby with a blanket. A piece of metal dug into my hip so my leg went numb, but I didn't move. I took shallow breaths. It smelled of old carpet and motor oil and I needed more air.

Finally the engine started and the car moved forward with no sirens or shouts. I stretched my legs as Ty screamed, "Whoo-hoo! That was crazy, dude! That was the craziest shit!"

I squeezed my eyes shut, willing him to shut up.

"Did you hear that, Loc? I drove the wrong way on the ramp?"

"That was crazy, *ese*."

"You want to be let out?"

"No!" I shouted. It was like this fool wanted to get us arrested. "Just get us out of the area."

The pawn shop had been in a small town a long way out of Portland, so I squeezed in the trunk for more than an hour, feeling every bump in my hip, stolen garbage scratching my skin, living the gangster life.

IT WAS THE FIRST TIME THE CREW HAD BEEN together in weeks, JBone, Donald, Mike and me. This was my family, but we were falling apart.

JBone had backed off. He was loyal when he had to be, but his heart didn't seem in it.

D didn't look good. Smoke puffed from his nose and drifted over his face. His fingers shook around a cigarette, coughing on it.

Mike was cool, sitting back, watching without emotion. He had gone in deep with Chavo's crew, even started dating the man's daughter. He still gave me my cut, but had stopped including me in most of the business.

LTD was dying and none of them wanted to do anything but hang in the basement.

I took my turn playing pool, stewing on all this. I had spent too much time in jail and no longer knew how I fit in. It depressed me so much I decided I couldn't handle it anymore that night. I figured I'd head back over to Becky's house - we were still together - to think about what I should do. But just as I was about to tell the crew, Brett stomped down the stairs.

With wide eyes, he yelled, "Loco! Ah shit!" He seemed smaller than usual. Thin wrists poked from his pockets. "I got jacked, *ese*."

I whipped the pool cue onto the table. "What are you saying to me?" An hour before I'd given him a $1500 bag of dope.

"I lost your weed," he stumbled over the words. "You know what I'm saying? I got jacked."

Fire crackled through me. I moved to him, almost hopping, and gripped his shirt. "You playing?" He shrunk as I shouted, "Somebody jacked me? Jacked me?"

"Naw, I'm not playing. That James Reed motherfucker. He took your weed."

I shoved him back and looked to my boys.

"I got the guns, you hear me? Let's go get this fool."

They stared back at me. All of them calm, none of them moving. No one even spoke for a moment until Mike raised a hand, still sitting.

He said, "Let's just think this through a moment."

It was like somebody poked a hole in me. I stared at him, not understanding but losing my energy, deflating.

"We'll get the money back, but let's make a plan, you know?"

JBone nodded and D had already left the room for another bump. I fell into a chair, shaking my head, not sure what was going on.

Mike spoke quietly, "Maybe we chill out and think it through."

"I guess," I said. "Yeah."

I started giving into the calm, figuring maybe I should chill out, think it through, like Mike said. I leaned back and rubbed my eyes.

But again the door banged open upstairs, and, like Brett had a minute before, Ty Angel broke into the room. He punched JBone hard in the shoulder, laughing at nothing. Talking too loud, he called Mike a fat motherfucker and grabbed a beer.

I nodded at him.

"What's up, Loco?"

I shrugged. "I just got jacked, *homes*."

Ty shot up, eyes wide. "What? Who the fuck would jack you?"

I leaned forward, heat rising, and told him about James Reed.

"Naw," he said. "Naw, that's not happening. Let's go get this motherfucker."

Mike, JBone and Brett shrank back; I didn't even see them anymore.

"Where can we find this fool?" Ty shouted.

The fire had relit in my gut, so by the time Brett muttered the name of the neighborhood, I was halfway out the door. It was late fall, cool and already getting darker. On instinct, I grabbed the shotgun from the trunk and laid it in the backseat. We started to move. As he drove, Ty screamed over the music, describing in sick detail what he was going to do when we found the man.

We looped around the neighborhood and it didn't take long before I spotted a *vato* wearing red. We pulled close and it was James Reed himself, standing on the sidewalk. He had a homie with him and they were talking to some high school kids.

Ty pulled over. I gripped the gun and leapt out before the car was in park, screaming, "Hey, motherfucker, you rob me?"

James stared at me stupid as the kids scattered off. He raised his hands. "What're you taking about?"

I closed in on him, shouted, "You robbed my boy, fool," and hit him in the forehead with the gun.

He clutched at his face as he fell to his knees. I busted him again in the mouth. Blood and teeth sprayed out as the momentum threw him onto his back. Ty had his homie laid out next to me. We had won, but it wasn't enough.

He moaned. "I don't even know who you are."

I said, "I'm Loco." I turned the gun around, finger on the trigger, had a slug ready to go.

"Gun!" Somewhere in the background a girl had been screaming but finally I heard it. "He's got a gun! Get down! Get down!"

It was like I woke from a dream. I blinked around, and saw the bus for the first time. I saw the flagpole. I saw the students.

"Aw shit," I said. My anger was immediately replaced by something close to panic. "We gotta move, Ty." I stooped to dig through James' pockets, grabbing a wad of cash before backing up and stumbling to the Impala.

He peeled away from the high school. "That was crazy, Loc." He was grinning, ready to celebrate. He didn't get what we had just done.

"Hide this car, *ese*."

"Yeah, of course."

"You got to hide this car."

"I got it, Loco."

I didn't know if he did.

He was eager to keep moving, go look for more trouble, but I had him drop me at Becky's house. I limped to her door. I wasn't hurt but felt broken, exhausted. I barely said hello, and moved straight to the bathroom. I rinsed the flecks of blood from my face and smudged it from my white shirt. Becky knocked quietly, asking if I was all right.

"Yeah," I said, but I was far from all right. I was coming down hard from the adrenaline and from the whole damn life. I sat on the toilet and counted the cash. I'd taken seven hundred dollars off James Reed but it was nothing.

I stepped out shirtless. Becky stared up at me. "What's wrong?"

I didn't know. I took down my enemy. I got my money back. Nothing should have been wrong, but for some reason I couldn't answer.

She said, "You okay?"

I didn't know. All I could do was shrug.

A HELLA-UGLY BUICK REGAL PULLED INTO THE driveway. Not Datsun ugly, but still not a car I'd want to roll in. I had been holed up at Becky's house for over a week, not feeling it, not into anything. I wasn't hiding, exactly. I didn't think much about what happened at the school. I was just exhausted.

But when I saw the car, I pulled on my shoes and hurried outside. I had figured who it was before he climbed out and didn't want Ty to come into the house.

"What you doing here?"

The fool didn't catch my mood and grinned. "We haven't hung out for awhile."

"Yeah, but what are you doing here?"

"Your homie Donald told me where to find you."

I twisted back to check if Becky or her mom were watching out the window.

"Come on, Loco. Let's go chill." He said chill, but he was grinning like he wanted to find some trouble.

I wanted to head back to bed, but that didn't matter. I was Loco; I didn't know how to say no to crazy. A few minutes later we were cruising across town.

Ty kept moving, dancing with the beat, pounding on the steering wheel. "I been thinking. We gotta start a gang, you and me."

"What are you talking about?"

"Let's start a Crip gang."

"Fool, I'm no Crip."

"Yeah, yeah, but we got to step it up. Start something against those West Side Piru motherfuckers. Throw down, you know?"

I knew that tone of voice. I felt it. I lived it. But I said, "Naw, man. I'm LTD."

"I know it, Loco, but maybe it's time to mix it up."

"You're not getting me. I'm Sureño. You hear me?"

"Chill, bro. I got you."

As he talked about it, he was driving us into a Crip neighborhood: the Rolling 60s. I didn't know what he was doing, but D slung some product around there and it was middle of the afternoon so I figured it shouldn't be a problem. We rolled into the Coffman Market to buy some forties. If Ty was smarter, I'd have thought he planned it, but when we stepped outside the store, we found the parking lot filled with bangers.

Ty started talking them up, like they knew each other. I watched quietly until he followed one of them out of sight. I leaned against the car. We had no beef with this set but a few were eyeing me, standing there alone.

I said, "Hey, you know my homie, Donald?"

They nodded, one of them grinned. "Yeah, we know Donald."

"He's my homie."

"Donald keeps us cool down here."

"Yup. I know it. I know he does."

These Crips liked rolling on bicycles. Hearing Donald's name, they relaxed and stopped mean-mugging. Instead, they cruised in little circles around the car, sipping on cokes, smoking cigarettes. Finally, Ty came around the side of the store.

The one walking next to him said, "You gotta come to our house down here and party."

I shook my head before he was done talking. "Naw, we're cool."

Ty said, "Come on, Loco, what's the problem?"

It was a stupid idea, dangerous, but they were all staring at me, waiting. I shrugged and climbed into the car. These bangers rolled around us in their bikes as Ty drove. One of them held a pistol, pointing it up at the sky.

"Ty, is that your gun?"

"Yeah, dude."

"What the hell?"

"He's just checking it out. It's cool."

"No, it ain't cool. He just jacked you."

"Nope."

"I'm not going to shoot this fool for you handing your gun to him, you hear me?"

We followed the pack of bikes a few blocks to a house tucked back next to the highway. Two stories tall, and ready to collapse in on itself. Half the windows had been boarded up. A slab of siding hung above the door like a scar.

There was no music, no girls, no party, just these crips staring at us as he parked. "Shit," I said. "Get your gun and let's roll."

"It's not like that Loc." He stepped out, relaxed and shaking hands. I touched the pistol in my jacket as I climbed out. My eyes bounced around the fools on their bikes to the windows then to Ty before he disappeared into the house. I could see my breath, and followed it slowly up the sidewalk.

It felt wrong, but I tried to relax. I had a reputation. I had respect. I was Loco. These *vatos* got their drugs from us and wouldn't want to start something with LTD. I told myself all of this, but still my heart was thumping hard as I opened the door into the house.

Place smelled of piss and dust. Bass thumped from another room. There was no melody, no music, just the deep pound of the beat rattling through my gut. Up a half flight of stairs, I found a few crackheads smoking from a pipe. Two sunk into a couch, one squatted on the floor. They stared up at me stupidly.

A chill climbed my spine, but I pretended it was all cool. I said,

"What's up, homies?"

"Just chilling."

"Yeah? You see a white boy around here?"

"Naw, we ain't see nobody."

I hurried back to the stairs. I was done. Ty could take care of himself. I planned on heading back to the car and waiting there until he was finished with whatever fool thing he was doing. But before I could take the first step, a billy jack slammed between my shoulders and I collapsed, rolling down until I came to a stop against a wall. I couldn't breathe but knew I needed to move. I started pushed myself up but a shadow kicked me in the ribs. It flattened me, so I crawled forward, moving by inches until I could push myself out the front door. I rolled down the front step. In the daylight I could see Ty taking his own beating by the car.

I tried to stand but another hit from the billy jack dropped me into the grass. I rolled over to see OG Bear, a huge man, the leader of this set, standing over me while one of his homies dug through my pockets, snatching my pistol and cash. Bear gave me one more kick without much effort, and the fools scattered off on their bikes.

More numb than anything, I stumbled to Ty. He was barely there, eyes heavy, muttering nonsense. I dug the keys from his pocket, and shoved him in the back seat. My face a mess, I could barely see the road for the blood.

THE DOOR RANG AND I BLINKED OPEN MY EYES. THERE was an angry pounding which shook the frame. I was still half-asleep, but alert enough to know it was nothing good. Becky sat up and wiped a sleeve across her face. Her dad was on the road, and her mom was visiting a sister, so it was the two of us alone in the house.

The knock came again even louder. I got on my feet, socks sliding on the floor, and lifted the window blinds with a finger. A cop car was parked out front. The sight of it landed like a punch, right below the ribcage, forcing air from my lungs. I scrambled back, not stopping to panic, and grabbed on my pants.

"Should I go out there?"

"No, no, no." I fell on my knees to search under the bed for a shoe.

"No, baby, hold on." I pulled my shirt carefully over my head - my face was still swollen from the beating I got from OG Bear - and gave her a nod. "All right. Go ahead."

I watched her walk down the hallway, then I slid the back door open real slow. It was a quiet morning, neighbors sleeping, no cops in sight. Frost covered everything, crunched under my Nikes. I knew this neighborhood. I could see the park - my park - and figured if I could make it there then I'd find my way. I was still fast, only nineteen years old, and felt the energy in my legs. I could make it somewhere safe, somewhere the cops wouldn't be looking.

I took a half a step, and a blur of blue stopped all my thoughts. There was a shout and I had a half-second to turn my head before a man in body armor tackled me to the ground. He pushed my head into the frozen earth. The grass scratched my cheek. I had a moment to wonder how it all went wrong before he yanked my shoulder, pulling me up in time to watch two cops give each other a high five straight from Top Gun.

I did my thing and sank deep. I went silent, and let time pass around me. I said nothing in the cop car, said nothing in the interview room, said almost nothing to the lawyer. In the courtroom, I pled guilty to the assault in front of the high school, but stayed deep inside myself even as the judge called me a terror, as he glared into my eyes and said they had to get me off the street.

But when he sentenced me to two and a half years, I couldn't help but hear. I came out of myself for a moment, but then sunk further down - not frightened, but finished. Distantly, I noticed the uniformed guards put their hands on me and I followed, thinking blankly of Brett getting jacked, of Ty Angel and James Reed, of the man's teeth tracing a little arc to the sidewalk.

I spent a few weeks in county jail before they shipped me out of town. My mom came to visit once. Metal seats, metal table, all cool to the touch. The room damp, smelling like middle school, of cheap meat and close bodies. I barely looked at her crumpled on the other side of the table. For ten minutes she sobbed, a tissue against her face. People talking around us, but she just cried until finally she flicked her eyes towards mine and then looked away. She shook her head, kept shaking her head, and said, "I can't do this any more, Bradley."

I sat deep inside myself, tossing it around, trying to figure what happened. I couldn't get my mind around it, thinking of Ty Angel, thinking of the dude's teeth and OG Bear, thinking through all of it.

"I'm done," she said.

I lowered my head, hearing her but far away like a dream I was forgetting. And she got up and left without anything more. I wouldn't see my mom again for almost twenty years.

I followed the guard, thinking of Mike, thinking of hiding in the trunk, thinking of Becky and the look on her face as they dragged me away in handcuffs. Locked in my cell, I fell back on the bunk thinking of everything, all of it; nothing else to do for two and a half years but think.

Hamilton,
Montana
2008

Homecoming
Fourteen years later

AFTER A STINT in prison, it was always strange to push on a door and find it unlocked, but there it was. I took a few steps out of the building and stood under a tree. The sun glinted off car windshields; a truck braked on the highway coming into town; the smell of hot asphalt mixed with trees and grass. I took another deep breath and started across the parking lot.

I was coming out of four years in prison, three in California and one in Montana. They had convicted me of a cocktail of crimes - a couple DUIs, an assault, a burglary. The final stretch was the toughest I'd ever done. Anger had burned through me until the guards couldn't handle it. They had to keep tightening security around me until I could barely move. But now, like a surprise gift, like I was getting away with something, they had let me out. And so, still dizzy from my change in circumstance, I started walking towards the little town of Hamilton, Montana.

I knew these streets; knew to cut through an alley and turn right to get onto Main Street where I followed the sidewalk. A little breeze ruffled the weeds growing in the cracks, and I gulped it in. The smell of mowed lawns mixed with fried meat coming out of the diner.

I passed the movie theater. It was closed for business now but had a movie showing the first night I came to town, ten years before. I had got off the bus with twenty dollars in my pocket and a garbage bag of clothes. I came for a girl, for Melody, with no idea what I was getting into. She had picked me up at a gas station and drove me the six blocks through town to her house. As we drove, I looked around, trying to figure out where all the people were.

She had thrown me a welcome party where I had met her little brother and his friend. These two fifteen-year-old small town kids kept asking about the gang life, and I had to prove I was the toughest, craziest fool they ever met. Three hours after getting off the bus, I had climbed ahead of them to the apartment over the movie theater and kicked the door open, the lock breaking easy under my boot. The kids faded back but I searched, tossing papers and tables until I found the wooden box, like they'd said, filled with a couple thousand dollars worth of quarters. I had lugged it by myself, quarters tinkling down behind me, falling between the slats on the stairs and leaving a trail all the way to the car.

I had taken the fall for that one too. That was what I did. In the fourteen years that had passed since I went to jail for the assault on James Reed outside the high school, nothing had changed. Sure, I had gotten married to Melody for awhile, and moved first to Montana, then to Sacramento, then into the California correctional system, but no matter where I went the stories were all the same. Drugs, petty crime, gang life, prison. I had been stuck in the same pattern my entire life.

But now I'd served my time. I'd been released. At thirty-four years old, I'd been given another fresh start.

Leaving the movie theater, I followed the sidewalk until it ended, then walked along a thinly graveled side street. To my left, a wide pasture was visible behind a little park; in the distance I could see a cow.

I stopped in front of a familiar house. It was smaller than I remembered. It needed painting and the garden had grown over. Ten years ago the lawn had been perfect, but now it was covered in weeds. It worried me, but I had no place else to go.

I rang the bell. When no one answered after a moment, I knocked. I thought I could hear a tractor in the distance but other than that it was quiet. I ran my hand along the cast iron railing. The wind pushed through the trees.

The deadbolt unlatched with a thunk. The door opened inward and revealed an old man in the doorway: Grandpa Bud. He'd been huge when I first met him, had paws for hands. But ten years later he'd gone bald, his face drooped, his back bent forward and he'd shrunk.

"What is this now?"

"Grandpa Bud!"

"They let you out, huh?"

"Yessir."

He scratched at his ear. "Well, you better come in then."

He had me sit at the kitchen table, brought me some iced tea without asking, and put the cordless phone in my hands. He waited as I made my calls. When I was done, he sat down close, pulling his chair right near mine.

Grandpa Bud was my ex-wife's grandfather and a retired pentecostal minister. Ten years earlier, when I was married to Mel, I'd come over most Saturdays. After helping his wife with the garden, I'd sit down at that same table. He'd push iced tea at me and start talking about the Bible. I'd nod my head, agreeing with every word, even as I was out causing havoc, selling drugs, living my gangster life in small town Montana.

Now the old man studied me. "You ready to change your life around?"

It was a question I'd been asked a hundred times since I was thirteen years old. "Yeah, Grandpa Bud. I am." Like every other time, this time I meant it.

"All right, Son. Give me your hand."

His hand was still big and rough, but it lacked the old strength. I closed my eyes as he prayed. Bud asked God's presence. He asked that finally Jesus would melt my hardened heart and help me change my ways. He asked the Holy Spirit to come in and turn me back to the Lord.

Amen.

ICED TEA AND PRAYER WORKED BETTER THAN A HOT shower. My time with Grandpa Bud left me feeling cleaner than I had in years.

175

Kicking a rock along my path, I crossed back through downtown and turned at the movie theater. There, a side street followed a gentle slope down towards the edge of town.

At the next block I stopped outside a corner bar. The place hadn't changed at all, down to the crack in the plastic sign. The smell of bleach and stale beer drifted out the open door. I figured I'd still know the drunks inside, and probably recognize the bartender, though it had been ten years since he kicked me out. I'd been so drunk that a minute later I couldn't remember why I was outside and had stumbled back in to order another drink. The bartender eighty-sixed me, screaming for me never to come back. Then he called the cops when I climbed into my car. It had led to my first jail time in Montana.

I rubbed a hand over my face. There was something broken in me, I knew that. But I was ready to change. I needed to - for real this time.

I walked on. After another block I came to the park. The old brick school stood next to it, casting its shadow onto the grass. The playground equipment needed a paint job and some lawn care around the edges. I ducked under the monkey bars and stepped onto the wide field where three ten-year-old boys were playing football.

I watched for a long moment. I kept my eyes on one of them in particular, a stocky kid with a baby face just like mine. He threw a pass. It missed its mark but I could see he had a strong arm.

Pride swelled up in my chest. My life had been a revolving door of drugs, crime and prison, but I had brought one good thing into the world.

"Chase!" I called the kid's name and he turned his head towards me. I watched as his surprise melted into a smile. He started running across the field at a full sprint, and I jogged forward to meet him.

"Dad!" he cried out.

I pulled him into a hug, and my son buried his head in my chest.

I SAT ON A BROKEN LAWN CHAIR ON THE PORCH WITH Chase on the steps near my feet. I marveled at the back of his head, damp with sweat. He kept swiveling around to tell me about some part of his life, trying to make me laugh.

The house sagged. The siding was covered with dirt. The sidewalk cracked. My son lived here with his two half-sisters and my ex-wife, Melody.

It was my fault. I hadn't seen Chase in four years. It had been longer than that since his mom and I broke up. Even when we were together I was either causing havoc or in jail. There was something wrong with me, and I had led them to this. I wanted to do better.

I listened to the sound of Chase's voice and it was like all the other times, like with my brother and Dave and Grandpa Bud. In the moment, I was all in, entirely committed to change. I was going to put all the criminal stuff behind me and become a steady father.

Chase laughed at a joke he had made and I shook my head. I'd made those promises before, and within days or a week I'd been back hustling drugs in some fool's garage.

It couldn't happen this time. I couldn't survive another stint in prison like the last one. I needed to get a legit job. I needed to be responsible. I needed to be a dad.

And maybe a husband. A car sputtered up the street and parked half on the lawn. Melody climbed out. She squinted into the sun.

"You found him," she said.

"Yup. We been catching up."

"Have you?" She gave me a hint of a smile layered with twelve years of disappointment.

We had met in Vancouver, Washington, after my old girlfriend, Becky, had moved away. Melody had two girls, babies at the time, and I created a bond with them. Soon, they started calling me Daddy and the word had stirred something inside me. For a time I tried to take care of them. Unfortunately all I knew was gangs and selling drugs which landed me in jail again.

For a few months, Melody had written to me, but then she moved back to the small town in Montana where she grew up. She asked in a letter if I wanted to join her, but I was a city guy, a Sureño. I answered something like, "Hell no!"

But when I got out, the Vancouver police wouldn't leave me alone. It seemed as I couldn't walk down the street without getting arrested. They backed me further into a corner until I had no moves left to make. Finally, figuring rural Montana had to be better than prison, I gathered all my stuff in a garbage bag and got on a bus.

That was ten years ago. Now, she walked towards me on the porch. Long blonde hair, pretty eyes, she stopped a few feet away and cocked out a hip.

"You can't stay here," she said.

I laughed. "Why you gotta be like that, Mel?"

"Don't. You can't stay here."

I raised my hands in surrender. "I'm just here to see my family."

"Mm-hmm."

"Come on. I just got out this morning."

"I know."

"I thought we could spend the evening together, you know. Have some dinner."

"Hmm."

"Then maybe I could spend the night."

She shook her head.

"Where are the girls?"

"They'll be home in a bit. Harli's at a friend's and Rachelle's got work."

"That's right. That's good. I missed them."

She shrugged.

It was her voice, her look. I felt the same I always had. I said, "I missed you too."

She rolled her eyes. "You can stick around for dinner."

"That's all I'm asking. Although listen, Mel. I gotta be in Sacramento in three days to meet with my parole officer."

Her eyes went hard.

"I could use a couch to sleep on for a couple days 'til I figure out what to do next."

A car crunched through the grit down the street.

"The girls," Melody said.

I grinned at her. "It's good to be home."

"You are not home, Brad."

"Come on."

"But I guess you can stay for one night."

I had already stood and was moving towards the car.

"That's right, Mel, thank you."

The girls were laughing as they opened their doors.

"How you guys been?"

I hugged them each in turn. The older one, Rachelle, smelled strongly of cigarettes. Last time I had seen her she was fourteen, eyes bright and full of spunk and sarcasm. But she'd become a young woman and there was a shadow over her face. She looked too old and too tired. "It's good to see you, Brad," she said.

I knew I deserved it but I forced the smile as the three of us made our way towards the house. With some effort I pushed it away, tried to enjoy the moment, but it stung. I had messed up too many times and my daughter no longer called me 'Dad.'

MY FEET FELT TOO HEAVY IN THEIR SHOES. THERE WAS a dull ache between my shoulders. I shuffled with every step, hating it, but had no choice. I had to visit the library.

The place was too quiet. It smelled of dust and an old woman's perfume. Still, I needed to log into the computer and check around, see what I could find. Chase had taught me how to use the internet. He pulled up something called Craig's List and showed me how to type in my search and click the links. Since then, I had made my way over every day. I'd type in construction. I'd type in handyman. I'd type in carpentry. Each time, I'd go down the list, but it seemed like no one was hiring within fifty miles.

I expected the same this afternoon, but hadn't quite made it into the building when a car pulled to the curb, a gray Buick, built for old women, covered in rust and in immediate need of new brakes. My daughter Rachelle leaned out the window.

"Hiya Brad," there was that name again. "What are you doing?"

I stepped close. The smell of weed poured out the window. There was a guy with her who was staring down at his phone. He was a white boy with a flat brimmed cap and a dark look on his face. I knew I couldn't judge. I had done more than my share of stupid and probably would have hung with this fool a few years before. Still, seeing Rachelle with him pissed me off.

"Trying to find a job," I said. I put an edge in my voice, directing it at this boy.

Rachelle tried to say something but started coughing and turned it into a laugh.

"Who's this dude?" I asked.

Her voice was too low from smoking, and her eyes drooped as she introduced him as her boyfriend, Dylan. I said hello, but he barely nodded, didn't turn his head, and started pulling the car forward before we were done talking.

Rachelle called out, "See you, Brad," with the old sarcastic tease in her voice. I watched the car until it turned down a far street.

I started walking, not sure where I was going any more. I couldn't deal with another hour with a computer, searching for a job which didn't exist. An old itch had came back, an irritation. I kept thinking of that boy's face. I wanted to lay my hands on him, but there was nothing I could do.

I was in a daze, not paying attention to my surroundings, just following the street next to the gas station, when a man grabbed me. Before I could react, he had pinned my arms to my side, lifted me in the air and screamed my name.

I wrestled myself free and turned on my attacker. A Mexican man smiled at me beneath a thick goatee. It was an old friend: my boy, Chavez.

He said, "How long you been out, brother?"

"A couple weeks."

"Yeah? What are you doing?"

I didn't have an answer for him.

"Let's grab a beer, Brad. Catch up."

I knew I should head back to the library, but I couldn't imagine spending another hour there when I felt hopped up like I did, so I let him take me to a place we both knew well: The Rainbow Bar.

It was a short drive across town. Inside, the familiar smell of stale beer mixed with fried meat. The midafternoon sun streamed dirty through the windows. The place was empty except for a man in the corner drinking by himself.

The bartender was a heavyset woman with wrinkles around her eyes. "Hey there, Brad," she said. "Long time."

I ordered a beer, first one I had in four years, and took it to a back table where Chavez was grinning like a fool. "Strain, what the hell, man? You're looking good."

"That's right."

"You're looking built. Holy shit. Been working out in prison?"

"Nothing else to do."

"Damn, it's good to see you." He leaned back and looked sly like he already had some scheme in his head.

I couldn't resist asking, "What you thinking, fool?"

"I'm thinking with you back, we could make a lot of money."

I snorted.

"Naw, listen to me though." He leaned forward. "Listen to me, this is different."

I waved a hand, still laughing. I said, "You still working at the shop?"

"Naw, Strain, now listen. I got friends up in North Dakota. They're telling me it is crazy up there." The bartender came close to wipe down a table but Chavez didn't stop. "It's crazy. Everyone is heading there for work and they need shit to keep them going, keep them awake working for the overtime."

"I'm not interested."

His eyes were wide, excited. "We get a few ounces of meth out there and we would make a fortune."

"I'm telling you I'm not interested." I ran the back of my thumb across my lips. "I'm done with that."

"What? You afraid of making some money?"

A hard flashback. Last time a fool asked me that question it ended in a high speed chase. I lost the smile and shook my head.

"All right. All right." He finished his beer and got up to order another. When he came back he said, "You working somewhere?"

"Naw. I couldn't find a job around here if my life depended on it."

"So what are you going to do? California?"

"My parole officer says I gotta stay in Montana."

"That's cool, man. There's money to be made around here too."

"Come on, Chavez, what's wrong with you? I'm done with that. I got to be around for my kids, you know what I'm saying? I can't do that shit no more."

"I got you, brother, I got you. Still though, what are you going to do?"

I had no answer for him.

"You should head out to North Dakota, for real."

"Come on."

"Not to sell, but if you're looking for a job, they got them."

"Yeah?"

"Serious. They'll hire anyone out there. Even an asshole like you."

I shook my head. I didn't have a car or a license or money for gas. If I got caught leaving the state I'd be sent back to jail. Overall, it seemed like a really bad idea.

DICKENSON, NORTH DAKOTA HAD ONLY HALF A MAIN street, no bars and two churches. It was much smaller than Hamilton, Montana, which stressed me out. For the first time in a long while I thought of Rocco and Miguel. I pictured them in the backseat, laughing at me, asking what I could be thinking driving out here. The idea made me want to turn towards the nearest city, but there was nothing else to do. I needed the job.

I followed the directions through town to a gravel driveway which led to a trailer home. A small sign stuck in the lawn identified it as the construction company. I stepped from my car and smoothed down my shirt. It was nothing nice, but the best one I had. I had kept my head bald from prison and rubbed my hand over it without thinking much.

Three sturdy steps led to the door. I peered into the window as I knocked. A woman sat behind a desk. She was younger, fairly pretty, and all alone. She glared at me as I entered, her eyes widening as they flicked from my bald head to the tattoos crawling up my neck to the ones covering my wrists. Most were dark blue from prison, designed to intimidate other inmates and rival gangs.

I smiled as wide as my face would allow and stepped back until I was half out the door. I would have gone further; I'd have retreated to the edge of the parking lot, but I didn't think it would help.

I said, "Mrs. Larson?"

"Yes," she stretched the word out, every part of it telling me to keep my distance.

I kept smiling until my cheeks hurt. "I'm Brad Strain. We talked on the phone."

Her shoulders dipped, not a lot but enough. Her face relaxed from a grimace into something more neutral.

"Mr. Strain," she said. "You made it."

"I sure did. It was a hecka-long drive and let me tell you, I'm glad to be here."

"Please, come on in." Her voice became overly polite and I could almost see her calculating the risks. I came off friendly, but there was still no one around if things went wrong. Still smiling, I carefully sat down in the folding chair.

"So," she said. "You're a carpenter?"

"Yes ma'am."

This was true. Ten years before, when I first came to Montana, Grandpa Bud had helped me get a job building log cabins. I had always been good with my hands and did well at it for about a year until the theft of the quarters and the DUI got me sent to jail. I had left some of these details out of our earlier conversation.

She said, "Good to hear. And the last couple years you've been a stay-at-home dad?"

"That's right. You know, with the economy it was all I could do." This, of course, was a straight-up lie. Hoping I wasn't pushing it, I said, "Best job I ever had."

"All right," she had relaxed and now sounded bored. She bent her head over a stack of papers. "Your references checked out, so we can get you started right away."

"That's what I'm looking for."

"We got a school to build out in Newtown. Hope you're ready to work hard."

I nodded with my whole body and said, "I sure am, ma'am."

This was true. Loco was dead. I was ready to work hard and send money back to Melody and the kids. I was ready for a new life.

The Fall
Five months later

I STARED AT the entrance to my apartment building. I'd cleaned my kitchen and gone for a drive and bought some things from the hardware store. Now I needed to get inside, turn on the TV and find a basketball game, kill a couple hours that way. I needed to chill out, drink some water, relax. Wind pushed against the windshield; clouds moved through the sky at a good clip. Still, I didn't move. It was too silent inside, too empty.

The itch in my chest started screaming through my body. Not for drugs as much as for chaos, for something crazy to go down. I needed to find a bar with smoke so thick I couldn't see the woman next to me. I needed music to smother the noise in my head. I needed some fool a little drunker than me to start mouthing off. I needed to go find my people and cause some havoc.

I squeezed the steering wheel. Most days it was okay. Most days I worked fourteen hours and passed out exhausted after a couple bites of dinner. But today was Saturday with no overtime available. A lot of weekends I'd drive back to Montana to see my kids and tell the parole officer that of course I'd been sticking around the state. But I had just made that trip the week before. I had nothing to fill the day or the next and the itch only grew stronger the longer I sat in my truck. I knew nothing good came at the end of the itch but I started to care less and less.

I couldn't imagine heading inside when there was a whole world of trouble available around me.

I swore and started the truck. I was ready to scratch the itch, but my phone rang, stopping me. I checked the screen. I was hoping it was my old friend Chavez looking to mix things up, but it was Wyatt.

I knew Wyatt from work. He had tattoos but they were different than mine. His were from a professional, a nice shop. He was thin, but tough. He worked hard.

"Hey Strain, Tonya and I wanted to invite you by the house tonight."

I'd met Tonya once or twice after work when she came to pick him up. She had big eyes under long, blonde hair. She gave me a bright smile the first time we met.

I said, "What you got in mind?"

"Nothing special. Tonya cooked up a pot roast. Thought we'd have you swing by and we could play a little Rock Band or something."

I had no idea what that was but I told him I'd be there. After hanging up the phone, I sat in my truck for a long time. I thought about skipping out and going to a bar, thought about taking a punch and throwing down. I'd slimmed down since prison, but I'd been working construction. I was ready for a fight.

I rubbed my face then pressed my fingers hard into my eyes. Finally, I backed my truck out of the space. It took effort, but I ignored the scream in my chest and drove a few blocks to another apartment complex not much different than mine. I walked down a dim hallway smelling of cigarette smoke. I knocked at the door and grinned at my hosts when they answered.

Their apartment had a warm afternoon glow and was filled with the rich smell of cooking meat. Tonya asked if I wanted something to drink.

"Sure, I'll have a beer."

She laughed, but not in a way that made me feel bad. "Sorry, Brad. We're not big drinkers over here. We could get you a soda or something?"

I thanked her and took a long drink of lemonade. The cool sensation sunk down my chest, soothing all the way into my belly. Wyatt passed a plastic guitar into my hand.

"What the hell is this?"

"We been waiting for you, Brad. Let's play."

The two of them grinned at me. A few months earlier, prison guards had kept me in lock down because I was a danger to other inmates. Now I sipped at my lemonade and stared at the toy.

The itch was still there. It still burned, but had grown quieter in their company. Tonya sang, and Wyatt banged on plastic drums. I didn't know if there had ever been anything less gangster, anything farther away from Verdugo than that, but I did my best to keep up with the guitar solo.

Later, during dinner, I talked about my daughter, Rachelle. Melody and I were hoping she could move out to North Dakota to get away from her boyfriend. Even when they asked to pray for her, even at the end of the night when they invited me to church, it was all right. I ate the pot roast. I had more lemonade. I told them maybe I'd see them at worship some other week.

Several hours later, I stepped outside and walked to my truck. I was in the middle of nowhere but I could easily find a bar within fifteen to twenty minutes in almost any direction.

Instead, I went home and crawled into bed.

JUST AFTER NOON, I STEPPED OUT ONTO THE PATIO for a cigarette. I had been working in North Dakota for almost a year. The month before I had moved into a two bedroom, ground level level apartment so Rachelle would have a place to stay. And it had been working out all right. She got away from her boyfriend; she got a job at the nursing home. She seemed to be doing better. I didn't worry about her too much, but I hadn't heard her come home last night.

A hot wind pushed through the trees on the far side of the parking lot. I ashed in a paper cup and wondered how the hell I got there. C-Loco, Verdugo for life, now a worried dad searching a line of cars for my daughter's. I finally spotted it in the corner, parked at a hard angle, its bumper too close to the curb.

From the apartment I heard a creak, a sign of life, and stubbed out my cigarette. As I stepped inside, the door opened to Rachelle's room.

She stumbled to the bathroom without speaking.

I sat at the table, sipped cold coffee and tried not to look like I had been waiting. When she came out, I pretended not to notice her swollen eyes, or how the skin on her face was red and tight.

"Good morning."

She yawned.

"You got plans for the Fourth?"

She shrugged.

"Working today?"

She shook her head, her hair in her face.

"I'm going to a barbecue near the park. You could come with."

"No thanks," she said.

I could tell she was done talking to me. Still, I felt this need to rescue her from something though I didn't know what.

I said, "No drugs, no drinking, no boys, right?"

She smiled without humor and barely nodded.

"Just remember why you're here." More than once I had given her the same talk I had received a hundred times. It was time to clean herself up, get her GED, and start fresh. But before I could get into it, she went back into her room and closed the door.

A half an hour later I left for the party. I was doing well; I had gotten out, was working hard. I was helping my step daughter, being a dad, saving money, sending cash to Melody, all of it. I still had no license but didn't think much of it. It felt good, driving through the summer afternoon, windows down, hot air whipping through the car.

I pulled down a gravel driveway already filled with trucks and bikes. These were my people now, rednecks and bikers - good people who worked hard and didn't take shit and laughed at my stories. They shouted my name when I stepped out of the car.

The owner of the house slapped me hard on the shoulder. He wore a trucker cap over a wide face, red from his cheeks down into his neck. He shouted into my ear, offering me a beer. I'd spent the past months playing video games with Wyatt and Tonya instead of drinking, but it was the Fourth of July. I took the bottle with a grin.

I finished my beer as I told somebody a story about San Bernardino, loving my audience when they laughed at the right parts. It was hot so I helped myself to another. I was off for a couple days; I could relax and let loose. I could be my old self, give them a taste of Loco. Not too much, I'd keep myself under control, but I had another beer as someone cranked up the music. It was Alan Jackson instead of 2Pac, but it was all right.

They lit sparklers. I found myself holding one, the world getting hazy, the sun beating down. An unsteady woman tossed firecrackers in the fire and squealed as they popped. I drank another beer, leaned on a stranger, and heard the whine of a two-stroke engine. Someone had a three wheeler, a souped up Honda, bright red. My host with the wide face, blotchy now with booze, was revving it up.

I finished my beer in three big gulps, not sure how many I'd had, not stumbling but feeling it. I hopped on; my buddy clapped me hard on the back, and like it was a horse, I was off.

The world turned blurry and soft at the edges and I was loving it, loving it, finally loosening up after months of hard work. It took thirty-five years but I had life figured out.

The party had spread a quarter mile down the gravel road to a city park by the river. I sped towards the entrance, a row of four pylons in front of me to keep the cars out. But I wasn't a car. The crowd roared as I came close, screaming my name over the engine as I gunned it.

A thud against my shin and I flew head first - like Superman - into the air. The ground came up fast and instinct cut through the alcohol so I tucked into a roll. The three wheeler stopped on its side ten feet behind me, smashed against a pylon.

I climbed to my feet, and it all rushed in: the shouts, the hiss of the motor, the roar of the river. I shifted an inch and an explosion of pain burst through my brain.

I collapsed, my face hit the ground and I blinked slow. The grass scratched hot against my face. Something bad had happened but I was too drunk to understand what.

THE NURSE TOOK OUT THE STITCHES AND TOLD ME my ankle was healing nicely from the surgery. I thanked her and hobbled out to my car. They had suggested I have a friend drive me home, but all my friends still had jobs.

I turned downtown, drove past the lone gas station which doubled as a grocery store. Next to that was a low building, more a shed, which housed some kind of church. My apartment was a block past that. The full drive was a little over a mile but my leg started to throb by the time I pulled into the parking lot. I took a minute in my truck. I knew I had to get out, get the crutches and make the walk across the pavement, but it seemed more effort than it was worth.

A couple years back I would've handled this kind of pain no problem. In prison at Susanville I had dived into a riot between the Paisas and the Norteños because the Paisas paid us for protection. I took some punches, grabbed a fool down and didn't stop even when I heard the gun shots. They came quick, the guards must have felt trigger happy, and something hit me hard in the ass. I'd gone to the infirmary. The rubber bullet had left a purple welt bigger than a fist. It had hurt like hell but I'd been back moving around within hours.

Now it had been more than two weeks since my accident and I couldn't face a hundred meter walk.

I didn't like it, but I had to keep moving. It was the one thing I could always do, no matter what: keep moving. Often it was in the wrong direction, but still, I'd keep putting one foot in front of the other.

Outside the car, the sun baked the pavement so I could smell the tar. I winced with every step, frustrated with my body. I had to heal up. I had to get back to work. I had bills to pay, the usual ones and now a medical bill. Surgery cost over twenty thousand dollars and I had no insurance. I stopped to catch my breath and tried not to think about it.

Before I could start moving again, I spotted a kid stepping out of the apartment complex. There was something about him, thirty feet away, hurrying at a bit of a jog.

I couldn't get a good look at him because he had his hat pulled low over his face, but I watched him to his truck. The plates were from North Dakota, so I wasn't sure. Still, I felt even heavier as I hobbled down the hall, the air too close, the hall light too dim for a sunny day. I found my apartment tidy, put together like I'd left it. Rachelle sat at the table with a spoon hovering over a bowl of cereal. She pulled her eyes from her phone to look up at me.

I said, "I thought you had work?"

"Not for another hour."

I stared at her. When she came to live with me I gave her three rules. Don't do drugs. Stay away from Dylan. And go to work. That was it. In return I didn't charge her rent.

I hooked my keys near the door and limped to the couch. It took me a long time to sit, lean back, lift my foot onto a pillow. Finally, I said, "Rachelle? That fool Dylan hasn't come around here?"

"Dylan?" She sounded confused. "No."

"And if he did?"

"I'd have nothing to do with him."

A UPS truck pulled into the parking lot and I watched it without really seeing. I tried to think of something else to say, but my mind went blank. I sighed, shook my head, and turned on the TV.

I GRIPPED THE ENVELOPE. I WASN'T SURE WHAT I WAS going to do after this, but I needed a place to sleep.

The door was heavier than I expected. It was a small office, close; the older woman who worked there didn't like it cold so never ran the air conditioner. She had thin hair, and a slight mustache on a pinched face. She never smiled at me, never used any extra words except for the ones she absolutely needed.

I took it as a challenge. I'd go out of my way to talk her up, see if I could get a response. I hoped one day to get her to smile.

"Can I help you?"

I waved the envelope, grinning even as I knew the check inside would empty my savings. Her eyes flicked at it then back to my face, her expression as always floating between annoyance and boredom.

I made the same joke I did every month. "I got your blood money."

Something changed in her expression: the hint of a grin.

She said, "I'm sorry, but I can't take that." She stared down at her computer, and started typing.

I felt a twinge of panic. "It's good, ma'am, I'm sure of it."

She arched an eyebrow at me. "I don't know about that." She pointed at her screen. "But see? I can't take it."

"What do you mean?"

She smiled now for real. "What I said. Your rent's already paid, Mr.

Strain."

I stared stupidly.

"Here..." She tapped at the screen. "Got a check a couple days ago. From..." she read Wyatt and Tonya's last name. "But they said it was meant for you."

I had to place my hand on the woman's desk to steady myself. They had asked me questions, I remembered, about my apartment and rent, things like that. But they said they had a friend hunting for a place and I didn't think anything of it.

My mind went blank. I always had something to say but for a long moment I couldn't speak. We listened to the country music come thin over a computer speaker.

"You have some pretty good friends," the woman said. She blinked at me until I smiled.

"Yeah, yeah," I said. "That's right. I guess I do."

An hour later, I found Wyatt by his truck outside a work site.

"It wasn't even us," Wyatt said. "It was the church. They took an offering."

"Still, man, I can't believe this." I was floating. "Thank you."

"You would have done it for me."

"Yeah, yeah, but... You don't know how much this helps."

"So how you holding up?"

I'd been out of work for almost a month. I had a huge medical bill and no way to pay it. I said, "I'm all right."

"Bullshit."

I laughed. "Yeah, well... Outside of construction, there's really only one thing I know how to do."

"Come on, Brad. Not that shit."

I shrugged. "What are you gonna do?"

"Listen, you got friends here. Going back to some of that crap... That's a bad idea." He gave me a hard stare. "We got this, brother. All right?"

I nodded. I thanked him again and watched him return to work.

Back in the car, my phone started to ring. Chavez's name appeared on the screen, his face grinning at me. I let it go to voicemail.

———

RAIN PISSED DOWN, ROLLING OFF MY HAT INTO MY face. I had parked close, only had to take a few steps to the door, but a few steps was all it took to soak into my shirt. Coming home after a nothing day, I opened the main door into the apartment complex and saw the kid. This time his face was turned to me, staring up, his eyes widening but frozen for a long second; long enough to see it was Dylan.

The kid pushed past me, and took off at a run towards his car.

"Hey!" I screamed after him. "You better not come back here."

I thumped down the hall feeling hot, not caring about my damp clothes anymore, gearing up for the fight. I started screaming before I had the door open. "You had three rules!" I could barely breathe. "What are you thinking?"

Rachelle looked up at me, again on her phone, again eating something - a sandwich this time. She tried the innocent look, opened her eyes wide, confused.

"That boy is no good."

Like a switch had been flipped, she lowered her shoulders, and her eyes pierced into mine. "You don't know him," she screamed back. "You don't know anything about him."

"I know that boy better than you do."

"You know nothing."

"I know I better never see him around here again."

"Who are you to tell me anything, Brad?" She said my name like she was spitting something out. Her disgust almost knocked me back. She pushed past, screaming, "You don't know anything."

I was stunned, but this wasn't my first fight. I could take a punch, even a verbal one, and I was quickly hobbling down the hall after her, telling her to get back in the apartment, telling her that she cannot see that boy.

She screamed back over her shoulder, "You got nothing to say that I need to hear," then disappeared outside.

I threw myself forward, not caring about the pain in my foot, pushed myself out the door into the rain but she was already at my car, my keys in her hand.

"I'm going with him. I'm not staying here, Brad."

Brad again, it sounded like a swear word. I kept moving towards her but the rain poured down making everything slick. I hit the curb wrong so my good foot slipped down to the street and my bad foot couldn't catch me. I threw down my crutches, my hands out, falling in slow motion, the concrete rising hard to meet my shoulder.

Pain streaked through my arms and hip. My pants were soaked through, my entire right side sunk in a puddle. It was a battle just to roll over onto my back. I blinked rain from my eyes.

I had sensed her near me before I saw her. She stood on the curb looking down. In her face I saw more pity than anger.

She helped me sit up, then lingered because I was no longer a threat. I had no authority, no anything. I couldn't stop her. I couldn't take care of her. Shoot, I couldn't pay my own rent.

She helped me stand. She grabbed my crutches and gave them to me.

"You're fine." She spoke quietly, almost at a whisper. The keys she placed in my hand. Then she tapped her phone.

"Rachelle..."

I heard the truck down the road, its broken muffler rumbling through the rain. I had nothing to say. I had no moves left. I couldn't catch the boy to lay my hands on him. I couldn't stop her from going with him.

I watched her get in the car. Dylan kept his face turned away, smoking a cigarette. As they drove off I felt like I weighed a thousand pounds and was a hundred years old.

I struggled back to the kitchen. I dug out my own phone, and wiped the screen with a towel.

"What's up, brother?"

Water dripped from my nose. A puddle was forming under my feet.

"Hey Chavez," I said. "We need to talk."

I HAD A HALF POUND OF METH HIDDEN IN A CUTAWAY compartment in the back of the Jeep near the spare tire. I had a baggie of it in my pocket for personal use, and I had just done a line with Chavez twenty minutes before. I didn't give a shit that I had my life in good shape a month ago. Chavez had said, "You want a bump?" and I said, "Yup." It burned in my nose and trickled down the back of my throat.

The drug heated my brain, pushed me forward out of Chavez's house and into my car. I took the highway north out of Sacramento, and thirty minutes later I was cruising through farmland, the full moon rising over a small California town. I was ready for this, feeling shitty and full of hate, but ready; the car rumbling underneath me, driving just at the right speed: fast but not crazy enough to be pulled over. Music on the radio provided the soundtrack, taken from CDs I found in the glove compartment. The Jeep wasn't stolen, but borrowed from a woman I had met online.

I nodded to the music, some pop-country bullshit, but feeling the drug, the excitement, feeling everything but the bad stuff which I shoved away. In the six days since I called Chavez, I hadn't thought about Rachelle, or my money problems or my family. I had barely thought about my ankle or the pain. I thought nothing but it was time to get a little crazy. I had lost everything going straight so if I acted loco, I'd get it all back. The drug worked my brain, filling me with unearned confidence, boiling away my doubts so I knew it was a good plan. The meth would sell easy, I'd get paid and it would be no problem. Smartest thing I ever did. No problem. No problem. No problem. I should never have given this life up.

I exited onto a two-lane highway. As I followed the ramp, the moon shone through the windshield, low to the horizon and huge. It almost outshone the stream of red brakes stretching a half of mile down the road towards flashing police lights.

My brain worked too fast. It wasn't a holiday, I figured, so it couldn't be a DUI check. It had to be an accident, so no problem; I took a slow breath. And if it was a DUI check, I'd be cool anyway since I hadn't been drinking. No problem. I didn't have a license; I'd never had a license, but no problem.

Ten cars back, I saw clearly there hadn't been any accident. Instead I watched a cop stop each car and lean in to talk to the driver before waving them forward.

Sweat started to streak down my back and pool under my arms. The drug made my brain fly but gave me nothing helpful. I had a baggie of meth in my pocket and a half pound in the trunk. I had enough to send me to prison for the next ten years if not longer. Enough for hard time, more time then I could face. A baggie in my pocket. A half pound in the trunk. Ten years if not longer. I kept pulling forward, trying to control my thoughts, calm down but I couldn't stop. Four weeks ago I had it all figured out. I was helping my family, putting away cash, and now I was two cars away from prison.

I thought about gunning it, forcing my way through. I thought about driving off the shoulder through the cornfield and the meth kept telling me it was time to let Loco out, but I swallowed that down. I wasn't high enough to be that stupid.

I wiped the sweat from my face. There was an old California ID in my wallet. It looked like a license in low light. If the cop was in a hurry, if he wasn't paying attention... maybe it could work.

I tapped it on the steering wheel. Everything was in order. I was cool. I was cool. I was sweaty and gang tattoos crawled up my neck. I had shaved my head and wore a tank top. I didn't look healthy. I didn't look right. But one car in front of me, I rolled down the window and a hot breeze hit my face. I gulped it down, put on a smile, acting cool, always acting cool and pushing ahead that was what I did and that was what I'd do now. Talk my way out of it, smile and charm.

I flashed the ID and tried to put it away, but the cop said, "Whoa, whoa, whoa. Let me see that again." He pinched it from my hands and studied it. He didn't betray nothing just waved me ahead, saying, "Pull over to the side, sir."

I crept ahead. The meth again cooking my brain told me to gun it onto the highway, but I knew there was no way, not with all the cops here, not in a ten-year-old Jeep, not on a two lane highway with no place to pull off and hide. They'd stop me within a half-mile and add a couple years of extra charges.

I needed to be cool. I wasn't drunk, that would help. I didn't smell like beer. I pulled over and watched the cop approach in the side mirror. An old man, tired, graying hair under his hat, long face, he asked if I had a valid license.

"No sir."

"You live around here?"

"No sir. I'm off work cuz of my broken leg. I'm here visiting friends."

The cop nodded. "Wait here," he said and he returned to his cruiser.

It was like the baggie was on fire in my pocket. One eye on the mirror I tore it out and felt around for a hiding spot. The cup holder between the seats lifted up and had an empty spot underneath. Moving slowly, trying to do it casual, feeling the eyes of the cop through the back window, I pulled out the cup holder and shoved the baggie underneath.

I replaced the cup holder but it wouldn't click down. It was a little more than a sliver off, but that was enough. I pushed down again, trying not to freak out, but the cop was coming any second.

"Cool it, Strain," I said the words out loud but they meant nothing and I tore off the cup holder. As I pulled the meth out of the hiding space, something snagged the plastic and the baggie ripped. Small brown shards scattered around the car, covering my pant leg, the passenger seat and the floor.

Behind me, the cop's door opened as I wiped myself down, trying not to move franticly. I brushed the powder off the seat feeling sharp edges cut into my skin.

"All right, Mr. Strain. I'm going to give you a citation for driving without a license and you'll need to be picked up. You understand? You cannot drive this car. Do you have anyone who can come pick you up?"

"Yeah, yeah," I said.

"Gather your things and step ahead to the side of the road. You can wait for your ride there."

I called Chavez, telling him to come pick me up, still playing it cool. I gathered a few things from the front seat, wanting to clean it up, wanting to shove the meth under the rug, but another cop had come up to the passenger side to shine a flashlight on me. I climbed out stiffly, closed the door and stepped ahead onto the highway.

The cop didn't wait to start searching. I watched the flashlights streak and drop through the windshield. On the curb where I stood a few feet away, it was a quiet night. Stars twinkled above me. Wind gently rustled the corn. The light of a farm house shone across the field. But when I looked back one of the cops held the baggie, shining his flashlight at it.

I stopped thinking, dropped my stuff and turned to run. I started hobbling on my crutches as hard as I could down the highway. Cars eased past me, but I barely noticed, moving crutch foot crutch foot but making no progress. Ten feet and my lungs already started to burn.

"Hey!" I heard them but ignored it. "Hey, come here!"

I limped another ten feet, knowing I couldn't face prison again. Footsteps came close behind me. I had been doing so well, four weeks ago I'd been doing so well. Arms grabbed me and I couldn't figure out what happened as I tumbled down to the gravel.

Another cop stood nearby, laughing. He said, "What in the hell were you thinking?"

I didn't have an answer.

Soledad
Three weeks later

I ROLLED MY shoulders forward, trying to get the pain in my back to go away, then took a long pull of pruno, a prison wine I brewed in a plastic bag from rotting oranges. That was my big luxury for watching the game, the first of the regular season, Raiders against the Colts. I was in jail, surrounded by nothing but gray cinderblock and hard benches bolted to the floor. I had to watch it on a television so small I could barely follow the action. So pruno; I figured I'd celebrate somehow.

I took another pull of the wine, gulping until I finished the cup. It was hella-sour and just as bad as I remembered. It burned down to my guts. I squeezed the cup in my fist, wanting to crush it and throw it against the wall because the Raiders looked like shit and this was my life.

I was facing three years. Only three years, Chavez had said, like I should be happy they didn't find the meth in the trunk. Easy for him to say, since I was the one drinking out of a plastic bag in the toilet. Just like every other time, I had kept my mouth shut.

Half time. The Raiders looked like hell and I got up feeling heavy, feeling like something was crushing my brain. I had hoped the wine would help but it hadn't touched me yet so I shuffled back up to my cell. I passed other inmates, but talked to no one. I had no friends there. Everyone hated me because I hated everyone. I dipped my cup in the bag, and came back, head down, trying not to think, trying to pull back into myself but it wasn't working.

The common room smelled like someone took a piss in the corner, and back at the TV I found a white boy on the bench. He was flicking through the channels looking for something. I knew this fool, never talked to him before and had no beef with him, but he killed his wife in a restaurant. A truck driver, never been in trouble with the law before, he found her where she worked and shot her five times dead. He was in county jail, on his way to prison like me. I knew his story but didn't care. I just wanted to be left alone.

I stepped close, violence crackling already on my skin. I said, "I was watching the game."

"That game's over."

"Naw, it's not."

He said, "It is for you."

A county jail was looser than prison and someone had left a mop bucket sitting near the bench. The man started standing, and I went from calm to crazy in an instant. I didn't think, just grabbed the plastic handle of the part that squeezes water from the mop, tore it from the bucket and swung hard at the man's face.

The fool was down before he knew he was in a fight.

CHIQUITA SAT ON THE BUNK WITH MANO, THE tattoo artist, leaning into his arm. He was using a pancake motor broken out of a CD player and rigged up through a Bic pen. The motor whirred quietly on the cot as Mano traced a line up my homie's wrist. Four of us in the cell with Sedio jigging at the door, keeping an eye for the guards.

Mano was quiet when he worked. He was a good tattoo artist, but the fool had been dipping into heroin. We were in Soledad prison, and drugs were flying through. Nurses and cops both were happy to bring the shit in for some side money. It was crazy easy to pass it around, and this poor fool was going at it hard.

Mano. The Hand. He was a good homie, pulled his gray hair back from a sagging face and big, droopy eyes. On the outside, he could almost pass as a normal old man, except he had bright red lips tattooed onto his forehead. He was stupid as hell but had been funny. He used to tell the story about climbing through a drop down ceiling in a Walgreens trying to get to the pharmacy. Halfway there, he fell through a panel into the tampon aisle. He used to laugh until he was wiping tears off his cheeks, but now he'd sunk into himself, turned into a junkie.

"Hey, Loco." He looked up at me. They all looked up to me. I was king of shit mountain. I was a Sureño with the age and experience, so I ran the tier. The big homies had given me the job before I even arrived over a year ago. They called role on my way in and put me in charge.

"Hey, *ese*, I need some shit."

I grinned at him.

"I need some shit. You got something?"

"I can get you some, homie, you want it."

"Yeah, yeah."

"All right."

A ringing sound signaled the end of rec time and we left Mano in his cell, the tattoo half done. I walked along the yard, time for lockdown then chow time. On the other side, another homie was crossing through, a tier tender from a different section. One of his set had showed me disrespect and wasn't listening to instructions.

I shouted, "You better watch your little homie, *ese*."

He nodded, said, "I know, I know, he's got it coming."

"He better watch himself."

"I told you, Loco. It's taken care of."

"Yeah, yeah."

I entered a low building, stepping on the smooth concrete floor towards the cell, narrow doors on each side. A big man with too much swagger came towards me, arms swinging wide. I'd never seen him before, a new inmate, but I knew how it would go down ten feet away. Kid probably got some bad advice from some some fool on the outside.

He stopped in front of me, leaned his face close to mine. "You don't look so tough," he said, and a fleck of spit landed on my cheek.

No guards in sight so I did the same thing I always did: acted first and hard and without warning. I hammered my head down on the bridge of his nose. Pain shot through my eyes, but the fool fell back, stumbling first then falling on his ass. Blood gushed between the fingers covering his face.

My brain felt too big for my head; it would ache for days. I wanted to wince and sit down and get a glass of water, but the fight wasn't done yet. I stood over him, grinning down, daring him to stand up, to say something. A guard grabbed me, pulled me back and pushed me against the wall but I was still talking, asking what smart shit the fool had to say as they shoved my face against the wall. The kid moaned, I raged, and it was like I had never been to North Dakota, I had never put in a good day's work, I had never drank lemonade and laughed when I screwed up a guitar solo. I wasn't that guy, not any more. I was Loco.

WE FOLLOWED MANO INTO THE SHOWER AND THOSE there by accident peeled off from the wall, leaving nothing but wet footprints. Mano turned his head, and I figured he'd catch us in his peripheral vision, but for a long moment he didn't react.

Sedio said, "Hey, *homes*," and Mano spun around. He saw us now, and stumbled back against the wall, a showerhead dripping onto his shoulder.

He raised his hands, the red lips on his forehead folded in on themselves, and he flicked his eyes to meet mine. There was no fear or anger in them. Instead, they were the eyes of a man who had given up, waiting for his beating, knowing it would come no matter what he did.

I lowered my fist on his face, careful, pulling my punch so I wouldn't hurt my hand. When I was a kid I had taken pleasure in this. I got into the power games, the gangster life, the violence, the discipline. Especially in prison, I always figured it was better than staring at a wall, but as I grew older I'd grown tired. I didn't want the bother. I didn't want to be there; I was sick of it, but the fool hadn't paid what he owed. He'd been warned. Sedio took him aside a week ago and Mano had sworn he'd have it. He'd said he'd do another tattoo, no problem - though it had been months since he finished the last one. He'd said he'd get the money to us in a couple days. But none of that happened, so there we were.

Mano whimpered, not begging but already hurting and knowing

what was coming. He was done. Empty just like I was. In the moment I could see no difference between me and my fists and him falling down underneath them.

It was meant as a warning, nothing too serious, and would buy Mano a week or two. Still, we weren't messing around and flecks of red landed on my knuckles. I thought I could smell his blood over the cheap shampoo. He had curled up on the ground, no longer moaning, just taking it.

I stepped back. The air was too humid and hot and I was sweating now. The others stopped too, following my lead. A little early, we'd gone too easy, but I didn't want to do it any more. I felt no pity - the fool knew how the system worked - but I looked in the man's eyes and saw he was beat down and done before we started.

I knew how he felt.

"Get us our money, fool," I said and I nodded at the others to follow.

My homeboys Chiquito and Sedio, they followed me out, but two others hung back. I heard the thumps, a whimper, but I barely noticed and didn't care; I wanted to get back to my cell and wash the man's blood off my hands. I wanted to close my eyes and wait this shit out.

I thought nothing more of Mano until the next morning when I learned in whispers that the damn fool was dead.

I WAS SINGING LOUDLY, BADLY, YELLING OUT THE words as I paced the cell. I didn't give a shit, didn't have to think about anyone listening; there was no one there. They'd thrown me in the hole, the O unit. We called it The Oil. I paced and screamed out the words to a song by 2Pac. The lyrics were rough against my throat but I kept at it until I got bored.

Then I sat talking to myself, having a conversation about some bullshit, about nonsense, a movie I saw twenty years before, that motherfucker Mel Gibson with that blue paint shit, that motherfucking blue paint... I let the words fall from my lips, not caring really what they were, but needing to form them.

I kept muttering as I did some push ups; then I'd nap. I tried to sleep my time in the hole. I'd been there for six months and had two months to go but when I slept right the days would slide out one after the other.

I'd close my eyes half awake and half dreaming of San Bernardino. Of my brother. Of Big Wheez and Rocco. Big Wheez was gone I had heard. I saw Little Weasel at a transfer center, talked to him through the fence for a few days, and I sat in the oil and thought about Little Weasel, his thick unibrow and bald head. Then I thought about Becky, my first love, thought of the time coming out of the bedroom with the hickie, everyone giving us a hard time, and I was singing again now, just shouting the lyrics getting them out feeling them rattle in my chest.

I was pacing again but stopped to look out the window into the unit. Sometimes I could communicate with the homies in the next cell if I screamed through the cracks in the doors. Or I could spend hours talking to the inmate across the hallway with sign language. I only knew the alphabet so we'd go one letter at a time. Or we'd pass messages, go fishing with a piece of string I made from my hair or a piece of blanket. Shoot out a note into the hall or try to catch one. Get a message back, get some news. Help make a call or two. But now no one was out there, no faces in the window. I was alone.

I stopped pacing and picked up the Bible. I had Where the Red Fern Grows in my cell but I already read it twice. I opened up to Exodus but the words were fuzzy so I thought about Jonah and the whale and sitting inside a fish's belly for a few days. It didn't sound that bad and I was doing jumping jacks now, leaping up and bending down. When I closed my eyes sometimes I saw Mano's face, his eyes staring at me, tired, just an old man, just got too deep into drugs, didn't deserve to die. I wasn't getting the murder charge. I left the shower and he was alive, but I had been there. I was responsible. I was screaming lyrics again and I thought of my son, of playing football with my son and I wondered what he was doing. Fourteen years old, my kid was a teenager and I was in the oil.

A letter came with my lunch and I tore it open. I read it slowly, forming the words with my mouth not thinking, then pacing, then push ups, then reading the letter again. Mano's eyes staring at me. The letter was from my aunt, Barbara. She wrote about her life, her regrets, her sins, confessing to me. I read it again and for a few moments I didn't feel alone. She told me I was still loved. She had sent me a rosary to pray.

I put down the letter and picked up the Bible and thought about Paul on the way to Damascus knocked off his horse with the shining light and the man was blind, and I started pacing and singing and I had two months left and couldn't not see that fools eyes staring at me in the last minutes of his life.

THE GUARD OPENED THE DOOR TO LEAD ME TO THE yard where I could walk around by myself for an hour. He gave me about a minute in the common area to take my turn at Trouble. The game had lasted weeks. I pushed down on the dice and moved, checking the board, doing some figuring. The next inmate would take a turn on his way to the yard. There was no way I would finish the game and I was good with that. I had three days left. Three days in the hole. Three days in prison, and I'd be out.

I followed the guard to the yard, did my lap, smelled the relatively fresh air. I came back to my cell and tried to stick to my routine; it had gotten me through eight months in the hole, but time was slowing down. I tried to focus on making a picture frame out of milk cartons, I tried to nap, tried to sing, but I was so close to moving freely, to having a beer, to talking to a woman, to sitting on a couch to... whatever, it didn't matter; I was so close to not being in this damn cell anymore, I couldn't focus on anything.

At dinner, the guard passed an envelope with the tray. It was thin, from the state of Montana. I opened it not thinking, not even curious, just passing seconds, waiting for my time to be up. I unfolded the cheap paper, but couldn't make out what I was reading the first time. So I read it again.

Then I screamed.

I didn't understand the details but they wanted me back. They said I had to serve time in Montana for something; it was all because I didn't register as a violent offender when I first moved there fifteen years before. Even though it was for the assault I'd done when I was 19 with Ty Angel. Even though I had served my time for it in Washington. Even though I hadn't lived in Montana, not really, for a decade.

The letter sat in my gut like I swallowed sand. The next day I talked to a lawyer then a judge, but there was nothing anyone could do.

Three days later instead of hugging my son, instead of getting a cheeseburger and taking a real shower for as long as I wanted, I was shackled up and put in the back of a van. It had no windows and two metal benches. They locked me to one side and drove for an hour until we stopped at a county jail. I wasn't allowed to move or adjust as we waited for some prisoners to get off and others to climb on. We drove another hour where they permitted me a few minutes to take a leak. I'd barely pulled up my pants before we were driving again.

The van was hot and smelled of sweat. The air didn't move even as the other prisoners pushed against me. We finally stopped in the evening and they put me in a holding cell. I asked for a toothbrush and a place to wash my face, but I got nothing but a peanut butter sandwich.

The next day they gave me a paper suit made of fabric as thin as a dryer sheet with paper boxers visible underneath. Then it was more of the same. Back of a van barely moving, we drove for another day, then two. Finally, I was allowed to take a shower then back in the van for two more days, crawling our way towards Portland.

From Portland it got worse. Now we rode for hours at a time without stopping. No one talked or looked at each other. If one of us had to take a piss we had to use a water bottle, pulling it out in front of everyone while still shackled to the bench. I felt less human the more we moved.

After two weeks of this, I arrived in Montana. After a night spent in a state facility, I faced one last drive to my final destination: the county jail forty minutes away. The ground felt spongy underneath me as I walked out to a police cruiser. A stony-faced cop pushed my head down into the back seat.

Soon after we pulled onto the road, the cop turned his head and spoke through the barrier. "Sorry, the A/C don't work."

I stared straight ahead. I was past feeling. Minutes passed, the air grew warmer and I felt more tired than I had ever been.

The cop turned again. "Sorry, can't open the windows."

I'd been looking forward to seeing the highway pass by, to seeing normal people in other cars going about their lives. I'd been looking forward to anything besides walls and gates and the back of a van. But this turned out to be worse than the whole two weeks before it. The sun beat at the roof of the car. The air grew thick. Sweat poured down my neck and covered my back down into my pants.

Time swam by, everything hazy. I breathed slow, my head drooping towards my knees. The cop drove down a ramp and spoke slowly into the speaker, "One for processing," but I heard it from far away. He parked the cruiser in the dark garage then disappeared. Minutes passed while I breathed in the heat, feeling it weigh on me, making me nauseous. Finally, the door opened and the cop half dragged me into the jail.

We were in Hamilton, Montana, and I knew the guards. They were men and women from town, some of them I'd known for years. On seeing me, one of them gasped.

"Strain? You okay?"

"He's fine," the cop said.

They had me sit down and the cop barked. "I told you, he's fine. What's the problem?"

It wasn't until the cop left that a guard held my arm and gave me a drink of cold water. It soothed it's way down my chest and for a few moments made me feel close to human.

The Train

One year later

I CLIMBED OFF the bus in Missoula and checked my watch. I had ninety minutes; plenty of time to do what needed to be done. Still, I hurried down the street.

It was my first taste of freedom after four years. The sun warmed my face while a breeze cooled the back of my neck. I made friendly eye contact with a passing jogger. No chains, no guards, no strict schedules. I trotted across an intersection, feeling the strangeness of it.

The bank was right where I had remembered. I waited at the line. Everyone in front of me were staring down at their phones, flicking the screen with their thumb. I felt dizzy, watching them. The world had changed since I'd been gone.

After a few minutes, an older woman called me up. She had her hair pulled back into a tight bun. She wore thick makeup which didn't quite reach the edge of her face. She glared at me impatiently as I dug out the only thing I had on earth besides the clothes I was wearing: a prison check for a hundred dollars.

I set it on the counter and the woman flicked her eyes at it. "Do you have an account with us?"

"No, ma'am."

"I'm sorry, then we can't cash this."

My shoulders tightened and I leaned in; I needed that money.

"But..." I started, not knowing what I could say.

The woman looked past me and said, "Next."

It was another six blocks to the next bank. I waited in line. I checked the clock. I was starting to run out of time.

It was a man this time, half my age and twice my weight. "I'm sorry," he said. "I can't cash this."

I shuffled out the door, feeling everyone's eyes follow me, thinking they all must know I had just gotten out of prison. I didn't belong in banks, didn't belong around normal people tapping at computers, using ink pads and wallets. I couldn't handle this. I wanted to give up, but I needed that money.

There was one more bank on the way back to the bus station. I pushed through the door feeling like I was slogging through water. I felt their stares before any heads turned. At the counter, I dug out the check, unfolded it, and smoothed it with my palm. I showed my state ID, my prison ID. A younger woman, barely older than my son, looked at me with big eyes.

"I'm sorry," she said.

"Please." I wasn't above begging, not for this. "I've been to two other banks and they said the same thing, but please."

The woman stared down at the check. She didn't look at me, just breathed at it for a long moment. "Could you wait a minute?" she asked, then disappeared into a back room. I was half convinced she had left to call the police, but she smiled at me when she returned.

"We will be able to help you, Mr. Strain."

The pinch in my chest released. I thanked her, gathered my hundred dollars, thanked her again, and returned to the bus station.

I sat on a bench. The place felt like prison, everything gray and hard plastic. The smell of bleach covered something worse. The bank teller's kindness faded and I again felt everyone watching me, glaring over their cell phones. I needed a shower. I was a menace, I was Loco, who knew what I was going to do. I was a danger to society, a shit of a human being. I was almost forty but still a throwaway kid.

An older lady shuffled past with small steps. She looked tired. Her purse sat unprotected on the suitcase she pulled behind her. It would be easy, I knew. I was getting older but I still had some speed in my legs.

I stood up. "Excuse me, ma'am," I said. "You can have this seat."

"Oh, aren't you sweet." She grinned at me like I was a regular human being, like I was her nephew maybe, and not an ex-con.

I felt lighter as I wandered outside. Dusk was coming and my ride was late. I watched a car pull up, then another, more anxious with each one. I wanted to pace, to move back and forth, maybe sing to myself, but swallowed down the crazy.

"Dad?"

He had come up behind me and I grabbed him, felt arms around me. I pulled him in close. It was the first contact, the first non-violent touch I had felt in four years. I held on until he laughed and told me to let him go.

He had grown so much. He was sixteen, had his license and had come to take me home. But first we walked to the sandwich shop across the street. Chase ordered a meatball sub and a large coke. He reached for his wallet but I laid my hand on his shoulder. I dug into my pocket and grabbed one of the twenty dollar bills I had worked so hard to get. I grinned. It was a small victory but it meant everything.

"Naw, Son," I said, "I got this."

I TOOK MY BREAKFAST OUTSIDE. THE SUN WAS shining, the lawn chair comfortable. Wyatt had set it up for me: a spare room in a doublewide trailer with a guy who wouldn't even charge me rent. All that, and I had a job lined up.

I took a sip of my coffee, feeling pretty good, when my phone rang. I didn't recognize the number, but had a few minutes before I had to leave, so I answered.

"Bradley, is that you?"

It had been over sixteen years and the voice had grown lower and rougher, but I recognized it immediately.

"Mom?"

"Bradley. There you are." Her voice was sharp with her Mexican accent. "Thank God!"

"Mom! How are you? How's..."

"Bradley, what have you gotten yourself into?" Her tone frightened me. "What did you do this time?"

"I didn't do nothing, Ma."

"What did you do?"

"I... honestly..."

"The police came here." We'd been talking fifteen seconds and already she was crying. "They tore the place apart, looking for you. They said to call as soon as I saw you."

"Mom."

"I can't have this."

"Mom, listen."

"I can't have this. I can't do it. I can't do it anymore."

"Ma, listen."

"Why are you like this?"

"Please, Ma."

"Why are you like this?"

"I just got out of prison. I didn't do nothing."

"I don't understand why you keep doing this."

"I'm in North Dakota. That must have been old stuff. That was old stuff. I told my parole officer I might head back to Vancouver, but I didn't. I'm in North Dakota." She could barely speak through her sobs, and I heard myself yelling, "Shit, Ma, I didn't do nothing. I haven't been to Washington for years."

"Oh Brad, I can't do this. I can't do this."

"You don't..."

"Please stop, please just leave me alone."

"Ma, I didn't do nothing."

"I can't do it. I tried my best but I can't do it."

"Ma..."

The phone went dead. I stared at it stupidly, in a daze. It laid heavy in my hand. My whole body ached. I needed to move but it took more energy than I had to bring my coffee mug back inside. I still had to bike into town to meet the boss. I couldn't drive because I had nothing. I was a full grown man without a car and an ancient phone with a cracked screen. I had nothing. I was nothing.

I moved without thinking, dull, the life drained out of me. I pedaled into town, and felt each mile, flat over a two lane road. I passed fields behind barbed wire fences without really seeing them. I tried to clear my head because I had to make a good impression, but I couldn't stop running the talk through my head, the sound of my mom's voice.

I was a teenager the last time we'd spoken.

I pulled into a gravel driveway, passed some parked cars and leaned my bike against a tree. I didn't even own a lock. There were about a dozen steps into the office, and each one was a fight.

The boss shouted my name as I came in. Another Christian from Wyatt's church, he smiled at me, and I felt his pity against my shoulders.

"Brad, I've heard good things. Over at construction they said you worked your ass off, always had a good word, always in a good mood. We need that."

I had a hard time meeting his eyes but forced another smile.

"Yes sir."

"Awesome. Now listen, this is just a formality. We need you to sign some papers, that kind of shit. Tomorrow we'll put you to work. Start making a plumber out of you."

"That's right."

"We'll get you trained in quick. You a fast learner?"

"Yes sir."

"How are you doing in the way of tools?"

I had a bike, a four-year-old phone, and a change of clothes. It twisted my guts and I braced myself, waiting for the door to close. "I don't have much."

"That's all right, we got some tools here for you."

He nudged his foot against a set of brand new tools, the tag still on the belt, easily seven hundred dollars of equipment. I stared at the man without understanding.

He grinned at me. "Can't work if you don't have tools."

I looked at the tools and around the little office. I knew what was expected and I thanked the man with a smile and a handshake. I told him a few times how grateful I was for the opportunity.

But inside all I could hear was my mom's voice. I was still nothing but a throwaway kid.

FIRST DAY ON THE JOB WAS COLD BUT I DIDN'T HAVE to bike at least because another guy gave me a ride. It was good to get to the worksite; I had had a bad night, had a hard time getting my mom's voice out of my head. I wanted to stop thinking about it, stop thinking about her and stop thinking about Soledad, Mano's eyes staring up from the shower floor. All of that was in the past. I was done with it for good. I had to be. But it wouldn't leave me alone.

It was better when I got to work. I got orientated and met the guys. They shook my hand, smiled when I talked, asking me what my story was. I could do that. I knew how to talk to men, knew how to make friends. That was my deal; I was your friendly neighborhood gangster.

But there was one guy who wouldn't look at me. His name was Derek. He said, "Hey," in a monotone but didn't engage after that.

I didn't think anything of it at first, but as the day went on, it started to bother me. He gave me nothing. Alongside the paycheck, I needed the company. I was empty, inside and out, so getting these fools to like me - getting this one fool to like me - was all I had.

The next day it was the same thing. I grinned at Derek as I greeted him, but he looked down, barely nodding like I'd pissed him off.

The day after that, no change. Breaking for lunch, I sat near him and asked after his life. He gave one word answers and choked down his sandwich to get away.

It continued like this through the end of the week. Last break on Friday I sat down opposite and looked the man in the eye until he looked up.

"Hey."

He quickly looked away, but in that moment I saw something I recognized in the guy's face.

That night a few guys invited me out to a bar. I was glad to go. The nights had been too long and empty; they gave me too much time to think. A few minutes after I arrived, Derek showed up. I started telling my stories, draining bottles, making the guys laugh. Derek, however, sat staring silently at his beer.

We went out again the next night. Again, Derek didn't say much but this time I watched the man drink. I tried to keep up with him and had to stumble home. Sunday, I went fishing with a buddy and Derek was there. He drank quietly, working through an eighteen pack. I did my best to match him, beer for beer. He didn't say much but didn't have to. I knew on instinct that we shared something, a similar history. He had made some serious mistakes and done some serious time. I cracked another beer, knowing we'd be friends. He was just as screwed up as me.

WE STOOD ON THE EDGE OF THE CREEK, THE WATER gentle past the rocks. We only caught a few little ones and threw them back, but it was a day I couldn't have imagined even six months ago. I hoped to remember it forever.

I draped my arm across my son's shoulders. He was growing smart and strong and I got to act - for a few days at least - like a real father.

It had been a few months since I got out of jail. I had a car now - no license yet but I had a car. I had money in the bank. I was paying child support and more. I was helping Melody with extras for the apartment, making it nicer for them. I had been talking to her on the phone and there seemed to be something between us again, a little spark.

It was all good as long as I kept a smile on my face and didn't spend too much time thinking about things, as long as I didn't close my eyes without several beers in me. I was moving forward.

Because that was all I could do: move forward. I made mistakes and kept getting beaten down. Sometimes it was bad luck, more often it was my own bad choices, but I kept getting back at it. As long as I had breath I would keep taking those steps, one at time, forward to the next day.

It got closer to noon so we packed up our gear and followed a deer path back to the car. Chase was heading home to Montana, but we still had a few hours. As we walked, he told me about his life, his girl-friend, school. I gave him some fatherly advice as best I could.

In the car, I asked the question I'd been thinking about for three days. "How's your mom doing?"

Chase said, "Fine, I guess. She's got a new boyfriend I don't like much."

A lump filled my stomach. There had been nothing said, no promises, but there had been more than hints. A month before I had gone with her on a weeklong trip to San Diego to help take care of her niece who'd had a miscarriage. Afterwards, I thought we had something started, and I'd been sending her little gifts.

"Dad, you okay?"

I felt like a fool, and for a long moment the car was quiet except for the gravel rumbling underneath us. Finally, I said, "She's seeing someone?" I couldn't take the anger out of my voice.

Chase answered quietly. "Yeah."

"How long?"

"I don't know. A couple months."

I thought back over the last two months, and it was all messed up. I tried to put on a show for my son, but I was twisted up inside.

Later, I dropped Chase off with his ride and gave him a hug. As he drove off, I tried to be grateful for our time but all I could think of was how far away I was from Melody. I got home and sat alone in the trailer.

Finally, I called her up. I told her what I knew and we yelled at each other for awhile. Finally, she said, "Who gives a shit? You're just going to prison again." And she hung up the phone.

The trailer was dead silent except for the tick of a wall clock. I stared stupidly at the television, thinking through my next move.

Derek answered on the first ring. Twenty minutes later we met at the bar. I had one beer then another and another, with no plans to stop.

FOUR MONTHS LATER I WAS REAR-ENDED BY A TOMB. I tried not to take it as an omen, but it was an honest-to-God graveyard vault on the back of a semi-truck. My boss had been driving through traffic and the driver of the semi didn't see him brake. The truck slammed into us and I flew forward into the dash then swung back with enough force to break the rear window. It left a mess.

It gave me a concussion and the doctor told me to take a few days, up to a week if I had to; he said I needed to rest before I came back to work. But after two days I was struggling.

On day three, I woke up ornery and looked down the trailer towards the kitchen. A stiff wind shook the wall and a scattering of acorns thunked against the roof. I couldn't stay here, not one more morning, never mind a week. I couldn't sit alone in bed. It was too damn quiet, too damn empty.

I forced myself to sit up until my feet touched the floor. My head still hurt enough to make everything unsteady, but that doctor knew nothing; I had to get back to work. All I had was work and beer, those things abided. The rest of my life was crap.

I should've been happy. I had built myself up from nothing. Six months after moving back to North Dakota and I had a job, a checking account, and a place to stay. I'd done all of it without drugs or gangs. I was moving forward, and it should have been enough. But in times of quiet like this, it all felt empty. Thirty years later, I was still the throwaway kid.

To get through the morning I tried to pace, tried to sing to myself, tried to keep moving, but it wasn't enough. I couldn't exercise. I couldn't drink - or I wasn't supposed to drink - and I couldn't help thinking I had nothing. I was worth nothing. I was nothing. It was all a lie and that damn Mano still kept staring at me under his tattooed lips.

I was out of my head. I was a gangster. I was a Sureño. I was a prison boss. I once dropped a guy with a single punch. I stabbed a fool in the neck with a pencil. I beat up a murderer and a pedophile. I was a monster, a menace, I didn't need a damn thing, but...

I wanted my mom.

It didn't matter what the doctor said, I could not sit there anymore. I tried to put on my pants and it went fine. Then I struggled to pull my shirt over my head and every movement of my neck made me wince. But I needed to get to work. If I had to stop for one more day, one more hour, one more minute, I'd go crazy.

I WENT TO WYATT AND TONYA'S AFTER WORK, HAD some dinner with them but I'd started feeling itchy almost immediately. I sipped the lemonade; Wyatt wanted to play Rock Band for old times' sake, but the the itch was strong and I was out the door before I was out the door. I hurried to Derek's ready to get my drink on, ready to smother the itch with alcohol until it was safe to go home and pass out.

I'd been drinking so much over the last few months the beers barely hit me. I felt immune to them, kept pounding them back. Before it got too dark, we drove down the gravel path around his property, letting his dog, Pepper, run ahead of us. We pulled beer out of the case between the seats. It was the lazy man's way to take a dog for a walk.

A half an hour later, back at his house, Derek felt restless. He said, "Let's go see if there're any girls at the bar." It was more of a joke than anything. There were never any girls there and if they were, they were sixty years old or older. But it was a little better than nothing.

An easy walk, we took Pepper and stumbled towards it. It was a nice night, cloudy but not too cold for late October in North Dakota. My breath came out visible in soft puffs.

We crunched through leaves without much to say. It was quiet except for some distant highway traffic. Pepper was a white blur in the corner of my eye. The booze swished around my brain, making everything soft.

We started across the tracks. The moon barely glowed behind the thick clouds. There was a single light over the bar, another light behind the grain elevator, otherwise it was dark. I heard the rumble, felt it in my legs, but had a hard time registering it.

Derek shouted, "Train!"

I grinned at him then looked around. I saw the three lights in the distance. The rumble grew louder, but it was nothing to worry about. Except, dammit, I couldn't see the dog.

I stumbled to a stop, checking around my feet for Pepper until I spotted her, fine on the far side of the tracks. But Derek was screaming something at me. The train. I didn't hear a horn but felt the thunder in my belly. The three lights were huge in my face.

I moved, but my foot was caught, like something held me and I fell across the tracks, smashing my head against the far railing. The world trembled as I climbed up, moving as fast as I could but the head slam and the drunk threw me off balance. The three lights on top of me; I scrambled, but not fast enough. The train scooped me up.

I flew again, like I did as a child stealing dope from a dealer, as I did on the three wheeler, as I had my whole waste of a life. A drunk, a hustler, a liar, a gangster, a thief, I flew through the air and slammed hard into the earth.

Everything went dark. I heard nothing, saw nothing and couldn't breathe. Panic finally cut through the alcohol. I gasped, gulping, but nothing worked. I opened my eyes wide, scanning the soft gray haze, but couldn't find any help. I panted desperately for air. I heard something - a roar, a shout - and took a shallow, ragged breath.

I was okay. I was going to be okay.

I rolled to my side. The signals my body sent to my brain made no sense. Everything was buzzing. Something was seriously wrong and I needed to stay awake. To stay awake I needed to stand up.

I moved onto my hands and knees. My leg was a bag of sand; it wouldn't move, but I felt no pain, just heaviness. I wobbled up to my knees, then my feet. More shouting, someone called my name. But I was up, looking around and breathing. It was okay. I was going to be fine.

This thought lingered as I looked down at my body. A mess of blood and spaghetti spilled through wide tears in my coat and shirt. My skin had been sheared away. I was looking at my own intestines.

The pain didn't come but still I tried to scream without enough breath. I sunk to a knee, then collapsed to the dirt. I laid back, everything going gray but I had to stay awake. I had to stay awake but it was all too heavy. I was flying for a moment, but it was all over now. I needed to stay awake but I closed my eyes, I had hit the earth and I knew it was over. Stay awake but I couldn't, not any more. Too much had happened and it was time to rest.

Bismarck,
North Dakota
2014

Cornflakes
Four days later

MY ARMS AND legs floated lazily, throbbing but disconnected from the rest of my body. My eyes wouldn't open and my mouth didn't move and something in my throat made it so I couldn't swallow.

Everything was dark, but I could hear voices in the distance. I cracked an eyelid and light poured in, too bright. The shadows were moving, breaking apart and reforming. I tried to focus on one but it slid down and swirled into dust.

"Brad?"

I tried to speak but nothing happened. Machines beeped in my ear and tubes and tape tugged at my skin. I opened my eyes again and the shadows cleared enough so I could see Rachelle, staring at me, running a finger under her eye. Next to her was Derek, his head blocking the light.

"Brad? You with us?"

I remembered the three lights coming at me. I remembered trying to stand. I remembered looking down at my body.

Rachelle's eyes were open wide so I could see the white all around. "Dad?"

The word warmed me.

"Dad," she said. "You got in a bad accident."

I tried to speak but could only grunt. I tried to nod but my head wouldn't move. Someone put a pen in my hand. I scrawled out, "Is it Saturday?"

Rachelle shook her head. Derek blinked. "It's Tuesday," he said. Like Rocco thirty years before, the way he looked at me told the whole story. It was bad. This was it. I'd really done it this time.

I almost smiled. I wasn't going to make it. And it was okay.

I WOKE TO PAIN SCREAMING THROUGH MY BODY. I was twisting in the bed. Hands on my back were pushing me onto my side.

"Hey, look who's awake."

The hands lowered me back to the bed and the pain dissolved into sweet relief. A large black man smiled down at me.

"You got some serious tattoos there, Mr. Strain. Those for real?"

I tried to nod but didn't know if it worked. My head weighed too much.

"We don't see that kind of thing much around here. You Sureño?"

His voice was thick in my ears and I struggled to pay attention. I tried to adjust my legs but they didn't move.

"So you Hispanic? I would not have thought it. I was here when they brought you in on the helicopter and you were pale. With a name like Strain, I thought for sure you were a white dude."

They had taken the tubes out of my throat but it still hurt too much to talk, so I followed him around the room with my eyes.

"But you're looking good now. You got some color back, but damn. You were a ghost. Looked like death. Maybe I shouldn't joke about that, huh?"

His dreadlocks were pulled back into a pony tail which bobbed as he moved.

"That train messed you up. They had me working your oxygen pump. I was squeezing that thing for... I don't know but my hands were wearing out." He showed me his hands. They were huge. "We were worried about you, bud. I thought 'this dude ain't going to make it,' but they kept at it. Miracle you're alive, honestly. Praise the Lord."

I pulled apart my lips to say something but the nurse kept talking.

"They said you kept sitting up." He chuckled at this. "EMTs were telling about it. Had your guts hanging open and they said you kept sitting up in the stretcher, talking. Not making any sense, but talking so they had to push you down. Crazy. I'm telling you, that train messed you up good."

The throb in my leg grew more intense; it pushed against my brain harder and harder. Pain started shooting from everywhere.

The nurse said, "You know, I was into that gangster shit for awhile."

I searched for a part of my body that didn't hurt.

"Yeah, I ran with a crew out on the west coast and, damn, I don't know. Maybe you wised up already and are out of it, but I've been out almost ten years, thank Jesus. And I know you don't know me from Adam, but listen: It's better when you get out. Get away if you haven't already. Hear me?"

It was all too muddy but I tried to nod. I noticed the pain had eased back.

"Gave you your pain meds so you might get sleepy again."

My eyelids grew heavy.

"Seriously though, there's a better life out there. You understand?"

I couldn't quite manage a thank you before I fell asleep.

I HEARD HER VOICE BEFORE I SAW HER. I WAS conscious which meant I had either just woken up or was just about to fall asleep. I knew I had been hit by a train, but couldn't remember much besides the three lights, and watching my insides tumble out.

I heard her voice again and turned my head towards the window. Sunlight streaked in from behind her head, creating a blinding halo, so I had to squint at her silhouette. When I heard my dad speak quietly and my son respond, I knew who the woman must be.

"Mom?"

I hadn't seen her for over fifteen years, but that was her long hair, I was sure of it.

"Mom?" The word made my throat hurt. "You're here."

Voices muttered around my bed but I couldn't understand what they were saying.

"Mom, I was hit by a train."

I heard her voice. She said, "Brad."

Someone squeezed my hand.

"It's Melissa. Mom's not here, Brad. It's your sister."

She moved away from the window so her face became clear. Her cheeks were damp. She had black smudges under her eyes.

Besides Melissa, my dad was there with my son and a doctor. The doctor was talking, but his sentences tumbled over each other.

"Cornflakes?" I said. It was the only word I understood.

The doctor raised his glasses to his forehead. "Yes, Brad. Your pelvis has been shattered. In your X-ray, it resembles cornflakes. It's beyond our abilities here to fix you, but we would like to send you to Regions in Saint Paul."

Cornflakes. There was more talking but I lost the thread. Everything was muddy, but I knew I had messed up. I figured it was about the worst thing I'd ever done.

I opened my eyes again. "Hey," I said. My sister looked up from her phone. She sat alone in the room. Night had fallen and lights from the city glowed through the window.

"You're awake," she said.

"Hey, don't tell Mom, okay." I closed my eyes. I had never messed up this bad before. "Please. Don't tell Mom."

"Okay, Brad."

"She'll be so mad. She'll be so mad at me."

"It's okay. No one is mad at you."

I was so tired, and I had screwed it all up again.

"Please," I said. "Don't tell mom."

MY SON STOOD BY MY BED, TALL AND STRONG. MY ex-wife slouched in a chair, smiling at me through tears. The sun turned her hair gold. My dad, stony-faced, shoved his hands in his jacket pockets, and shifted his weight.

"You need to go to St. Paul, Brad," Melissa said for the third time. "They have a doctor there who thinks he can take care of your leg."

I nodded. It had been ten days since the accident. There was always pain and I was always confused, but I understood enough. I'd be leaving the hospital in Bismarck. I'd be traveling solo. I didn't know anyone in Saint Paul so I'd be facing surgery by myself. I was nervous but I didn't need anyone. I'd do it alone, like I'd done before, just me against the world. I'd face it no problem.

Except there was a problem. My pillow and sheets were soaked with sweat. A high fever wrestled with pain medication and it felt like giant spider legs wrapped around my chest. It scattered my thoughts and emotions so that one moment I was fine, the next I couldn't handle facing surgery in a strange city alone.

I groaned quietly. I could face the recovery, the pain, the drugs, the fever, as long as I knew someone had my back. But they all were leaving me. Feverish, I tilted my head from face to face, seeing Melody, then my dad, then my son.

I closed my eyes. When I opened them there was a man in the room talking to my family.

"We do have space for one more if anyone wants to accompany Mr. Strain."

My sister said, "We can come with?"

"One person can, yes ma'am."

There was more talk I couldn't follow, but then Melissa said, "I'll go."

I turned towards her voice and became aware she was holding my hand. I squeezed back.

"Oh wait, no. I don't know what I'd do about the kids."

"Don't worry about that, Punk'n." My dad's voice was a low growl. "We can take care of that. Between me and your mom, we'll figure it out."

"Thanks, Popps."

"You just keep an eye on your brother for us. Keep him out of trouble if you can."

It was too blurry. Even as she walked next to me towards the Lifeflight, even as they loaded me up on the gurney, I didn't get it. My sister was afraid of flying. She'd be so scared, and would have to sit up front in the little plane next to the pilot.

I couldn't fully track what was going on. All I understood - underneath the fever and the drugs - was that I had a family. My sister was there and my dad was helping. I had people watching my back and because of them I wouldn't have to make this trip alone.

THE FLIGHT WAS A HAZE, A STREAK OF COLOR AND fever dreams. A stern-faced nurse welcomed us to Regions Hospital in Saint Paul and wheeled me into the building. But a few minutes later, something must have happened because the nurse trotted off, leaving us in a hallway by a closed fire door. Around us was chaos. A gang member must have been in one of the nearby rooms. I figured he must have been well-respected because it was all noise and heartache. Kids in gang colors shouted at each other, everyone miserable and stressed.

Next to me, my sister pressed her hip against the gurney, trying to get as far away from the chaos as she could.

I watched from my sickbed fascinated but frightened. I had been flown here for healing, but I couldn't even figure out where I was. There were no staff members around to make sense of it. Everything I had seen so far had been under construction. And it felt like my old Sureño life was screaming in my face.

I glared at the fire door. In my fever, I figured we needed to get to the other side of it. I stared up at the false ceiling.

"We could crawl through."

"Did you say something, Brad?"

I nodded up at the tiles. "Crawl through."

"You want to crawl through the ceiling?" She grinned. "I'd like to see that."

"I knew a guy once. Had these red lips tattooed on his forehead. He fell..." I started laughing a little, then huffed because the laughter hurt, then winced because breathing hurt. I closed my eyes for a long moment, but I tried to finish my story. "Tampons," I said.

"I have no idea what you are talking about."

I shook my head. It was all confusing. The fever made the sounds around me drip too loud, then too cold, and there were too many voices, like the gang member's whole family was yelling in my ear.

Finally, the door cracked open from the other side.

"I'm sorry about that."

The nurse gave us an apologetic smile.

"This way," she said and started pushing my bed.

Behind us, the voices grew to a murmur then went silent. We moved outside of the construction area, and the walls grew softer, the lighting more natural until finally the nurse brought us into a room with a giant view. We were on the ninth floor and could see a cathedral rising over the city of Saint Paul.

"Wow," I said.

Melissa thanked the nurse, then sat down and grabbed my hand. When she was a teenager, she had some experience with the gang life. She'd hung out with Los Tiny Dukes until she got help and cleaned herself up. It had been twenty years, but even with a fever I knew what she was going to say.

"Brad," she said. "There's a reason for you to have survived that train."

I stared out the window. The blinds were knocking gently against each other.

"Listen to me. God saved you for a reason." She leaned towards me. Her voice grew louder. "That was a miracle, you understand me? That was an absolute miracle. A blessing from God."

I couldn't quite follow her words, so I said, "I got hit by a train."

"That's what I'm saying. No one survives that. You are here for a reason. A reason from God. You hear me?"

Her face kept blurring and I was so tired. When I shut my eyes I started to float, but I couldn't keep them open, so I stopped fighting. When I opened them again, a doctor was in my room.

"This room smells like death," he said.

"Does it?"

"Mr. Strain, you're awake! I'm Dr. Cole."

He had a lively round face and bright eyes behind his glasses.

"I'm going to do your surgery."

"Yessir."

My eyes fell closed and I listened to the doctor talk to Melissa about an infection.

"Doctor," I said. All of it - the train, the flight, the fever, the gang members - it swirled so I couldn't get a proper hold on any of it. "Doctor, I'm worried."

The doctor grabbed my hand. His was warm and dry. I opened my eyes to look at the man's eyes, but he had squeezed his shut.

"Holy God," he said. "Watch over Brad. Bless this surgery. Heal him, Lord. And give him peace."

I gazed stupidly at the top of his head, it bobbed gently as he talked. His hair was thinning. It felt so strange, these people praying, so much talk about God.

"Amen," Dr. Cole said.

"Amen," my sister said.

I closed my eyes and fell asleep.

DRESS

Three weeks later

"I TOLD HIM, I said, 'You have the gift for this. God gave you the gift for this, to do this surgery.' And he held my hand, right with you lying there. He grabbed my hand over your bed and we prayed for you, me and Dr. Cole."

My sister had been talking for awhile. She was going too fast and crying, of course, but I did my best to follow.

"So he did the surgery. We all talked about it and thought..."

I raised my hand slowly to stop her. "Wait... what do you mean?"

"Dr. Cole. He did your surgery, Brad. On your pelvis."

I remembered cornflakes and blinked. "Right."

"There were complications."

"Okay."

"But the surgery went really well, that's what I'm trying to tell you."

I closed my eyes and was somewhat surprised when they opened again. I had woken up a couple days before and was becoming alert for longer periods. Still, I'd been in a coma for over two weeks. It was a struggle.

Melissa had been trying to explain what happened. "The surgery went fine, but your... they said the stitches in your colon came loose. I didn't... It was a problem. There was feces they said in your..." She patted her belly. "It was really bad."

I remembered the Life-flight to Regions in Saint Paul. I remembered the visit from Dr. Cole when he had told me my room smelled like death. I'd had a fever of 105.

"Dr. Cole prayed over you, like I said."

It sounded like everyone had been talking to God about me. I had no problem with it; they could do what they wanted, but I figured God had better things to do than mess with an old gang-banger like me.

Melissa said, "He was amazing. He put you back together."

"Humpty Dumpty."

She grinned. "That's right. But I think you're going to be okay."

I blinked at her again. It didn't feel like it was going to turn out okay. I had a roll-cage around my pelvis which I'd have to live with for the next three months. I couldn't even move from one side of the bed to the other.

"It's a miracle, Brad," she said. "You been saved by God. And Dr. Cole."

I WAS UNDERWATER FLOATING FAR FROM MY BODY. I tried to surface but for a long time I couldn't quite get there. I couldn't remember where I was, or what had happened to me.

Slowly, the room came into focus. I was in a hospital bed. I'd been in an accident. I'd had surgery. I'd had a lot of surgeries.

My room was dark. Out the window gray clouds hung low over the city lights. A winter storm was coming. It was day, I figured, but I couldn't tell if it was morning or evening.

I closed my eyes. When I opened them again a woman was sitting next to my bed. She had long red hair and a kind face.

"Hello, Brad." She leaned her elbows onto her knees. "I'm Ellen." The skin around her eyes and mouth crinkled deeply when she smiled.

I whispered hello.

"I'm Bill's sister," she said. Bill was a friend from North Dakota. "He told me you might be down here for awhile and you might need visitors."

I nodded. She had a soothing voice and there was something motherly about her which made me feel safe.

"I don't live too far away so I told him of course I would."

"Thank you," I said.

"I've heard you're a wonderful man."

I tried to laugh but didn't have the energy.

"Where did you hear that?"

When she shrugged, she looked familiar, but I couldn't place it.

I said, "Have we met before?"

"No, I don't think so."

My sister stepped in from the hallway and knocked gently on the door. I pointed at her stupidly, still not fully awake.

I said, "Do you know Ellen?"

"I do. She came to visit when you were in a coma."

"That's nice," I said. I wondered if that's how I recognized her. It had happened a few times. I was able to recognize some nurses who took care of me while I was in my coma. I thought about this as my eyes again grew heavy.

"I'm sorry, Brad, I have to go."

My eyes fluttered open. I didn't know how long I'd been out.

"I'll be back in a couple days."

Ellen grabbed my hand. With a voice as warm as my grandma's meatloaf, she said, "Lord Jesus, take care of Brad. Watch over him tonight. Help his body to heal. Amen."

Melissa, on the other side of me, echoed, "Amen."

I had closed my eyes. It seemed like every day someone was praying for me. I had started to like it, these people talking to Jesus about me. It made me feel warm.

When I opened my eyes again, Ellen and my sister had both left. The room was dark. The hallway was quiet. The windows were black. Still, I whispered, "Amen."

DR. COLE KNOCKED ON THE DOOR, INTERRUPTING my thoughts which was fine since they weren't any good. I'd had two weeks to recover from the coma so I was more alert, but that just made me more aware of my situation. My body was wrecked. It looked like I'd never walk again, which meant I'd never be able to work again. I couldn't even go back to my old life. No one had use for a crippled gangster. And with tubes coming out of me, pooping in a bag, I figured I'd never again be intimate with a woman. I was barely a man any more. Most days I didn't know what I was.

Usually, Dr. Cole would come in smiling, but he looked grim as he sat heavily on the chair next to my bed. He took a deep breath, released it, then leaned in.

"Brad," he said. "I think we need to amputate your leg."

There wasn't enough air in the room.

"It's not healing like we want it to. And I'm afraid it's going to cause you some serious issues down the road.

I already felt like I was under water but now I was drowning.

"You don't have to make the call right now. We got time. Think about it. Talk with your family about it." He shrugged. "Maybe try praying about it."

I got lost in my own head and said nothing. Soon Dr. Cole excused himself and left.

I had nothing, but somehow I was going to lose even more. I felt the weight of my leg under the covers; it gave off a low throb. It was messed up but it was still part of me. I couldn't imagine not having it.

I closed my eyes and waited for the pain medication to kick in and put me to sleep.

"Brad!"

One of my surgeons stood smiling over my bed. His name was Tom Blee. He had the thick arms of a gym rat, and a startling energy. When I was in a coma and the stitches in my colon came apart, he was the one who put it back together. The man had saved my life but he kept talking about miracles and God. He kept talking about hope, which I figured was easy to do when you hadn't been hit by a train.

Dr. Tom had an intense way of looking straight at me. He said, "Hey man, I heard about your leg."

I was sure he had. They probably all stood around and talked about it. Heat rose in my chest and I didn't know what to do with it. I wanted to rage and curse, throw a punch at someone, but I barely had the strength to feed myself.

Tom must not have read my mood because he sat down.

"Listen, I got a guy I think you should talk to."

All I wanted was to be left alone.

"He was the leader of a gang back a few years ago, but got out of it. His name's John Turnipseed."

I had no interest in a guy who turned his back on his homies. I had loyalty unlike some of these other fools, walking around acting like they were real gangsters.

"He's got a son who got shot fifteen times. The kid survived, but lost his leg."

This got my attention, but I refused to show it. I gave him nothing.

"All right, Brad." Dr. Tom sighed. Like Dr. Cole, he soon excused himself, and left me to my dark thoughts in an empty room. I figured that would be the last time I saw him, but he came back to visit the next day. And again a few days after that.

I LAID IN MY ROOM ALONE, STARING AT THE CEILING as dusky light filtered through the window. There was a gentle knock on my door, and I scowled up at it. A man stepped in from the hallway. He was tall, wore a fine suit and tie. He removed his hat as he approached my bed and gave me a slow smile.

"Good afternoon," he said. "I'm John Turnipseed."

He skin was a dark, chocolatey brown. He had shoulders and a bearing that suggested he had once been an imposing presence, but had since earned a bit of a stoop.

"I'm a friend of Dr. Tom's."

I liked him immediately. He had a kind of voice I wanted to listen to and an easy grin. I could tell he had some stories I'd want to hear, but another part of me immediately shoved all that away. It had been almost two months since the accident, and I felt awful. My sister had gone home. Ellen hadn't been able to visit in several days. They had sent me across town to Bethesda hospital where they specialized in rehabilitating complicated patients and I didn't know any of the doctors or nurses. I didn't like myself or my situation. I was miserable and wanted to stay that way.

"How you doin' today, Brad?"

I had a bag of my own waste attached to the side of the bed. I shrugged.

"Dr. Tom told me you might like a visit."

My leg was throbbing. I had decided to keep it. Dr. Cole warned me that it might give me troubles down the road, but I didn't care. My body was a wreck but at least it was in one piece. I didn't want to explain any of this to the man. I shrugged again.

"That's all right. That's all right. Can I sit with you a moment?"

I told myself he was another Montoya, another man who'd pretend to be down, but would just tell me the same thing I had heard my whole life. One more person who had never been there, not really, and could stand up and walk out the door no problem when he was done.

I said, "I'm not feeling so good today."

John nodded. "I hear that. I hear that," he said, but didn't leave. He seemed at peace the way he was standing, like it was fine if we talked or if we didn't. He was fine no matter what happened. He had some kind of serene glow.

"Well, Brad, if it's all right with you, I'll stop by another time and maybe we can talk then."

"Yeah, all right."

With that, he left me staring up at the ceiling. And like I had with Dr. Tom, I figured I'd never see John Turnipseed again.

EVERY DAY I HAD TO SIT UP IN A CHAIR FOR FORTY-FIVE minutes.

I used to be the toughest gangster in the room. I'd thrown down with anyone. I was Loco. When I worked construction I'd spend sixteen hour days in the sun then bike home in the dark. My whole life, being tough was who I was.

But now I needed a nurse half my age and half my size to move me into the wheelchair. Then I needed to dig deep in order to bear the torture of sitting - just sitting. Most days I could barely handle it.

And today was worse than most days. I had been sitting for barely twenty minutes, but something was wrong. There was a heat in my chest, which felt different. I sipped at some water, but the heat kept spreading slowly down to my stomach and up into the back of my throat. I tried to swallow but it didn't feel right.

I started to sweat. The heat spread to my forehead and down my arms. I checked the clock. Barely a minute had passed since the last

234

time I looked. It had come on so quick I didn't know what was happening. I called out for the nurse, but my throat was tight and my voice came out raspy.

A fever quickly followed the heat. Within minutes, my head grew so heavy I'd have tumbled out of the chair if the cage around my pelvis hadn't kept me in place. Pain began to streak over my skin like I was sunburnt. It radiated from my guts, intense enough to take my breath away.

Finally, the nurse walked in. She had a smile lingering on her lips as she entered, but lost it as soon as she saw me.

"Oh my word!" She hurried to my side. "What happened?!"

I moaned. She seemed impossibly tiny, and I wanted to ask for a bigger nurse, but my brain was frying and I could only mutter as she started to move me. She tried to pull me towards the bed but when her fingers touched my skin I screamed.

I was boiling from the inside. Other nurses flurried into the room. They talked in hard sentences to each other, then gently to me. I could only whimper.

My fingers and feet and neck, everywhere started swelling, stretching my skin. EMTs arrived. They moved me and every touch was fire.

In my fever I heard Melissa telling me I was alive for a reason, telling me I was blessed. I saw her wide eyes, smudged mascara, damp cheeks and cried out. Every moment was punishment. I knew I wouldn't survive the next breath. I didn't want to take another. It was hell. It was the only thing I understood. I knew I was in hell.

WEAKLY, I THRASHED IN BED, CRAZY WITH PAIN, crying and panting, trying to find some comfort. In the hours since it started, it only grew worse. Every inch of skin had turned dark red and tight as my body swolled up. My fingers grew fat, my testicles grew to the size of a cantaloupe. Nothing touched the pain. They pumped me full of steroids but it didn't help.

I wanted to pass out. I wanted to disappear into nothing, but I was conscious of everything happening around me. Every nerve ending was on fire. I felt every movement of the sheet against my skin, every flutter on my face. I winced at every sound, and every smell because it all hurt. Breathing hurt. Blinking hurt. Squeezing my eyes shut hurt.

"Brad?"

I heard the voice but couldn't track it.

"It's Dr. Tom."

The voice rattled in my ears and made me queasy. He dimmed the lights but it didn't help.

"Hey Brad. I just heard they brought you back to us."

I groaned.

"Can I sit with you?"

I had no answer. If he sat or not it would make no difference.

"I know you're hurting, man. But you're not alone."

I lolled my head over and glimpsed his eyes staring at me. There was only one thing he could do.

"Please Doc..."

I paused to catch my breath.

"Please Doc..."

As he leaned close his hand brushed my sheet and a fresh wave of pain flashed through me.

"Kill me," I said.

"Brad."

"Kill me, Doc."

"Brad, I can't do that."

"Tom, you know me."

"Brad, listen..."

"You know me."

"I do."

"Please."

"I can't do that. I can't."

I closed my eyes. I had no strength left to speak.

Tom began talking, his voice low and soothing. He spoke quietly about his life, about his journey. The words were jumbled in my head but I understood enough. He told me how he had been broken once, how he had been lost and hurting, but he had found some kind of peace.

"Hey Brad?"

I tried to answer but my lips weren't working so I nodded. The movement of my head sent a jolt of pain through the back of my head.

"Can I pray with you?"

I was sick of prayer. I was sick of positive people who thought they had the answers, who thought that God cared about crippled gang bangers. I had heard it all before and thought about telling him that, but at the same time I didn't want him to leave.

"Yeah," I said.

Gently, he grabbed my hand. I felt warm fingers touching the one spot on my body which didn't hurt - an inch of skin in the middle of my palm.

His voice grew even quieter as he prayed. It sounded like he was talking to someone he knew well, someone he trusted, someone he could be cool with. He said, "Dear God, watch over Brad here. He's in a lot of pain, God, and needs your help."

The words settled on me like a blanket. I floated in and out, listening as best I could, holding on to the sound of his voice.

He kept praying and the pain eased back, from a scream to something almost tolerable, like someone turned down the stereo a few notches. I felt peace wash over me and a sweet relief.

I took a few breaths, feeling more aware as I listened to his voice. He was telling the Lord about me, a lowly piece-of-shit gang-banger ex-con in need of healing, and I felt a gentle pull away from his voice, away from the pain, away from the world until gently I fell into a deep and peaceful sleep.

I Got You

Eight days later

I SAW JOHN Turnipseed out of the corner of my eye, more a blur than a man. He had his hat in his hand, talking low and smooth and I cut him off with a wave before he could come in the door.

"Not today," I panted, and I squeezed my eyes shut until I was sure he was gone.

It hadn't gotten much better. One day then the next and little had changed. It wasn't as bad as that first night; they had some of the pain dialed back, but every morning I woke up - if I slept - feeling boiled from the inside. My body swolled up: my belly, my legs, my neck, it all hurt. I had no appetite but if I did I couldn't do anything about it since I couldn't even hold a fork.

It hadn't been that long, maybe a week, a little more, but since the doctors couldn't figure out what the problem was, I figured I was done. This was the rest of my life: constant throbbing pain everywhere. I wasn't begging my doctors to kill me anymore but I wouldn't have stopped anyone either.

This was my mindset when the phone rang. It was near enough I could grab it, but it hurt to touch. It hurt to bring it to my ear. When it touched my cheek, it burned.

"*Mijo*! Bradley? It's me."

My mom had called a few times while I'd been in the hospital, but

I'd always been feverish or knocked out on pain medication.

I whispered, "Hey, Ma."

"Bradley, it's so good to hear your voice."

"You too."

"Melissa says you're a miracle."

"I know she does."

"She says it's a gift from God that you're still here."

"I know, Ma."

Melissa wasn't the only one saying it. Many of the nurses, Ellen, Dr. Tom, even my old friend Chavez. He had come to visit a few weeks before and though he was an atheist he said I must be here for a reason. He even called it a miracle.

"Bradley?"

"I'm here, Ma. I just don't feel too good."

"I know. *Pobrecito*. Is there anything I can do?"

"Pray for me."

The words just slipped out. I had never asked for that before, but I surprised myself by meaning it.

"I will, Bradley."

"Just pray," I said.

Something had happened to me. Something with Dr. Tom in the Emergency Room when his praying over me allowed me to sleep. I had felt a peace I didn't understand. I felt different, even as sick as I was, even as I suffered, my whole body hurting as I felt so lost like I would never feel better again, still just saying those words gave me some small stirring of something in my chest, to think my mother of all people would turn to the Lord and bring up my name.

I COULDN'T REMEMBER WAKING UP. THE ROOM WAS dark along with the whole hospital, and I was completely alone. I couldn't even hear the nurses in the hallway or any of the machines that were always beeping. There was no one around to help, no one caring for me in any way. I felt like the throwaway kid.

I was recovering from DRESS syndrome. That's what the doctors had named it. It meant my body had had an allergic reaction to one of the antibiotics. Once they figured that out, they started treating it and it got better.

The pain had started to fade and my head began to clear, but I was still in a bad place. I had spent the last several days turning over the choices I had made, where they had led me, what I had to show for it. It all came up to nothing. I had nothing to my name. And now my body was broken and I faced a lifetime of hospital rooms, wheelchairs and boredom.

I laid in that strange darkness and blinked up at the black ceiling. I couldn't figure out what time it was, whether it was day or night. Everything was in shadows, but I barely noticed beyond my own self-pity.

My whole life, it always came up to nothing. I was always the one who got into trouble, got thrown out, got hurt, got left behind - even when others were doing worse than I was. It was me that took the fall, no matter what.

The injustice of it became an agony. I didn't want to be alone anymore and tried to cry out for a nurse, anyone to come sit with me, but there was no one.

I've shown you.

The voice vibrated through me. I couldn't sit up but I swiveled my neck around, searching the room but there was no one there. Even my window was blacked out.

I've shown you.

The voice said again. It was terrifying, but still, I felt a strange, low warmth spread into my belly.

You have nothing to fear.

The words fell over me. I laid in my bed, abandoned, my body broken. I had nothing to my name. I faced years of disability and pain.

I've shown you.

But in that place I heard the voice of the Lord. He spoke one more time.

You have nothing to fear.

I closed my eyes and shuddered. I listened for the voice to speak again but it had gone quiet. In the silence, everything felt different. In the darkness I felt full of light. Alone in my hospital room, I felt connected to the Lord of everything.

When I opened my eyes again the sun was streaking orange through the window. The hospital was full of noise: the sound of nurses chatting in the hallway, the whirring of machines, the distant beeps from another room.

It was disorientating. I had had some kind of dream or vision. I didn't have words for it, but I knew it had been something real. I knew I wasn't alone. He showed me, Jesus said. The Lord was there.

And so was Ellen. She looked up from her magazine, wearing the same purple sweatshirt she always wore, and smiled.

"Good morning."

I had a hard time speaking. The dream laid on me thick like a blanket. He showed me. He was showing me. Ellen laughed gently at the look on my face.

"You need to eat."

She had worked in a nursing home before she retired. She had helped people just like me. And she just happened to live nearby and was my friend's sister. For the first time, I saw God's hand in it. It was the first of many miracles I began to see, big and small, all around me. The Lord had showed me, kept showing me all the time.

Ellen lifted a bite of scrambled eggs to my lips since I had been too weak to do it by myself. I chewed as she talked in her soothing voice, telling me about the day before, what she had done and who she had seen. I listened as I took another bite.

"You're looking better," she said.

It would still be a few days before I started to gain my strength back, but I felt much more than better. I had nothing to fear. The Lord had showed me.

I had hope.

IT WAS GOOD TO BE SITTING UP IN BED AND THE PAIN was better, but nothing had changed. My body was still wrecked, I had nothing to my name, and no way of making a living. I might never walk again, but still I had never felt more grateful.

Three days ago my eyes had been opened to the Lord and now it was undeniable, the miracles I kept seeing around me. I started being able to move around in my bed. I could raise a fork to my mouth. It was amazing. The nurses poured light in my room whenever they checked in. I thanked God constantly even when I couldn't have less going for me, because wherever I looked, I saw Jesus.

John Turnipseed grinned at me from the doorway. He'd visit at least once a week and I saw Jesus in him too. I invited him in. He settled himself on the chair with his hat on his knee and grinned at me comfortably. He always seemed at ease, like it didn't matter if he was talking to the President of the United States or a broken old drug dealer - either way he'd be cool.

"Mr. Bradley, how you doing this morning?"

"You know me, John." I gave him a big grin. "I'm just living."

We started talking, not about anything, just clowning, chatting about the Super Bowl coming up, about his grandchildren and his wife. It was nothing serious but as we talked I could see something in his eyes.

It reminded me back to Ty Angel or TJ from my days in Portland. I saw something I recognized when they looked at me. The hate and chaos in their eyes was reflected in my own - and it would rev me up so I was ready to cause some havoc.

In some ways, it was like that with John Turnipseed. Staring in this man's face, a former gang-banger like me, I saw something familiar and got revved up. But in an important way it was the opposite of Ty Angel. With John, I saw peace. I saw love. I saw Jesus.

It had only been a few weeks since I first met the man and sat in judgement like a fool. I'd figured John had turned his back on his gang to get where he was. But after hearing the voice of the Lord, I saw him for real. He hadn't turned his back on nobody. What he had done is turn himself towards God. And because of that Turnipseed had something different about him. It was like he glowed.

I wanted that for myself. I wanted to plug in to whatever made Turnipseed glow. I wanted to take it into the world and spread some of that light around.

After an hour Turnipseed said a little prayer and shuffled out the door. I laid in my bed for awhile after he left, thinking about these two men: John Turnipseed, the former gang member and now preacher, and Tom Blee, the surgeon. I thought about how they acted, excited about everything, enthusiastic about life. I thought about Ellen and Dr. Cole and my sister.

I wanted what they all had. Like them, I wanted to glow.

"YOU GOING TO BE OKAY?" IT WAS ABOUT THE THIRD time my sister asked the question. She bustled around the room, not doing anything helpful, just fussing with things, turning my water cup, adjusting a sheet, moving to move.

I watched her, grinning, feeling so grateful she could be there. She had raced out again when she heard I had DRESS syndrome and had given me another two weeks of her time.

I had nothing to my name, but since I started trying to follow Jesus, it felt like I had everything I needed. It felt like Jesus just kept putting things in my path, little blessings, big blessings, all kinds of things.

She gathered her magazine, her phone, her purse. She wiped a finger under her eye. "Bradley, are you going to be okay?"

"Aw, Sis, you know me."

"Humpty Dumpty."

"That's right. And I'll just keep moving forward."

She gave me a sweet smile with her eyes.

It was all impossible. It was all a miracle. That's what my sister kept saying and I saw it now. The train took a lot away but God gave me back everything I needed. I had my family around me. Popps taking care of her kids so my sister could be with me. My brother calling. My mom calling. I had aunts and uncles sending their prayers. I had my family. I had nothing to my name but I had Jesus pouring out these blessings on me and I couldn't help thinking how much easier this life was because of it.

In my old life, everything was a struggle. Getting out of bed, going to work, it was all struggle. All hard. My body was healthy and strong but it didn't matter, every day felt like I was moving through a swamp. But with the Lord, even in the midst of the pain, even with a hernia taking up most of my midsection, even with surgeries ahead of me, even more confined than I had been in the hole, even with all of that, I found it easy. Easy to get up in the morning, easy to face the day because I knew the Lord would put something new in my path: a nurse to give me encouragement, Ellen calling me wonderful, my body doing something new it hadn't been able to do the day before.

"Thank you for all this," I said.

Melissa leaned in, wrapped her arms around my neck and squeezed.

"HOW DO YOU LIKE PEANUT M&MS?"

I muted some professional wrestling on TV.

"I love them," I said.

Dr. Tom handed me the bag and I tossed a handful into my mouth. They tasted amazing. There was that word, Tom and I both scattered it through everything we said. I followed an amazing God. My body was healing in amazing ways. I popped a couple more M&Ms and grinned up at Dr. Tom as I chewed. He kept showing up. Ellen kept showing up. Turnipseed kept showing up. I had amazing people in my life.

All I wanted to do was give thanks. Didn't matter much what was going on. Three nurses would hold me up, pain screaming in my legs, and I'd give thanks. It was strange, but I was like a newborn baby discovering the world for the first time.

Tom said, "I brought you something else."

He gave me two books. One was a Bible, and one was a devotional named, Jesus Calling.

"A couple days ago God told me to bring these books to the guy from North Dakota."

The spine crackled as I opened the book.

Dr. Tom said, "But it was a different dude I thought God was talking about. And then I forgot them at home and that guy was gone by the time I remembered. Then I figured you were a North Dakota guy too."

"That's right."

I opened the Bible and found Tom had written something in the front flap. I read it through slowly as he sat down near me.

What a blessing God has given me in getting to know you, it said. *I struggled for so long trying to be a good man. This book introduced me to the greatest man ever - Jesus!*

Following Him has led me to another great man - Bradley Strain! Thank you for your courage, strength, and for showing me how to 'Fight the fight.' Stay strong!

I looked from the words to the man who wrote them. It took me a long time to speak.

"Thank you," I finally said.

"You got a minute to read with me?"

"You know me, Tom. I got nothing but time."

We paged through the Bible and talked about what we read. Tom told me about his struggles. He talked about his failing marriage, about feeling empty and desperate, but also about how Jesus showed up when he fell on his knees.

And he told me about reading through the book of Matthew, about how he hit this part where Peter was sinking into the water. Jesus had reached down, grabbed his hand and said, "I got you."

I nodded with my whole body.

I got you.

My whole life I'd been running from the Lord. I'd been a tough guy, the first to throw a punch, the first to do something crazy. I had been Loco since I was fifteen, but I didn't have to be that any more.

"I got you," Jesus said. My whole life I'd wanted to hear that from someone: my mom, my older brother, my dad. Then Big Wheez, then Melody. I was always searching for someone to have my back and I'd always been let down.

And through that whole time, God kept trying to show me: I was never alone. I was not a throwaway kid. "I got you," Jesus said.

I crunched on some Peanut M&Ms and nodded with the doctor.

"That's right," I said.

I got you.

"That's right."

I LAUGHED AT THE PHYSICAL THERAPIST. THIS WAS stupid, crazier than anything I ever did as a kid. She was a nice young woman and didn't laugh back. Instead, she tugged at the belt she had around my waist.

"You can do this, Brad."

I laughed again.

"You're crazy," I said, but it was clear she wouldn't leave it alone. "This is impossible."

245

"You got this."

I shook my head but lifted my leg to the first step. Expecting nothing, I pushed down, leaning heavily onto hers. Slowly, like a miracle, I raised myself up.

Cheers echoed down the stairwell. I looked up to see Dr. Tom and a nurse grinning down at me.

For thirty years I'd do just about anything to get a reaction from a crowd. I'd be stupid, mean, reckless, whatever it took, as long as I got a response. I didn't care that they were reacting to the spectacle, to the crazy. It all felt the same to me at the time.

Now all I was doing was raising myself up a few inches, but these nurses, this therapist, Dr. Tom, they were cheering for me. They were on my side. I took another step and it was amazing the way they shouted my name. I couldn't help but thank God, the words pouring straight from my heart.

Dr. Tom shouted, "You're doing amazing, Brad! Amazing!"

I laughed. Before my train accident three months ago I could have run up those stairs, but that didn't matter. It was in these small things, these little moments that I kept seeing Jesus. Before, I'd always want something huge. Like all criminals, I'd bargain with God, tell him I'd follow him if he made it so I didn't get caught, or changed around laws or evidence so I didn't have to go to jail. I wanted the oceans to part and would turn my back when God didn't deliver. But now I saw Jesus in all the little things around me - and he made them huge. I was doing nothing but climbing a single stair, but Jesus made it among the biggest moments of my life.

I called up to Tom, "This is a God thing, isn't it?"

"It's amazing, Brad."

My legs were screaming, sweat poured down my back, but I couldn't help but grin. "Dr Tom," I said, "I think I got that thing that you and John have."

"What's that?"

I raised my foot up to the next step and laughed when my legs held my weight.

"That glow," I said. "I got that glow."

———

AN AIDE PUSHED ME DOWN THE HALLWAY. EVERYONE was smiling at me, these nurses and doctors I came to know as family during my time here. They said good-bye, grinning at me, telling me to take care of myself, telling me I was looking good and they hoped to see me again.

I felt full. I could walk with a walker, I could get out of bed and feed myself. I was getting stronger every day. It had been an amazing journey.

The aide pushed me into an elevator. We talked about nothing as we went down, then we came out into the main lobby. I hadn't left the floor - barely left my room - in weeks. Down here, everything was bright and smelled good and clean. The aide patted my shoulder at the door as we waited for my ride.

It was only a few minutes before Derek pulled up in a van, rust creeping up the bottom edge, a cloud of exhaust tumbling from the back. The sky was a dull gray, the color of nothing, and snow fell around him as he hopped out.

I took a last look at the hospital. After almost four months there I found all of it comforting: the light, the chatter, the people moving. Everyone was smiling; everyone was positive. Yesterday Ellen had come to say goodbye and Dr. Tom had visited the day before, each of them telling me I was wonderful or special and that God had something big planned for me. Turnipseed had come a week earlier, listening to me like I was worth something.

But it was time to leave, time to head out into whatever the Lord had planned for me, so I turned back to the van. It was the middle of the afternoon, but dark and cold: February in Minnesota. I couldn't remember the last time I'd been outside and I told myself it'd be like getting out of prison. I'd have a real meal for once; I'd get some freedom.

It didn't feel like that, however, as I sludged through the snow. The cold bit at my face and the few other people outside had their shoulders hunched against the wind.

"You all right?" Derek asked.

I nodded as we pulled away. Derek had been driving through this snow for twelve hours but he was in a good mood. He chattered at me about North Dakota, about the job site, about the people we both knew.

We drove first to the restaurant. All morning, I had been excited about my first good meal out, but my leg started aching as I wrestled my walker out the back. Then, as I ate, I worried how my body would deal with the rich food. I worried about what I'd do if I had any troubles. I worried if Derek would be able to do anything to help.

I left unsatisfied and we were out in the snow again, slushing through to the hotel. I kept telling myself it would be good to stay somewhere where it got fully dark and quiet. It would be good to sleep a full night without being woken up by a nurse checking on something. But when we shuffled into the room, we found a layer of grime covering everything. It smelled off, like they sprayed air freshener over a dead animal. We'd asked for something handicap accessible but the doorways were narrow and the toilet low and nothing about it was helpful or comfortable.

With some effort I sat on my bed. Derek sat on his and gave me a shit-eating grin before pulling out an eighteen pack of beer. He cracked one open and handed it towards me.

"Time to celebrate, Brad. You're out!"

"Naw. Thanks though," I said.

I had told myself a lot of things about leaving the hospital and heading home to Portland, but none of it was turning out like I'd wanted. It gave me an uneasy feeling as I'd gone through this before. I'd get out of prison thinking I had things figured out. I was done with that old life, I was going to be a new man. But then I'd find myself back doing the same old stupid stuff.

Here, I hadn't been out of the hospital for a full afternoon and already I was in a hole being offered a drink. I shook my head again and closed my eyes. The positive buzz from the hospital had dimmed, but I thought about Dr. Tom and Ellen and the nurses. And I thought about the Lord.

The moment passed. I'd had a rough start but that didn't mean anything. My situation had changed but that didn't mean I had to go back to the old Brad.

"Naw, man," I said, "I'm not getting back into that."

I looked back up at Derek. He had a sad-sack look. He was always apologizing, always feeling bad. He kept telling me how sorry he was for everything.

I said, "Hey, thanks. Thanks for all this. For coming to get me, for all of it. You're a good man."

He had a spark in his eyes for a moment. His mouth twitched. He had been beating himself up his whole life over a mistake he had made when he was a kid and for a moment I thought maybe we could talk about it, maybe I could do for him what Dr. Tom and John and Ellen had done for me.

But then he shrugged and grunted, "You'd do the same for me."

"Maybe, but you were the one who did it. And it was amazing."

Derek took a pull from his beer and turned his eyes to the television.

I rested back and said a quiet prayer. It didn't sound as good in my head as when Dr. Tom prayed or Ellen, but it felt right enough.

Home
Eighteen hours later

A PALE, THIN-BEARDED airport worker pushed me to the security gate then placed his hand under my elbow to help me up. I had grown used to strangers touching my body, giving me help, but he surprised me and I had to fight the instinct to pull away.

When I was on my feet, he handed me my walker. I thanked the man and started shuffling with my luggage through the security gate and into baggage claim. My head ached and I had no confidence in my legs. It had been a six hour flight, by myself. I had an open seat next to me, but it had been a small space and I spent the time worried about my colostomy bag and what would happen if I had a problem. But that was done. I was out, and on my feet. Pain throbbed from different areas of my body at different intensities, but I was home.

"Brad!"

My sister, Melissa, was the first to see me. She started crying immediately as she grabbed me for a hug.

"You're walking, Brad! That's so great!"

"Easy there," I said.

"You look so good."

I had a poop bag on me and I could barely stand, but I grinned at the lie.

"So do you, Mel."

My dad stood behind her, with the hint of a smile. He nodded at me as my nephews brought up a wheelchair. I felt better when I sat down, but there was someone missing.

"Where's Mom at?"

They told me she was waiting back at my dad's house, and that was okay. They wheeled me outside into the sun.

We drove through Portland. I hadn't lived in the area since I was twenty-one, hadn't been back to visit in years, and I felt the low glow, excited to be back. It was true that I was returning with nothing. I was achy from the flight and needed to lie down and take some pain meds, but through all of it, I still had Jesus. I'd been given a fresh start. I had been shown the light and I was going to follow it this time.

We stopped in front of a tidy rambler with a perfect lawn. My dad dug his hand under my arm and pulled me out of the car with a grunt. He had turned into an old man at some point but he was still strong.

I shuffled through the front door then stopped when I saw my mom. She too had grown older. The dark skin of her face had grown lined under blonde hair. She had always been small but now she seemed frail.

"Oh my baby!" She laid her palm on my cheek. "Oh my precious baby!" She leaned into me and held on, crying into my chest.

My back ached. "Ma, I gotta..."

"Come sit on the couch." Gripping my arm, she pulled me to the living room.

The sun poured through the windows. It felt good to sit. It felt good to have my mom next to me. My sister sat on the other side, making the same high-pitched sounds, both of them crying and making a fuss. I felt warm all over.

I showed them pictures from the hospital, of the nurses, of Dr. Cole and Dr. Tom. I told a few stories, but was just getting into it when my mom stood up.

"Ma?"

"I got to get going, Bradley."

"I just got here!"

"I know."

"You're not staying for dinner?"

"No, baby. I have to go home. I'm not feeling too good."

Her voice had become whispery. Her head was turned in my direction but she wouldn't quite look at me. It was the first time I had seen her in forever, and it had only lasted a few minutes. The warmth drained out of me, but I was too tired to argue.

My sister and nephews followed Mom out so it was just me and my dad. He got me a glass of water and turned on the TV, but the house felt empty and quiet.

When I had to go the bathroom, I glanced over at Popps staring stony-faced at the basketball game. He was a strong man, but a hard one, and I couldn't bring myself to ask for his help.

I struggled to stand, my legs screaming, the pain in my belly pushing out, and I hobbled to the bathroom. It would be a process, but I hoped I could finish what I had to do in time for dinner.

I'D SPENT THE MORNING SITTING IN THE GARAGE with the door open, staring out into the gray drizzle, trying to keep my spirits up, trying to feel positive, trying to feel like I did in the hospital, but nothing was working. I'd been alone all morning, nothing to do but wait for my dad to come back after an errand.

I'd been home for three weeks. A few people had reached out in that time, mostly from my old life. Some of them had cleaned themselves up and wanted to reconnect. Others... I didn't want to know what they are after, but it was hard to feel optimistic. A darker part of me even thought maybe there was something to that life, some way to make a hustle even as a cripple, but I'd push that thought away as soon as it came. I'd shake my head and think back to Turnipseed and Dr. Tom; I'd think back to my time following the Lord. I knew Jesus was there. It was undeniable that there was a God. Still, He felt so far away, and I didn't know what to do about that. It hadn't been like this at Regions.

My brain was churning with all this when my dad pulled into the driveway. I had to stand up and shuffle over, moving too slow. My dad got out of his truck and with a grunt helped me into the house.

He closed the door hard on his way back to his truck. In the last week there had been an edge to everything he said or did, even when it was something helpful. He'd ask me if I needed a glass of water but make it sound like I just cut him off on the highway.

I settled onto the couch. After a few minutes he barreled back into the house and grumbled to the kitchen. He banged around the cabinets, then muttered, "You can't wash a plate, huh?"

I didn't get why he was being like that. I had my faults but I wasn't a messy person; it was just that I could barely walk to the kitchen much less do the dishes.

I decided not to answer and let it go. We had church that night so I figured I should take a shower. It would get me out of his space.

I gathered my things and started the process. Some time later, the water turned cold while I was still rinsing off soap in the shower chair. I didn't know how long I'd been in there because everything took forever. I shut off the water then struggled to stand then pulled the towel off the hook and carefully dried myself. I dabbed at the tube coming out of my body and prepared myself to change the colostomy bag.

All this and I hadn't even started the hardest part: dressing myself. I had laid out my clothes and necessary tools on the bed ahead of time, knowing it could take all afternoon. But when I shuffled into my room I found the bed made and all my stuff had been moved. The clothes were put away in a dresser. My tools were laying against the wall.

In my towel, water dripping down my neck, I stood quietly, trying to breathe. A familiar heat rose in my chest. Dad had come into my room and tossed my stuff aside and now I had to, what, I had to spend a good thirty minutes finding it all. I'd need to ask the man for help as I stood naked in a towel and it was too much. I rubbed at my face with a damp hand. I'd been trying so hard, taking all his shots, my dad picking at all the little crap that I couldn't do anything about. It took an hour to cross the damn room to the bathroom, for God's sake. I would have made the bed myself if the old man would just let it alone.

The old Brad, the old Loco rose up crazy and ready to throw down. It was easy to let it take control, and I heard myself screaming for my dad.

He stood like a rock in the doorway.

I spit out, "Why are you moving my shit?"

"I was making your bed."

"You can't just come into my room and move my shit! I need that stuff!"

"I'll go wherever I want in my house."

253

"This is my room, Popps. You can't just - I had all that stuff set up..." I hated the whine in my voice. "You can't fucking do this!"

He threw each of his next words like a fist, "This is my house!"

I wanted to burn it to the ground but I had no strength so I picked up my walker and hurled it across the room. It glanced against the wall, leaving a scar. I panted from the effort.

My dad looked from the walker back to me. "Get out of my house."

With the last energy I had, I screamed in frustration.

He grunted. "You haven't changed at all."

With that, he left me alone to wonder what the hell had just happened. I found myself standing naked, somewhere in the fight I had lost my towel. I struggled to lean forward and picked it up with the ends of my fingers then wrapped it around my waist. I glared at the hole I'd made in the wall, knowing the man was right. No matter how hard I tried, nothing would ever change.

NOTHING HAD CHANGED SINCE I WAS A KID gangster running around San Bernardino. That same rush of red heat, followed by that insane moment when it faded, leaving me spent and disoriented, trying to figure out what I'd done.

Right on time, the regret swelled through me as I struggled with my socks. I thought I had changed. I thought I was following the Lord, but apparently not. Apparently I was just the same as I always was, which meant I'd follow the same path as I always did. I'd never get out of it. Eventually I'd do something stupid, and end up back in prison or the hospital or dead.

But before I could do any of that I had to get out of my dad's house. I heard him watching television in the living room and could feel the tension through the door. I couldn't go out there. I couldn't stay in my room. I literally had no place in the world to go.

Like a child in trouble at school, I called my mom. I bowed my head as the phone ring, then squeezed my eyes shut when she answered.

"Ma, you gotta come get me."

"What's wrong, baby? What happened?"

"You gotta get me." Weakly, I pounded a fist again my knee. "I gotta get out of here."

"Slow down, Bradley. What happened?"

"Dad went off on me and I can't stay here no more. We got into a big fight and... I need to get out of here. I need to come live with you."

My voice sounded pathetic and my room was dark and I couldn't get my own socks on and I didn't know how I got there. It wasn't more than a few weeks since I saw Jesus in every corner of every room, but now He didn't seem anywhere. I was all alone.

"Okay. Just stay in your room and I'll be there soon."

"All right. I gotta try to get dressed, so all right."

I pulled on my socks then wrestled with my pants, all the time hearing the color commentators ramble on the game. Finally, I pulled my shirt down over my tubes and sunk into the edge of the bed to wait.

It wasn't long before the doorbell rang. The TV muted, and I listened to the low thud of my dad's footsteps followed by my mom's voice.

"Keith, what happened?"

"I went in there to make his bed," my dad was already shouting. "I moved some of his things and then he flipped out on me."

"Okay, calm down."

"He's the same damn kid as always, throwing stuff around. I'm not putting up with that."

I was a forty-year-old man and my parents were arguing about me in the other room. I felt no miracle in that moment. I saw no evidence of God.

There was a knock at my bedroom door. My mom opened it before I could stand up to answer.

"Bradley?"

"Mom, I'm just trying to get dressed and dad moves my things. I don't know why he comes in here and tears down what I already got set up. It's already hard enough for me to do this stuff."

She sighed. "What do you want to do?"

"Why is he making it so much harder for me? I'm crippled. I can barely walk."

"Bradley?"

"I want to come live with you."

I had to ignore the look on her face.

"I have a one bedroom, baby."

"I know, mom."

"You'd have to sleep on the couch. And it's up a flight of stairs."

"I don't care. I have to get out of here."

Her hands were clenched tight, but she said, "Okay."

"I can't stay here, Ma."

"I know. Come along then."

I gathered my stuff. I didn't have many personal items but I had a lot of equipment. It took a few trips, mostly my mom walking between my room and the car. My dad sat dead silent on the couch, glaring at the TV. Neither of us said good-bye.

BLUE LIGHT GLOWED BEHIND THE BLINDS AND MY mom was thumping around her room. I couldn't remember sleeping but apparently it was time to get up. I lowered my legs to the floor and pushed against the couch until I was sitting. Every part of my body hurt in different ways.

Four weeks ago I had seen my mom for the first time in eighteen years. She had called me Bradley in a tone of voice no one else used. She had given me a hug and cried, smiling through it, so happy to see me. But that was then and now I woke up after five days on her couch and knew I couldn't make it another night. I was sleeping in the living room like I did when I was seventeen. I had gone all the way back. Nothing ever changed. Nothing ever got better.

And like a teenager I felt like my parents just didn't understand. I had gotten hit by a train. It took me an hour to put on my pants. I had to clean my own waste out of a plastic bag every day. So, yeah, sometimes it took awhile before I could get around to clearing the coffee table.

But I had no place to go so I shuffled into the kitchen. This was going to be my life: pain, hospital visits and getting yelled at by my parents.

"You're up," my mom said, and since I was feeling sorry for myself, I heard it as a criticism. "You have any plans for today?"

I shrugged.

"Well you gotta find something to do."

I let that one land as I swallowed one of my pills.

"Ma," I said, "I think I gotta go back to Dad's."

"Yeah, I think you do."

"I need a bed."

"I know that. I told you it's a small place."

"Right."

"You'll have to apologize, but he'll take you back."

"I have to apologize to him?"

She was behind me and didn't respond.

"I have to apologize, but he's not saying sorry to me?"

"If you want to move back in with him, yes."

I couldn't remember a time in my whole life the old man ever apologized for anything. It burned so I couldn't stop shaking my head.

"It went both ways, Ma. It was a double situation."

She shrugged.

"I have to poop in a bag, Ma. I don't... What's wrong with you people? I was hit by a train."

"This is how it is, Bradley. Your dad has lived alone for a long time. He's not used to this."

She shrugged again and disappeared into the bathroom. I returned to my couch and grabbed the phone. I had to fight to keep from whipping it against the wall. I didn't know who I was anymore. I wanted to gather my stuff in a garbage bag and get on a bus and head out for wherever. The whole Jesus thing felt like something that happened to somebody else, like a story I was told once. Now, I wanted to return to the life I understood, have some beers, get a little high. I wanted to get things going, start throwing down, find myself in violence. The miracles, the amazing moments, seeing Jesus in everything, that wasn't me. I was the same old Brad; I was still Loco, and ready to get crazy.

The only thing keeping me back was everything. My body was broken. I could go nowhere without help. I could do nothing. Big Wheez, if I could find him, wasn't going to let me stay at his place. He wasn't going to take me to my doctor appointments and make sure I got my meds. I only had the one option.

I gripped the phone, swallowed my pride, and swiped around for my dad's number. I muttered, "This ain't right," as I listened to it ring. I half wished he wouldn't pick up, except, as bad as this was, I couldn't spend another night on my mom's couch.

He answered with a grunt.

"Hey, Popps."

"Yeah?"

"Hey, I just wanted to call and tell you I was sorry."

"Are ya?"

It was a punch in the gut, but I tried to roll with it.

"Yeah. I'm sorry for losing my temper."

"Yeah, well..."

My dad stopped there and I waited for a moment, listening to him breathe, thinking he was going to say something back.

When he didn't, I said, "All right, so... I'd like to come back to your place."

"I bet."

"This isn't working out."

The door to the bathroom opened behind me and my mom stepped to the back of the couch.

With another grunt, my dad said, "Door's unlocked."

And that was the end of the conversation. I put away my phone and nodded at my mom.

"Gather your things," she said.

She returned to her bedroom and my head drooped towards the floor. With my eyes squeezed shut, I tried to pray but all that would come out was, "What the hell is happening to me?"

MY DAD WALKED IN FROM HIS SATURDAY ERRANDS and eyed me sitting on the couch.

"You going to church tonight?"

We had gone to Mass together a few times on Saturday nights but I had forgotten about it so it felt like a surprise, an alien thing he was asking. But I nodded.

"All right." He checked his watch. "I got to head out again. You need anything? A sandwich or anything?"

"No thanks," I said.

He grunted, said, "Well, you got my number." He scratched the back of his neck for a moment then stepped out the door.

I listened to the quiet apartment for a long moment, then picked myself up and shuffled to the bedroom. Those words had been the most we'd said to each other since I'd come back a couple days ago. I didn't really know what to make of it but didn't have the energy to give it much thought. I had to get ready for church.

I planned through the steps I had to take and it exhausted me. I was sick of it all. I had sunk down into myself. I hadn't talked to anyone but my dad and my mom in over a week. I spent all my time sitting staring at the TV or out the window at the empty streets, just wallowing in my thoughts which were all negative all the time.

Checking the clock, I considered a shower; I wanted one before church. It was a few hours away so as long as I hurried, I'd be fine. But when I opened a drawer for a change of clothes I found my Bible shoved towards the back, laying on its spine. I hadn't opened it for weeks and it felt like a relic from another time. I sunk onto the bed with the book resting in my hands. I turned it over, then turned it over again.

The Bible reminded me of Dr. Tom, the way he would talk to me, the way he'd look at me, the way he'd listen when I had a thought about the Lord. It had been only a couple months since Tom and his son, Jack, had thrown me a Super Bowl party for no reason at all, just because they knew I liked football. John Turnipseed and his grandson, Devon, had been there too. They had got some snacks and a couple other friends together and we watched the game. It had felt so good laughing about whatever. It felt so good being around those positive people.

The blinds were closed, but there was just enough light so I opened the Bible to the first page, and read the dedication.

To: Brad Strain

On: January 29th, 2015.

On the occasion of: A new life!

I reread Tom's note: *What a blessing God has given me in getting to know you. I struggled for so long trying to be a good man. This book introduced me to the greatest man ever - Jesus!*

Following Him has led me to another great man - Bradley Strain! Thank you for your courage, strength, and for showing me how to 'Fight the fight.' Stay strong!

A great man, he'd called me. I shook my head; I barely felt like a man at all. I felt like nothing, empty, but Tom's words hit me somewhere deep. I remembered the light. I remembered the feeling of God being close.

I paged open to Matthew and started reading. I didn't have a lot of time, but I figured I'd read a chapter or two. But when I finished those I kept going, feeling my heart warm, feeling my shoulders relax, feeling my spirits rise, feeling Jesus near me for the first time in a month. Finally, when I reached the end of Matthew, I stopped.

I didn't understand all of it, but I got enough. I went back and read Matthew 14, where Peter tried to walk on water but sank. Jesus reached down and grabbed him. I remembered Dr. Tom talking about this verse, talking about how Jesus said to Peter, "I got you."

That I could understand. I knew what it was like to try following Jesus only to find yourself under water.

I got you. I showed you. You got nothing to fear.

I tried to believe. I tried to believe the Lord was watching out for me just like he watched out for His disciples, even crazy Peter sinking in the middle of the lake.

Tom had also given me the devotional, <u>Jesus Calling</u>. I found it shoved in the same drawer and paged through it. The devotions were short and written as if Jesus was talking directly to me. I read one slowly. It said that Jesus was there even when I couldn't feel it.

That was enough. I flipped my hood over my head - it made me feel quieter - and said a prayer. I asked God for help. I asked to feel better. I asked for faith.

I squeezed my hands together and thanked Jesus for my dad who hadn't had to live with anyone in almost thirty years. I told the Lord that the old man was trying and it was hard for him too. And I thanked God for my mom who wasn't a paid nurse. She wasn't able to leave at the end of the day to get a break from me.

I asked God to bless them. And I asked for the strength to stand up and make it one more day, Lord, just one more day.

When I opened my eyes I felt more like myself. I felt lighter and closer to God. I wasn't glowing exactly, but I wasn't all dark either.

I prepared for my shower, gathering my stuff carefully on the bed. An hour later, when I came out of the bathroom, I heard my dad watching TV in the living room. And I found my stuff exactly where I left it.

Fireworks

Three weeks later

DAD LET THE truck idle in the parking lot. The smell of exhaust and damp cushions was making me queasy, but I wasn't ready to get out.

"You sure you don't want to come in, Popps?"

He shook his head. "I don't think the priest could handle the both of us."

I chuckled. "You got that right," I said. Then I took one more deep breath before opening the door. I was stronger, but still had to wrestle my walker from the back of the cab. I entered the sanctuary alone.

A light told me the booth was occupied so I sat down in the pew to wait. The air in the sanctuary was warm and I had to wipe sweat from my forehead with a sleeve. My chest was tight around to my shoulders. It was hard to get a good breath.

I hesitated on the edge of it, ready to leave. I could come back next week, I figured, or never, but the light went off before I could move and an old man stepped out. He shuffled to a pew in front of the altar. With his back bent at a sharp angle, he was moving even slower than I did.

My brain got jumbled up as I made my way to the confessional. I was going in there to cleanse myself. I was going in there to shock the priest. I was going in there to be allowed to take the Eucharist. I was going in there to kill time on a Saturday afternoon. I was going to confess. It was a mess as to why I was there, but it seemed too late to turn back.

Inside, the booth smelled like a wood-paneled basement - damp and oaky. My shoulders could touch either wall without much leaning. Through a screen I could see the movement of the priest on the other side.

He had a good voice. It was low and steady, soothing like Dr Tom's had been when I was suffering from DRESS syndrome.

The memory felt right for the moment. I had some kind of sickness. I didn't know what it was, but there was something wrong with me. I'd done bad things all my life and couldn't stop. But I didn't want to make excuses any more. I wanted to empty myself from my sins and let Jesus take their place.

I panted through the first words, struggling to get enough air. But I'd always been a talker and it got easier. I'd told these stories before - in prison yards mostly or at chow when there was time to kill.

I liked having an audience, even if it was a priest, and I liked remembering my old crew. But I also knew I'd done terrible things. I had stolen from my father. I had stolen from my grandmother. I had brought havoc into good people's lives. I had frightened strangers. I had been cruel to my sister. I had hurt people with drugs. I had hurt my family with my addictions. I had not been there for my wife or my children.

The longer I went, the worse I felt, until a sickness started creeping up into me. I knew I could have sunk into it, but Jesus was there gripping my hand. Like Peter in the lake, the Lord had me, so I told the priest everything. In the end, I even told him about Mano staring at me from the shower floor.

The priest must have been an old man as I had to listen to him wheeze for a few long moments before he began to speak. He told me I wasn't alone. He told me I was forgiven. He told me my record was clean. My penance seemed light for what I had done. Thirty years of sin and all I had to do was a few Our Fathers and a couple Hail Marys.

I thanked the priest and hobbled out of the booth. I sat at the pew because it was physically impossible for me to kneel. I stared up at Jesus hanging on the cross.

It was because of Him that my penance was so small. Dr. Tom,

Grandpa Bud, Dave, all of them kept telling me. And God had shown me: That man hanging there, Jesus, he'd taken my punishment. All my sins, all that bad stuff I did, had already been dealt with - by Him. Because of that, I had nothing to fear.

It seemed too good to be true, but, for me, it was undeniable. I was there taking breath. I had woken up that morning. I had fed myself. My body continued to work. As long as I kept my eyes open, watching for it, I could see Jesus in a thousand small miracles every day.

It was undeniable that He was there so I said the Our Father without problem. At my first Hail Mary, however, I had to stop. I couldn't remember anything past the opening line.

Another failure to add to the list. Not sure what to do I grabbed a nearby hymnbook. I didn't know what I would do with it, but it fell open to the perfect page. There it was, printed in full: *Hail Mary, full of grace, the Lord is with thee...*

Another gift. Another reminder: Jesus was there, still showing me, still saying, "I've got you, Brad."

IT WAS RIDICULOUS HOW LITTLE WEIGHT IT WAS. A year before I could have done this no problem, without breaking a sweat, but now I had to work just to curl it a few inches to my chest.

Still, I'd moved the bar, and that was all that mattered. And I was able to do one more rep than I'd done the last time. I was moving forward, however slowly, and that was all I had. It had been over a month since the fight. Things were better with Popps, but I was still a forty-year-old man with a broken body living in my dad's extra room. I had nothing but that extra rep, that bit of strength that wasn't there the week before.

I wrestled my bad leg off the bench and shuffled with my walker across the room to do some shoulder presses. I grunted, pushing up hardly any weight at all - but I did two more reps than I had the last time.

I dropped the weights and had to laugh, thinking about Rocco, the weight room in his garage. Fifteen years old, hella-skinny but we spent hours there acting the bad-ass gang-bangers. Drinking, getting high, looking to cause havoc, we saw ourselves as soldiers for the Sureños.

Twenty-five years later, it was still soldier time - I started another rep - but now I was a soldier for the Lord. I was a weak-ass soldier but that was all right. Jesus didn't care much about strength. I'd learned it was when I was at my weakest that He showed up the most.

When I was broken and dying, it wasn't my old gang who showed up to have my back. No, it was the Lord and the people who followed him.

I shuffled over to another bench. The weights seemed small in my hands but I knew it would be a struggle to lift them. Still, I was going to keep at it. Every day. Being a soldier for the Lord wasn't about weight. It was about showing up in weakness. It was about showing up with the love of the Lord in my mind, body and soul. It was about showing up to help the people around me.

The last rep didn't go well. I barely moved the weight, but that was all right. I'd be back again tomorrow. And the day after that. I was a soldier for the Lord, and I was in it for life.

ON MY LEFT WAS MY BROTHER. HE HAD BEEN CLEAN and legit ever since leaving the neighborhood for the Air Force. I hadn't seen him for over ten years, but here he was sitting in my dad's garage, clowning with me like it was 1984.

On my right was my dad. Quiet, but enjoying himself, laughing at the kids and their water balloon fight.

Ellen was there. Tonya and Wyatt. Derek. Other friends like Bill and Ryan.

And my sister, Melissa, was in the back of the garage helping my nephew with a plate of food. As she scooped macaroni salad, she talked to my son. All of us were together. I'd been out of the hospital six months and we were celebrating the Fourth of July.

It had often been an unlucky day for me. I'd been run over by a car one year and had rammed a three-wheeler into a pylon another. But this year I felt blessed. God had been so good to me, putting things in my path. It was far better than I deserved.

But I had one thing I needed to do, a question I needed to ask before I could really celebrate. I didn't know what the answer would be, but I wanted to try. It was time finally to be a better father and a better man.

My brother stood up for a brat and my son took his seat. The kid leaned back in the chair, laughing still about something his cousin said.

"Hey, Son. I was thinking." My stomach floated for a moment. "You should think about hanging around here for a bit."

"I'm not going anywhere."

"Yeah, yeah, yeah, but I meant this fall."

He raised his eyebrows and lost the grin.

I made my pitch. "We could get you into school here. Maybe get you a job. Save up some money and we could look into getting you a car."

"That sounds great, but Mom..."

"I'd talk to your mom."

He started scratching at the back of his head. It made him look so much like his grandpa, I had to laugh.

I said, "Think about it, okay?"

He nodded and promised he'd give it some thought. A few moments later a water balloon landed too close to grandpa which ended the game. Chase went out onto the lawn and the party rolled on.

At dusk, we moved chairs into the driveway and waited for the sky to turn dark. The air turned cool and we all stared up at the sky. There was a low poof, a boom, and everyone cheered.

This was so much more than I deserved. I'd been nothing but a gangster, a drug dealer, a drunk, an ex con, a broken man. If there was any justice I'd be rotting in a cell. Instead the Lord, in his wisdom, hit me with a train. He'd been showing me my whole life, but finally it took losing everything before I turned to see.

Colors drifted across the clouds. My family surrounded me. It was beautiful. I was blessed by God and completely at peace. In my own way, I glowed.

I STOOD UP AGAIN, GRABBED MY CANE, AND LIMPED to the window. Spring sunshine spilled over everything I could see. Fresh leaves were bursting from their buds. Life was spreading back into the grass.

"Stop it."

"I can't just sit there, Popps."

He muttered something I couldn't hear. I moved into the kitchen and leaned into the fridge, searching for something to distract me. But there was nothing good to eat so I went back to the living room.

"Just sit your ass down and watch the game."

I lowered myself back to the couch and stared at the TV without paying it any attention. I checked the clock on my phone for the tenth time in as many minutes. They should have been there already.

"They're on their way, for cripes sake."

"Yeah, yeah, yeah," I said. "I know it." But I stood up again.

I started back towards the window but heard the low rumble of the engine before I got there. With a swelling of pride bigger than my chest, I watched the car pull into the driveway. It was a piece of crap, but we had bought it together, and spent hours working side by side to keep it running.

My son spotted me in the window and gave me a big smile. His girlfriend stood from the passenger side. He in his tux and she in her prom dress, they came in giving hugs. I barely knew how to handle it. Love and amazement made it hard to breathe. But this was my life, somehow. This was how good God had been to me.

In the backyard we took a few pictures. The cool Portland air made me shudder, but there was nowhere else I'd rather have been.

He had decided to stay, of course. Back in August we had moved the queen bed from my room into the basement and replaced it with two twins. It was tight sometimes and I'd joked that Chase was my new cellie, but the reality was the opposite of prison. I had felt free for the first time in my life. I felt free to be who God made me. I felt free to be a real father for my son.

I was crippled and slow and beaten up, but none of that mattered when every day I could be there when he got home from school or work. I was able to help the boy with his car and give him advice about life. I was able to watch him play ball, make friends, get a girlfriend, live his life. I was able to bring my son with me to church and talk to him about the Lord. For the first time in my life I got to be a positive influence. I could shine some light instead of darkness.

It had been amazing.

When it was time, Chase led his date back to the car. They smiled at me standing in the doorway. He promised to be safe, to have a good time, and to act like a gentleman. I waved at them as they backed out, then followed the car with my eyes until it disappeared down the street.

THE PEOPLE SHUFFLED IN THEIR CHAIRS BEHIND ME, although I felt them more than heard them. The ballroom was full, I knew that. And Doctor Tom was up on the stage, talking about trauma surgery then talking about me.

I had a huge grin on my face as I listened. It had been almost two years since my accident, and I was supposed to be there, I knew it. I had a word to say to these good people.

Dr. Tom had invited me. He made presentations at health care conventions all over the country and since this one took place in Bismarck, North Dakota - with nurses and doctors who had first treated me after I got hit by that train - he had invited me to come along.

He finished his talk and introduced me, inviting me up to the podium. I nodded over at Derek before hobbling up. Dr. Tom had invited me as his guest and I invited Derek as mine. It was an easy drive for him from Dickinson.

I could move pretty well at this point, but I was still slow so I started talking as I climbed the three steps to the stage. The words came easy. I told them about myself, about my history: the gang life, the drugs and addictions. I looked over at Dr. Tom smiling up, and positivity rolled over me. In that room were the men and women who saved me, who knit me back together again. Because of them I had life and hope and light. I wanted to return to them the same gift they gave me and shine the love of Jesus back at them.

It wasn't that everything was perfect. I still was living with my dad, and that could be hard. My son had moved back to Montana after he graduated and I missed him. I still had a major surgery ahead of me to fix a massive hernia. I was still struggling to get a driver's license and, since I wanted to do it right, this meant I had to rely on friends and public transportation to get around.

But in that moment, talking to those people, it all made sense. I was doing what God wanted from me: spreading some light.

I had nothing to my name but that was all right. All the Lord wanted was for me to be me. I didn't need to be Jesus. I didn't need to be

Dr. Tom or my sister or anybody else. God wanted me to tell my story, to take some of that hope I had been given and share it with the world.

And that's what I did. I told them my story and ended with this:

"I never expected to be where I am today. I was a piece of crap. I spent most of my life in jail. I didn't deserve it, but still so many of you worked so hard to keep me alive.

"Why you would do that for someone like me, I don't know. But you gave me a second chance and I want to take advantage of it. If I didn't change? If I went back out there still doing the same stuff? That would be a slap in the face for you great people. And, trust me, I definitely don't want to slap anyone in the face anymore.

"But today my life has totally changed. I don't know if anybody here believes in God, but I do. I believe the Lord set my life up to give me the strength to overcome something traumatic. And that train was traumatic. It wasn't easy, but God gave me the strength and the power to make it. God carried me through.

"I believe the Lord had a plan for me. I didn't always see it, but now I do. And now I'm in it for the Lord. Now I want to tell my story, which is God's story. I want to share it with those people who are living like I was. I want to help the young men causing havoc in the streets and in and out of jail. I want to show them that there is a better way.

"You saved my life. The Lord changed my life and put me on a path. Now I want to honor what you all did and honor the Lord. Now I want to try and make the world a better place."

I grinned at their applause and felt I was glowing when I left the stage. Back at the table Derek shook my hand, and Dr. Tom brought me into a hug.

"That was amazing, Brad," he said. "Amen!"

Epilogue
2019

Glowing

MY FAMILY:

My daughter, Rachelle is doing great. She lives in Michigan and works as a housekeeper. Three years ago she had a son and named him Allen, which is both Chase and my middle name. I call him Big Al.

My son, Chase, is back in Montana studying to be a registered nurse.

My daughter Harli is our free spirit. She lives in Montana.

Melody still lives and works in Hamilton. She and I have become good friends.

My sister, Melissa, is happy and healthy. She lives in Vancouver, Washington with her family.

My dad is in his mid-seventies. He lives in the same house and continues to work part time.

My mom still lives in Vancouver, but has had some recent health concerns. We are praying she will be okay.

My brother, Eric, lives in Las Vegas where he drives for a limosine service. He comes to visit us all in Washington often.

MY FRIENDS:

Chavez is clean and sober. He has a good job and lives with his girl-friend and their children in Montana.

Wyatt and Tonya are all still living and working in North Dakota and still doing great.

Derek lives in North Dakota and calls often to check in on me. Sadly, his dog, Pepper, died a couple years ago, but he has new dog - a big puppy named Toby.

MY OLD CREW:

JBone cleaned up his life. He is currently a father and works as a welder.

Last I heard, Rocco was serving time in California State Prison.

THE OTHERS:

Becky, Ty Angel, Mike, Big Wheez, Donald: I lost contact with them a long time ago, and I don't know where any of them are now.

AS FOR ME,

I lived with my dad for two years. It wasn't always easy. We had a lot of bad days. I struggled with my temper. I struggled with stress. But I kept trusting Jesus and focusing on the things I could control. I am very grateful for the patience and care he showed me.

I had more surgeries and eventually I was able to get rid of the colostomy bag. I struggled with pain, but I was able to finally wean myself off pain medicine.

I got my drivers license. After three years of rides from family and friends, after three years of waiting for buses, after three years of paperwork, I opened an envelope and a card fell out with my picture on it. For the first time in my entire life, I could legally drive a car.

I grew strong enough to get a job. I work with my brother-in-law almost full time. I have found the more I am able to work, the healthier I feel.

And now, a little over four years after the accident, I can walk without a cane. Like Dr. Cole had warned me, my bad leg still gives me problems, but I'm glad I kept it.

In the end, the Lord has been so good to me, showing me his love day after day after day. God keeps shining light into my life even when things get dark. Now it is my greatest hope to be able to shine that same light into the lives of others. I want show up for hurting people, just like Dr. Tom and John Turnipseed and Ellen did for me. I want to walk with people stuck in darkness and show them the love of Jesus. I want to keep sharing my story for the glory of God. It has been an amazing journey, and now I want to glow.

Afterword

Melody

A message from Brad's former wife

Brad and I had a rough go at it over the past 22 years. It hasn't always been easy for us to talk or even look at each other. So when Brad asked me if I would write something for his book, I was glad he did it in a text so he couldn't see the tears in my eyes. I was surprised, of course, but also honored. Surprised because we have both placed a lot of hurt on each other. Honored because after everything that has happened, we are still family. For him to include me out of all the wonderful and amazing people that have made a positive impact in his life, well, I can't even begin to express my feelings in words.

When I met Brad almost 23 years ago, he was intoxicating with long wavy hair falling over his face, baggy clothes, and a grin from ear to ear. Over time as I got to know him, I could see hurt in his eyes. The hurt was something I knew he often struggled with, but never talked about.

Knowing Brad as I have, and after reading his book, I can say his story is about much more than gangs, drugs and violence. His story is about a boy who couldn't connect with his family. He didn't feel wanted and didn't seem to fit in. Turning to the "dark side" wasn't what Brad felt was a choice, but a need to find a new family. He was taken in and cared for by gang members and drug dealers until their world became all he knew. He began to crave the thrill of violence or the high of a drug, just to feel something, anything - or the numbing of alcohol so he could feel nothing at all.

Brad's life saw a lot more crime, violence, and pain than he has revealed in this book. He has lived an extreme life, full of crimes and jail time, struggles and hardships, paths unknown and paths that seemed to be hidden from him. As he grew older, Brad had thoughts of going to school to be a counselor of some sort. He wanted to be someone who could contribute to the troubled youth out there, be someone they could listen to, look up to. But he couldn't seem to stay out of trouble of his own. He was a magnet for the troublemakers and the thrill of it was too tempting. It seemed at every turn Brad was going to jail or prison.

Still, he has never been without love in his heart. It wasn't always easy to see from the outside. At times, I doubted whether that love was still there at all for anyone, including himself. But now I know that Brad has never been without love. He has loved truly, madly and deeply throughout his life and continues to do so with his friends, his family, his kids and even me.

The night my daughter called to tell me her dad had been in a terrible accident was the worst one of my life. I wasn't even going to answer my phone because I was out celebrating a friend's birthday at a local bar. I had stepped outside to smoke a cigarette when my cell phone rang. I can remember my daughter scolding me, telling me to listen carefully because she had something important to say. She described the accident and Brad's condition. My son was staying the night with a friend so I had to find someone to give me a ride so I could tell him in person what happened.

The next few days were terrible as we waited each morning to find out if Brad had made it through the night. I can remember lying on the living room floor with my son, talking and crying, wondering how we would ever make the drive so we could be by his side. Brad was living in North Dakota and my daughter had just moved to be with him not long before. My son and I lived in Western Montana, over 700 miles away.

It was the scariest thing any of us had ever been through. Not knowing if someone you love is going to live or die and watching them suffer in the most excruciating pain anyone could ever imagine... it was something none of us will ever forget. It hurt to see my children struggle through the emotional stages of fearing they might lose their dad. It was also the moment I knew without a doubt that I needed Brad to always be a part of our life. I could not bear the thought of losing him - for my kids or for me.

I can remember talking to Brad often while he was on his long road of healing, starting in the hospital in Minnesota and as he moved home to Washington State. There were days he would be so angry and hurting he couldn't talk or think positively. There were days he would sink into himself and refuse to reach out to people. But he worked hard and pushed through it to heal his body, surgery after surgery. As time went on, I noticed a change. Brad seemed to be counseling me - and anyone else that would listen - on staying positive and how to be healthier. He would talk about God and how prayer can change your life and how it had changed his. He had said things like this before, of course, but this time seemed different. It wasn't like the old Brad who meant it in the moment. This time, he truly believed it.

Close to two years after Brad's accident, our son moved to be with him for his senior year. I was nervous as I had never been without my son for that long. But he wanted this time to be with his dad. They both knew it might be the only chance they had left to build a stronger bond before our son was grown.

They had their struggles. Sometimes I would get calls from Brad or my son angrily complaining about the other. Other times they would call and tell me funny stories or send me pictures. Brad made our son get a job and save money for a car and he took on the challenge of keeping him focused when he became interested in a girl.

It hadn't been easy, but I still feel the emotions well up inside me when I think of the bond they were able to build. And I am so proud of our son. He was learning to be strong and keep pushing forward - just like his dad.

After everything, a life of crime and violence, love and hate, after being hit by a real-life freight train, Brad Strain stands to tell his story. His prayers and perseverance have lifted him up and given him the strength to continue. It has been a gift to watch him live his life to the fullest and to make a positive difference in the lives of others.

He is our Superman.

How to Save a Surgeon

An excerpt from Dr. Tom Blee's 2016 memoir

The orthopedic surgeon pointed into the man's abdomen and said, "Hey, Tom, I can't make heads or tails out of it. What is that?"

I looked where he pointed and said, "That's poop."

"Why is there poop?"

Having just arrived in the operating room, I didn't know a thing, but I couldn't imagine it would matter much if I did. Half of the patient's body was missing from hip to ribs and he had feces throughout his pelvic region, I assumed he was septic and damn near dead. I asked the anesthesiologist, "How's he doing?"

"Stable," the anesthesiologist said. "He's doing fine."

He was stable, maybe, but fine was a stretch. The patient, I would later learn, was a thirty-nine year-old man named Brad who had spent most of his life in and out prison. At the age of 36, he decided to start over in a new part of the country, away from familiar, destructive patterns. He moved out to the North Dakota plains where he met some good people and started a decent job.

Things were looking up until he shattered his leg in a four wheeler accident. He was an uninsured felon; he lost his job, and had nothing saved up, so he returned to what he knew: selling drugs. It was essentially the same business in North Dakota as it was anywhere else, but it carried the same risks. It wasn't long before he was busted back to prison for three more years.

When he finished his time, he returned to North Dakota. His leg had healed up and his friends gave him a second chance at another job. Again, things started looking up. He liked the work and met more good people. He was on his way to a better life until one evening after dinner out with a friend he was walking with his dog towards home. As they crossed the railroad tracks, Brad noticed the train coming toward them, but it was too far away to put them in any real danger. The movement of his dog, however, worried him and he stepped in a way that trapped his foot. His momentum made him fall and slam his head against the rail.

The train rolled towards him. Brad wrenched his body up, but he couldn't move fast enough and the train impacted him at close to full speed. The steel frame of the train's engine threw him to the side, peeling the skin from his abdomen in the process until his bowels were exposed. He had been eviscerated.

Many weeks later he described the next horrifying moments. "I was surprised to be alive at all," he said. "Then somehow I stood up. Then I saw my intestines hanging out... I don't remember anything after that."

They raced him to a hospital in North Dakota. There they found his pelvis had shattered, he had lost his abdominal wall and a large portion of his colon. It took several hours of surgery to wash him out. Then they closed him up and hoped for the best. Somehow, he survived the next few days, and even grew stable enough for the trip to my hospital in Saint Paul.

When he arrived his abdomen was a mess, filled with broken bones and organs - and there was the poop. It was because of this last that they paged me. When I joined them in the operating room, his abdomen was exposed so I could see parts of his bowel. I asked, "Where's your incision?"

"We don't have one," the orthopedic surgeon gestured to an area that stretched from hip to armpit, "That's all missing skin."

His body was twisted onto his side. The orthopedic team worked above on his pelvis so I had to move along the edge of the table, almost underneath him in order to get to his abdomen. As I removed staples I realized his wound was just skin to skin. I slowly moved organs away to the point where my hand came out the very wound they were working on in the pelvis. I checked the colon reconstruction and found it had broken down - as a few percent do - and its contents were seeping into the belly. At this point I was able to form an idea of the injury. I understood the source of the contamination and I understood what I needed to do to stop it. But, given the way Brad was positioned, I would need to work upside down with my body twisted to get where I needed to be under his injury.

I was able to staple off each end of the colon which stopped the contamination. I brought the colon up through a separate wound in his upper quadrant and attached a colostomy bag. We dumped liters of saline in the wound then suctioned out the poop. We scrubbed the area until it was clean. We were successful, in that his colon was no longer leaking and his abdomen was free of poop, but now we had to find a way to close the wounds if he were to have any chance of surviving.

Everyone has a big sheet of fat in their belly called the omentum. Vascular and full of lymphatic tissue, it is the watchdog of the abdomen. When we get infections it moves and covers the problem area. If you get appendicitis, for example, the omentum will shift in order to protect you. If you had a perforated ulcer, the omentum will wiggle over and stick to it.

Brad was missing much of the inner structure of his abdominal wall, so we spread the omentum out as much as possible to cover his abdominal contents. We then used what skin we could find and tugged and stapled it together to make a temporary closure. Finally, when we had done all we could, we sent him to the ICU. He was in rough shape but still alive.

Brad would go on to have fifty-five more operations. His pelvis and abdominal wall needed to be reconstructed. His belly and side were covered with skin grafts. He constantly battled infection.

In our trauma system, we bop around. Sometimes we will spend the week covering surgical ICU. Other times we will cover true trauma or emergency general surgery. Our connections with specific patients can be sporadic, so I only saw Brad a couple of times as he went through this process. After several months had passed, he had almost fallen off my radar when a nurse came flying into a workroom where John Turnipseed and I were having a conversation with a young man about LIFEteam. She yelled, "Oh my God! They're going to cut Brad's leg off!"

Brad's bones had shattered and most of the nerves to his left leg were ruined. He couldn't feel anything. He couldn't use the muscles. He was essentially dragging around a forty pound dead weight. Therefore the orthopedic surgeons had recommended amputation in order to prevent future wound issues like infections or ulcers.

John Turnipseed knew none of this, so he asked, "Who's Brad?"

I gave him the short version, "He's spent most of his life in prison for selling drugs. When he got out, he was hit by a train which shattered his pelvis. Now it looks like he might lose his leg."

"Hmm," John said. "My son lost his leg after being shot seventeen times. I have an idea of what Brad would be facing. Maybe I should talk to him."

The nurse said, "Well you better get in there now. It's so bad the orthopedic surgeon is praying for him."

We hurried to visit Brad but found the situation not quite as urgent as we were led to believe. Brad was a wreck, grieving over his leg, but the decision to remove it wasn't one he needed to act on immediately. He decided to wait, and, after some time passed and more healing, they ultimately made the decision not to amputate at all. But this episode led to John meeting Brad; and during that time I got to know him better as well.

I had been working with a different man from North Dakota at this same time who had been struggling with meth and crack cocaine. One afternoon I was reading and praying at home when my eye landed on the books sitting on our coffee table: a Bible I couldn't read because the print was too small, Fight: Winning the Battles That Matter Most by Craig Groeschel, and Jesus>Religion by Jefferson Bethke. I had been working on following prompts from the Holy Spirit so when something came to me that said, "Bring those books to the North Dakota guy," I listened.

Except the next morning I forgot and left the house without them. It wasn't until two days later when I was doing a 24 hour shift that I brought the three books with me. I went to the guy from North Dakota, the man addicted to Meth, but he had been discharged. I had been sloppy the day before and now he was gone. Angry with myself,

I cursed out loud to the empty room. Then, with those three books in my hand, I prayed, "Sorry God. I missed that one," and went on with my call shift.

Twenty hours later, after three o'clock the next morning, my resident called. "You need to come to the ER," he said. "This guy from North Dakota wants to talk to you."

I hurried downstairs to find 'the guy from North Dakota' was Brad - and he was in rough shape. He had a drug reaction called DRESS syndrome which shut down his bone morrow so he had no platelets in his blood. His kidneys were in failure. His heart rate was 140. His blood pressure was 80. The reaction had inflamed every inch of his skin. He was bright red, like he had been boiled in a microwave. His tattoos looked like they had been rubbed with sandpaper. He could tolerate contact with one square inch of skin on the palm of his hand, otherwise any touch caused him excruciating pain. He couldn't even bear bed sheets.

It was torture. In between sobs, he whimpered, "Tom."

I had to lean in to hear him. "Yeah, bud?"

"Kill me," he muttered. "I'm done."

"Brad, you know I can't do that."

"You know me. You can do it."

"Brad, we're at the point where there's only one thing I can offer."

Gently, I touched his palm. At this point I had never prayed out loud with another person, but I closed my eyes - I figured that was what you were supposed to do - and bumbled along using some of the words I had heard at church. I asked God to be there. I said something about Jesus. I mentioned healing several times. It was probably a 28 second prayer though it felt like a half hour.

When I looked up I saw Brad's face had relaxed. His eyes were shut. He was breathing softly. His pulse went down and his blood pressure went up so both were normal.

He had fallen asleep, and was - impossibly - at peace.

Later, Brad talked about this moment. "That was a point when nothing was working - not in my body, not in my life. It was all pain. When we prayed together, that was all I had. In that moment, I had to let go. In order to get through it, I knew I had to submit. I had to give up, and release everything to God."

In his hospital room, every inch of his skin inflamed but one, Brad was also forced to surrender - and he also experienced a closeness with Jesus. Through a stumbling prayer, in the midst of tremendous pain, the peace of Christ enveloped him so fully he was able to sink into a blissful sleep.

I was away from the hospital for several days, but the day before I returned I heard a prompting from God: "Brad is your boy. He is the 'guy from North Dakota' who needs those books." It made sense so I grabbed them as I left the house. Later at the hospital I found Brad moving through dialysis and on a powerful antibiotic.

I asked, "How was the week?"

He had gone through hell, walking every day along the edge of the canyon of death. "It sucked," he said, but he was smiling. The inflammation had lessened and he wasn't in nearly as much pain. "But I'm doing okay."

Brad was with us for months, and as he slowly improved, I would visit him whenever I was on call. We discussed the books I had given him and had long talks about the Bible. I was no expert but shared what I knew. I started on page one: God made the earth. God made Adam and Eve. They ate the fruit which screwed everything up, but God immediately started to fix it. He made the tree grow in the distance and then came down as Jesus.

Both of us looked forward to our talks. Brad soaked it up, hungry to learn all he could. Others often would listen in on our conversations and occasionally join in with a comment or question. It was a good time.

One afternoon, I was paged by the rehab unit. A nurse spoke in an urgent voice, "Doctor Blee, Brad needs you to come down here."

I was in the midst of a trauma resuscitation, but I ran down to him as soon as I was free. He wasn't in his room so I searched the hallways, but he wasn't anywhere I could find him. Finally, a nurse with a sly grin told me to check the stairwell.

I opened the door she had indicated and there was Brad. He needed help from a therapist and a brace but he was climbing up a flight of stairs on the same leg that at one point was scheduled to be cut off. He beamed up at me, "Look doc!" he shouted. "Isn't this amazing?"

It was more than amazing. I said, "That's unbelievable."

He laughed, "It's a God thing, isn't it?"

It absolutely was.

Later, back in his room, he told me he was finally going home - which wasn't necessarily good news. His personal life was still a mess. He was divorced. His son didn't like him. His step-daughters wanted little to do with him. It was going to be a rough road, but in that moment he was at peace. He had an inner light which brightened the room.

"Tom," he said, "I've got that same glow that you and John have - I can feel it."

Brad had to lose everything: his family, his livelihood, and his health; he had to be stripped down to nothing before he finally surrendered. "In order to get through it," he reflected later, "I knew I had to let go. I had to give it all up to God."

When he did, he found Jesus waiting there for him. "I was such a piece of shit my whole life but you and John just kept coming back. You just kept showing up and telling me about Jesus. And because of that, I knew Jesus cared. I knew he loved me and I wasn't going to let him down."

Surrender. Letting go of yourself and trusting fully in Jesus. It may be the most difficult part of following him, but - when you finally lose yourself in him and feel him catch you, hold you, lift you up - there is nothing more glorious.

You can read the rest of Dr. Tom's remarkable journey in his 2016 memoir, How to Save a Surgeon.

About the Authors

Brad Strain

is an author, speaker and leader. He lives in Vancouver, Washington, surrounded by his family and friends.

For more information, check out:
www.bradstrainforlife.com

To contact Brad Strain, please send a message to:
bradstrainforlife@gmail.com

Brian Scott

lives with his family in Red Wing, Minnesota where he is the director of 9 Foot Voice, a Christian publishing company. His previous works include <u>Six Years Lost</u> with Benjamin Schmidt and <u>How to Save a Surgeon</u> with Dr. Tom Blee.